JEWISH FARMERS

OF THE CATSKILLS

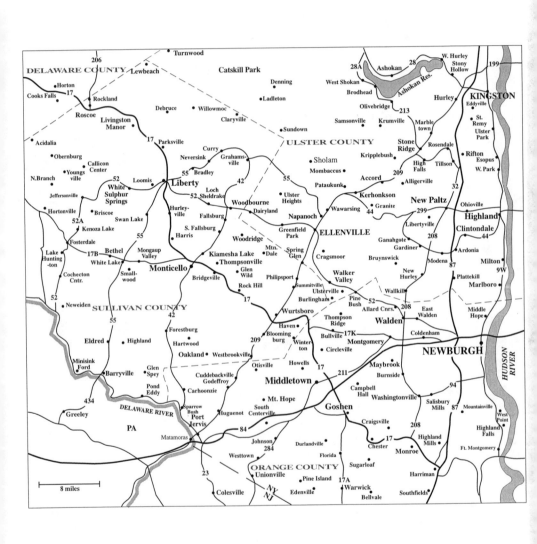

JEWISH FARMERS
OF THE CATSKILLS

A Century of Survival

by

Abraham D. Lavender

and

Clarence B. Steinberg

University Press of Florida

Gainesville   Tallahassee   Tampa   Boca Raton

Pensacola   Orlando   Miami   Jacksonville

00 99 98 97 96 95 6 5 4 3 2 1

Library of Congress Cataloging-in-Publication Data

Lavender, Abraham D.
    Jewish farmers of the Catskills : a century of survival / by
Abraham D. Lavender and Clarence B. Steinberg.
        p.   cm.
    Includes bibliographical references and index.
    ISBN 0-8130-1343-7 (alk. paper)
    1. Jews—New York (State)—Catskill Mountains Region–
–History—20th century.   2. Farmers, Jewish—New York (State)–
–Catskill Mountains Region—History—20th century.   3. Catskill
Mountains Region (N.Y.)—Ethnic relations.   I. Steinberg, Clarence B.
II. Title.
F127.C3L38   1995   94-39645
974.7'38004924—dc20

The University Press of Florida is the scholarly publishing agency for the State Univer-
sity System of Florida, comprised of Florida A & M University, Florida Atlantic Uni-
versity, Florida International University, Florida State University, University of Central
Florida, University of Florida, University of North Florida, University of South Florida,
and University of West Florida.

University Press of Florida
15 Northwest 15th Street
Gainesville, FL 32611

In Memoriam

Judith Serrae Steinberg

March 3, 1931–September 6, 1992

Who loved and wrote and waited well, but not quite long enough.

Contents

Illustrations

Preface

Most current impressions of Jews are that they are an urbanized and industrialized people. While this impression is true in general of today's Jewish communities in most of the world, it is incomplete.

Ancient Jewish history has major references to the importance of agriculture in Jewish life. In Eastern Europe, the homeland of most American Jews, there were a large number of Jewish farmers. Many early Sephardic Jews in the Americas were in agriculture, and there was an organized Jewish agricultural movement in the United States at the time of the Great Migration from Eastern Europe.

While comprising a small percentage of the total Jewish population, these farmers have nevertheless played an important part in the Jewish community. The information in this book helps to correct the incomplete impression and to analyze in detail the largest concentration of Jewish farmers in the United States—in the Catskill Mountains in New York state.

In chapter 1, "Jews and the Farming Tradition," we discuss the historical importance of agriculture to Jewish life, briefly review the history of Jewish farming in the Americas and in Eastern Europe in the century before the Great Migration, and describe the organized efforts to encourage Jewish farming.

In chapter 2, "Settling in 'The Mountains'," we describe the Catskill Mountains where Jewish farmers began moving around 1880, the early years of the interaction of farms and boardinghouses, and the beginnings of a Jewish religious, institutional, and farming community. The chapter covers Jewish life in the mountains through the 1920s.

We cover, in chapter 3, the Jewish farming community in the Catskills as it faced the depression in 1929, the continuing dilemma over how much to mix farming and resort keeping, and the major parts played by co-ops, mutual aid societies, and the Jewish Agricultural Society. The chapter narrates Jewish life in the Catskills until 1940.

In chapter 4 we consider the Jewish community's reaction to World War II, from the Victory Farm Cadets to settling of refugees from Nazism, and then describe how the farmers expanded their operations and the resort keepers their facilities in to the prosperity following the war, through the 1950s.

Completing the years through the 1950s, we describe in chapter 5 the Jewish farmers' improving social life, expanding religious life, attempts to develop a cultural life, and improving relations with Christians.

We relate in chapter 6 how Jewish farming began to decline in the 1960s and continued to decline through the 1970s and 1980s as Catskill farmers no longer had a captive market in New York City and could not compete with larger farming operations in a national market. We also show how the Catskill farmers suffered as the Catskills lost their allure as a resort area. Finally, we portray the Catskills today and describe how a remnant hangs on—witnesses to a unique century of rugged individuals with a vision.

Acknowledgments

We are grateful for many people's help. First among these, of course, are the splendid souls we interviewed over the decade the book was being researched and written. Their names are in the list of interviews. Special thanks go to Herman J. Levine, not only for his extensive interviews but also, and especially, for his suggestions and encouragement. We also express our appreciation to the Orivitz family for a Max Orivitz Grant and to Sharlyn Pearlman of Miami Beach, both of whom provided travel funds for Abe Lavender to interview Herman J. Levine, then in his eighties, at his home in New York City, and to go over his collection of photographs, taken when he headed the Jewish Agricultural Society's Ellenville, New York, branch office. We thank Mr. Levine's daughter Maryland Delegate Helen Koss for inviting Clarence Steinberg to her home to talk with her visiting father about old times and old photographs. Appreciation is expressed to Andrew, Daphne, Brett, and Nikki Pariser of Wayne, New Jersey, and to Harold and Vivian Hertz and Mark Hite of Fort Lee, New Jersey, for their hospitality to Abe Lavender on several trips to New York.

We also thank the staffs of libraries where we conducted research: the YIVO Institute Library in New York City; the Ellenville, New York, Public Library; the Library of Congress in Washington, D.C.; the University of Maryland Library in College Park; the Francis Marion College Library in Florence, South Carolina; the University of Miami Library; the Florida International University Library; and the Miami-Dade Public Library in Miami, Florida. Thanks are also expressed to Rabbi Herman Eisner for a copy of his manuscript on early Jewish settlement in the lower Catskills, and to the Ellenville Hebrew Aid Society for a copy of its own history which covers some of the ground we traverse. Special thanks go to Florida International University for word processing and copying facilities and for support for photographic and cartographic work.

We also thank Edward Koenig, the society's field agent for the Catskill area in the late 1940s and early 1950s, for his copy of Gabriel Davidson's *Our Jewish Farmers,* and for his sobering comments about the limits the Jewish Agricultural Society had set in its programs.

Thanks are also expressed to Rabbi Joseph Levine for encouraging us to pursue publication, and to Lillian Solomon, who helped us find certain interviewees.

We also thank several uninterviewed people for their forbearance. Most significant of these are Ellenville's Harold Sashin and Glen Wild's Meyer Kaplan. We had hoped to have their insights especially regarding the turbulent expansions and then consolidations of farms in the 1960s. Unanticipated problems on our part kept us from planned trips to speak to them and others.

Our earlier version of the manuscript benefited from the objective comments of four outstanding scholars in the field of Judaica. Rabbi Jacob Rader Marcus, Ph.D., founding editor of *American Jewish Archives,* Dr. Abraham J. Peck, managing editor of *American Jewish Archives,* Dr. Gerald Sorin, director of the Jewish Studies Program at New Paltz, SUNY, and Dr. Murray Binderman of the University of Alabama in Birmingham, founding editor of *Contemporary Jewry,* were all most helpful and gracious in giving their time and incisive suggestions. To Dr. Walda Metcalf, associate director and editor-in-chief, to Alexandra Leader, her assistant, and to Judy Goffman, editor, at the University Press of Florida, we express our appreciation for their understanding, helpful suggestions, and patience. We also thank Rand McNally for permission to adapt a map of the Catskills.

Chapter 1

Jews and the Farming Tradition

The term *Jewish farmer* usually brings to mind biblical visions of pastoral ancient Israel or of a present-day Israeli *kibbutz* (collective) or *moshav* (cooperative). From earliest Jewish history, the Hebrews were portrayed as a pastoral people. Most of the patriarchs were herdsmen, pasturing their sheep and cattle. The Torah, especially Genesis, Exodus, and Leviticus, repeatedly refers to Jews herding and tilling, both activities underscored by references to solemn pastoral holidays. Passover (Pesach) starting wheat harvests, Pentecost (Shabuoth) closing that harvest seven weeks later, and Succoth coming in the fall and celebrating the harvest of other crops, illustrate the importance of agriculture in Jewish holidays.

Jewish law required that the gleanings of the harvest, the vineyard, and the olive grove be given to the poor and the stranger (Leviticus 19:9–10, Deuteronomy 24:19–21). The sabbatical year of release required that land, vineyards, and olive groves be left fallow every seventh year and that the needy and the animals have the right to the produce that year (Exodus 23:11). The jubilee year allowed for agricultural land that had been sold because of hard times to be redeemed after fifty years (by the original owner or his heirs) if the land had not been recovered earlier (Leviticus 25:28). The Sabbath had major importance to a people "that had passed the pastoral stage and that employed man and beast in agricultural labor."[1] Many other examples show the importance of farming to the early Hebrews, but the Jewish interest in agriculture continued beyond the biblical era. For example, except for the first treatise, the entire first section of the Mishnah (written in the third century C.E.) is devoted to agriculture. Maimonides, the Jewish

1

Talmudic scholar born in Spain in the twelfth century, who lived most of his life in Egypt, devoted one of the chapters of his exposition to agriculture, giving details of proper farming methods.[2]

Glimpses of modern Israel show irrigation, hydroponics, figs, olives, wheat, egg factories, and grazing sheep. This vision of Israeli farming goes back a century and a half to the first recorded modern-day Jewish agricultural settlement in 1845, on the outskirts of Jerusalem. Warder Cresson, in 1844, became the first U.S. consul accredited to the Turkish court in Jerusalem. In 1845, he converted to Judaism, changed his name to Michael Boaz Israel, and founded the settlement called God's Vineyard. The settlement did not last, but major changes occurred in a few decades.

Between 1882 and the early 1900s, over twenty rural settlements were founded in Palestine by Jewish immigrants from Eastern Europe. They were largely unsuccessful, and many of these Jewish farmers who remained in agriculture became a gentry subsidized by European Jews and employing Arab laborers. Successful collective settlement began in 1911 when the village of Degania was founded. Labor-Zionist kibbutzim and moshavim were established after World War I. American and Canadian Jews moving to Israel had an above-average interest in the visions of Jewish farming. A 1965 survey of 1,428 Americans and Canadians in Israeli agriculture showed that about 9 percent were farmers, a figure above the average of other nationalities. About 55 percent were on kibbutzim, 17 percent on moshavim, and 28 percent in private agriculture.[3]

The image of Jewish farmers hardly ever shifts to the United States, much less to the state of New York. A mention of Jewish farmers usually gets a look of amusement or disbelief from both Jews and non-Jews. The generally accepted image of the American Jew is that of a city dweller, a business person or professional, and a descendant of immigrants who were peddlers, shopkeepers, or garment workers, who knew nothing of farming. For example, in *A New Life*, Bernard Malamud's Seymour Levin, a Jewish professor from New York who has moved to rural Oregon, looks at cows in a field and says that it is the first time he has seen cows in the open and the first time that the cows have seen a Levin.

The image of American Jews as nonfarming urbanites is usually correct. About 85 percent are descendants of Jewish immigrants from Eastern Europe who came to the United States during the Great Migration, the largest in U.S. history. From 1880 to 1914, about two million Eastern European Jews—one-third of the region's Jews—migrated: 158,000 in the 1880s, 314,000 in the 1890s, 945,000 from 1900 through 1909, and 499,000 from 1910 through 1914. The migration ceased during World War I, then resumed after the war for several years on a small scale before being stopped in 1924 by anti-Jewish and anti-Catholic immigration restrictions.

About 2,378,000 Jews came to the United States between 1880 and the end of 1924. During this period, the Jewish population increased from 280,000 out of 50 million (0.5 percent) to 4 million out of 115 million (3.9 percent). In the 1880s, 25 percent of the Eastern European Jews returned to Eastern Europe. By 1908, only about 8 percent returned, and after 1919 less than 1 percent. Irish-Catholics were the only immigrant group who had a lower rate of return.[4] Over 90 percent of the Jewish immigrants who left Eastern Europe came to the United States. Nearly all settled in big cities, mainly on the Atlantic coast, with over half settling in New York City.[5]

The Jewish immigrants of the Great Migration were mostly poor small-town *shtetl*-dwellers; smaller numbers came from large cities such as Odessa, Russia, and Lodz, Poland (Lodz was part of Russia from 1815 until 1919 when it was returned to Poland). A few of those who came from shtetls (small Jewish Communities) and were involved at least partly in farming are pictured in *Fiddler on the Roof*. Tevye was a milkman (a small dairyman) who sang that one thing he would do when he became rich would be to fill his yard with chicks, turkeys, geese, and ducks. Most of the immigrants, however, have been celebrated in nostalgic histories like Irving Howe's *World of Our Fathers*[6] and the film *Hester Street*,[7] histories read and viewed recently by those immigrants' suburbanized grandchildren or great-grandchildren. These descendants might remember tales of rickety assembly line looms housed beneath elevated trainways, of cotton dust clouds over dimly lit sewing machines, of thimble, needle, and thread in a stooping man's hands tracing a suit of clothes around another man's form. Others might picture awls, foot-treadled leather sanders shooting leathery powder, or pushcarts of bloomers, cloth bolts, shoelaces, buttons, and pins, or candy, ice cream, and newspapers, or stacks of canned fruits and vegetables on the shelved perimeters of oiled four-inch board floors. Most would see religious books in Hebrew, caressed Yiddish newspapers, perhaps a Yiddish theater program, pianos or violins. It is a world moved intact boat by boat from I.J. Singer's mirror of Jewish Poland in the nineteenth century, *The Brothers Ashkenazi*.

New York City blended its Eastern European Jews, whether from shtetls or big cities, into an urbanized world. Immigrants from Lodz, Poland's city of weavers and hovels, were blended with a bit of Odessa, where Jews had lived well enough long enough to produce Leopold Auer's virtuoso violinists (Jascha Heifetz was one) who played just a subway ride away. Former shtetl dwellers, many of whom probably had owned a cow, some chickens, and a small garden, also merged into the new urban mass. New York was not only the main point of entry for immigrants, but it also attracted many immigrants who had entered through Philadelphia, Baltimore, and other ports. It was the special area of settlement for Jews partly because of its size and importance as a port of entry but also because of the Jewish life already existing there.

But the squalor of New York's Lower East Side was not the Golden Land dreamed of by victims of pogroms when they had packed sacks and satchels for the steerage trip to freedom. An 1888 description of Lower East Side tenements would remain an accurate description of the living conditions for many immigrants for several decades:

> They are great prison-like structures of brick, with narrow doors and windows, cramped passages and steep rickety stairs. They are built through from one street to the other with a somewhat narrower building connecting them. . . . The narrow court-yard . . . in the middle is a damp foul-smelling place, supposed to do duty as an airshaft. . . . In case of fire they would be perfect death-traps, for it would be impossible for the occupants of the crowded rooms to escape by the narrow stairways, and the flimsy fire escapes which the owners of the tenements were compelled to put up a few years ago are so laden with broken furniture, bales and boxes that they would be worse than useless. In the hot summer months . . . these fire escape balconies are used as sleeping-rooms by the poor wretches who are fortunate enough to have windows opening upon them. The drainage is horrible.[8]

Moses Rischin noted that "conditions became almost unbearable in the summer months. Bred in colder and dryer climates, tenement inhabitants writhed in the dull heat."[9] Certainly, the squalor into which ships dumped more mortality did not please those arranging the exodus; to such philanthropists as Baron Maurice de Hirsch, there was no progress in desperate souls struggling in ironically named Orchard Street's and Grand Street's tenements and dank shops, hauling and hawking needle trade piecework, steering past or slipping on street garbage, nursing or ignoring tuberculosis, fending off unending petty debt, and being reduced to begging for alms.

It was infamous Lodz all over again, except for one crucial difference. In Eastern Europe, the safety of Jews was precarious: there were pogroms against Jews, for example, because there was a Jew among the radicals who assassinated Czar Alexander II.[10] In New York after 1882, a poor immigrant Jew's life was difficult but at least predictable. Although Sephardic Jews had been prominent in the founding of Tammany Hall in 1794, a hundred years later Tammany Hall food baskets rarely appeared on Orchard Street doorsteps. By this later date, Tammany did not consider Rosh Hashanah as important as Christmas, did not respect *kashruth* (kosher requirements), and did not like the old-country clothes, alien language, and alien religion of the Eastern European Jews. No one gave these Jews patronage in the way of employment, and corporate recruiters certainly did not seek them. No affirmative action programs helped them. No charitable health agency nursed them. Nevertheless, in 1882 there was a reversal of U.S. policy that excluded Eastern European Jewish immigrants when the mayor of New York City, W.R. Grace, and at least eight other Anglo-Americans, having noted Alexander III's pogroms, echoed the German-American Jewish position that the United States would profit from Alexander's victims. Thousands like them issued from Ellis Island weekly.

Almost none of the Eastern European Jews enjoyed the small reliance comforting poor Italians then arriving. Italy would take back any Italians who were rejected at the island, who were homesick for people or places, who were disappointed in the new land, or who wanted to return "home" once they had saved enough from their labors in America to ensure a better life for themselves in Italy. There was no special peril to Italians repatriated, and about a third returned. Members of most other immigrant groups could and did return to the Old Country. It was otherwise for the Russian Jews whose return to Czarist Russia was as unlikely as a return to Pharaoh's Egypt after Moses' Exodus.

The need to survive forced immigrants to apply immediately whatever skills they had instead of taking time to learn new ones. Lodz and its counterparts bred needlecrafters, and a flood of them filled New York. Many went into the garment industry, but what they had done in Eastern Europe was not important. What was important was to survive. As Stephen M. Berk noted, "They were 'greenhorns' desperate to do anything to survive, and as a result were frequently exploited by Jew and Gentile alike. The immigrants entered into a variety of occupations. They labored in factories, producing cigars, shirts and other clothing, and worked at anything having to do with the garment industry. Some were self-employed tailors working in cramped apartments under contract to small manufacturers."[11]

About three-fourths of the immigrants worked in shops and factories, mostly in the garment industry.[12] So many women, men, and children came so fast, all needlewise and belly hollow, that the Iron Law of Wages began claiming their bodies. They were victims of industrialization as much as if they had run the Manchester looms that the English poet William Blake had termed "dark Satanic mills" a century earlier. They were victimized in America as much as they had been in Lodz when Alexander was assassinated, when modernizing competition and alien workers made kopeks in a worker's home scarcer, and when pogroms cheapened life even more. But there were crucial differences between Russia and the United States, for although there were anti-Semitic incidents in the United States, there were no pogroms—and there was hope for change.

America's homesteading provided a valve for some European victims, but most would not or could not homestead. For nearly all Jewish immigrants, liberation did not rest in owning land and working it. Most Jews wanted a trade: as Gerald Sorin observed, "It is certainly true that the Jews, denied purchase of land and proscribed from participating in a variety of occupations and fields, had worked in trades for generations and came to believe that a *'melokhe iz a malkhes'* (a trade is a kingdom)."[13]

If the Jewish immigrants could not succeed at a trade, then wages—not farming—were next in preference. Wages meant freedom. Wages got what land produced, and to get more of what land made meant simply getting higher wages and shorter hours. And so they stuck with factory work, striving to better their circumstances collectively through strikes, parliamentary participation, and social revolutions. When the first boatload of pogrom victims arrived in New York in 1882, they were led immediately to scab against the striking Irish longshoremen but quit when Am Olam members explained to them in Yiddish that they were indeed scabbing. (Am Olam, "The Eternal People," was a society founded in Russia in 1881 to establish agricultural colonies in the

United States.) As the socialist Abraham Cahan wrote, "This was the only time when Jewish laborers threatened to come in serious conflict with the cause of American workingmen."[14] Many of the Jews then joined the Irish workers in street demonstrations. This collaboration is considered to be part of the beginning of the Jewish immigrants' participation in working class struggles.[15] The history of the organization of the needle trades, with unionization and fights to improve their conditions, accurately reflects the direction of the Jewish immigrants' efforts to improve their labor conditions.

But the notion of American Jews as urbanites and professionals whose immigrant ancestors were peddlers, shopkeepers, and garment workers is only partly accurate. There were a few disheartened Jews who dreamed of haystacks and cows. For those dreamers, translating even the vision of the dream into an American setting was almost as remote as their picturing colonial Sephardim in their mansions in Newport and Charleston.

The Eastern European Jews did not enter an area with no history of Jewish farming. There had been some Jewish farming in the Americas, including the United States, from the earliest period of European settlement. In the century preceding the Great Migration from Eastern Europe, a significant minority of Eastern European Jews had tried farming with mixed success. Moreover, during the time of the migration there were Jewish agencies that actively encouraged Jews to become farmers, partly to escape the sweltering cities and partly to counter popular perceptions of immigrant Jews as "parasites."

The farmer version of the American Jewish success story has been ignored in standard academic visions, in Hollywood movies, and even in myths. That is unfortunate, for we miss the tale of a leap from the Middle Ages to the twentieth century, apparently accomplished, according to popular thought, in several weeks of a steerage boat trip. That tale is a kind of parable speaking to all without means and despised but determined to prosper, those who can, with wit and some help, succeed.[16]

In the remainder of this chapter, we will review the history of Jewish farming in the Americas, Jewish farming in Eastern Europe in the century before the Great Migration, and organized efforts to encourage Jewish farming. Then we will begin our history of the area that had the largest concentration of Jewish farmers in the United States—the Catskills area of New York state.

Jewish Farming in the Americas

By the mid-1600s, there were Jewish farmers in Latin America and the Caribbean. In 1644, some Jews from Brazil went to Surinam, where other Jews had already settled, and colonized what later was known as the Joden Savanne. Jewish colonies were also founded in this time period in neighboring Cayenne and in Guiana and Curaçao. There are indications that a shipload of Jews came from Morocco to Guiana around 1659, and 153 Italian Jews came in 1661. Many of the Jewish settlers were farmers or planters and are credited with introducing indigo and sugar in these areas. Jewish farming colonies also existed in Tobago, French Martinique, and Guadeloupe. These Jews did not come from the shtetls and ghettos of Eastern Europe but from Spain and Portugal, where they had been integrated into the larger culture before the Inquisition. In 1654, when the Portuguese finally began to enforce the Inquisition in the New World, Jews in the Portuguese colony of Brazil went into exile again. Some went to Guiana, Surinam, and adjacent islands where some of them founded agricultural settlements.[17]

In fact the first Jewish settlement in the present-day United States was in New York City in 1654, made up of twenty-three Sephardic Jews escaping from the Inquisition in Brazil. They settled in the small Dutch town, then called Nieuw Amsterdam. Undoubtedly some of them raised a few small animals and garden items for themselves, but unlike many of the other Portuguese Jews they did not enter farming.[18] In 1687, Jacob and David Robles came to New York from France with "some necessarys for husbandry [and] designe to plant and settle here." Robles is a well-known surname of Spanish and French Jews, but some scholars suggest that by the time Jacob and David came to the United States this Robles family was French Huguenot rather than Sephardic.[19] One of the next references to individual Jewish farmers in the United States is to Mordecai Nathan and Simon Valentine who jointly owned a farm in Charleston, South Carolina, in the early 1700s.[20]

Individual Jewish farmers were not infrequent, and some had sizeable farms. As early as 1726, Moses Levy farmed seventy acres in Rye, New York, and by 1733 Abraham de Lyon was cultivating Porto and Malaga grapes on his Georgia plantation. In 1769, Mordecai Moses Mordecai, the son of a Lithuanian rabbi, joined the rush to the virgin land west of Lancaster, Pennsylvania, becoming the first Jew to farm in what was then called the West.[21] In 1774, Francis Salvador was sent by his uncle and father-in-law, Joseph Salvador, to inspect Joseph's 100,000 acres in South Carolina, in an area that later became known as "Jews' Lands." The Salvadors were members of a prominent Portuguese Jewish family originally named Jessurun Rodrigues (Salvador probably was the converso name). Francis, "the former London dandy, discarded his fine clothes for the homespun shirt and leather jerkin of the Carolinian men of the soil."[22]

David Hays was a farmer in Westchester County, New York, before the American Revolution. During the war, David and his brother Benjamin "herded their livestock from their Westchester County farm in Bedford, northeast of New York City, through English lines to reach the Continentals."[23] In the 1780s, Benjamin Monsanto, who could speak French, Spanish, and English, was a prestigious planter in Natchez, Mississippi.[24] In the Richmond, Virginia, area, brothers Moses Núñez Cardozo and Abraham Núñez Cardozo owned sizeable farms by the 1790s.[25] In the early 1800s, Ezekiel Block acquired a plantation near Cape Girardeau, Missouri.[26] In 1827, Jacob Bodenheimer, from Germany, cleared a farm, opened a country store, and operated a ferry in Moscow Landing, Louisiana.[27]

In 1783, a German Jew proposed a Jewish farm-colony in the United States and wrote a letter to George Washington requesting a grant of land to provide for two thousand families.[28] Nothing came of this request, and Jewish farming remained an individual undertaking in the United States for decades longer. In 1819, William Davis Robinson, a Christian American then living in London, wrote a pamphlet asking wealthy European Jews to invest funds to buy a large tract of land on the upper Mississippi and Missouri rivers for Jewish settlement. Robinson's plan failed. The Society to Meliorate the Condition of the Jews attracted a large following in the early 1820s and bought large farms near Harrison in Westchester County, New York, and New Paltz in Ulster County, New York. However, the leader of the society was a former Jew who had become a Christian missionary, and this caused alarm among potential Jewish recruits.[29]

The best known of the early Jewish settlement plans was Ararat, proposed by Major Mordecai Manuel Noah. In 1820, Noah, later an ambassador, thought of settling Jews on 17,000 acres of land on a Niagara River island. He laid the cornerstone in 1825 but could not persuade Jews to settle there. Eastern European Jews were then enjoying somewhat improving circumstances; the potential for recruitment was reduced, the plan rendered unnecessary.[30]

At the same time that Noah began his plan, Moses Elias Levy, born in Morocco where his Spanish-Jewish family had sought refuge from the Inquisition, began acquiring land for a Jewish settlement in Micanopy (near present-day Gainesville), Alachua County, Florida. He eventually acquired a total of 59,000 acres in different parts of Florida. According to Henry Green and Marcia Zerivitz, Levy's "intent was to establish a Jewish colony as a safe haven for refugee Jewish families. Levy's European travels had made him keenly aware of the contrast between the freedoms enjoyed by American Jews and the hardships of their European brethren."[31] Foreshadowing the migration of Jews from New York to Florida over a century later, between 1820 and 1823 Levy settled seventy families from New York and New Jersey. On New Pilgrimage, his plantation, which resembled kibbutzim later established in Israel, all the farmers worked the land and studied Hebrew. Although not yet as well known as Ararat, New Pilgrimage appears to be the first actual Jewish farming settlement in the United States. But the hot climate and disease caused it to fail. Levy's dream also failed with his son (who changed his name to David Levy Yulee to honor his Sephardic ancestry): Although his father had been an abolitionist, David became a slaveowner. He was the first U.S. senator from Florida and later a member of the Confederate cabinet.[32]

Other organized efforts at Jewish farming continued, all unsuccessful. In 1837, the Association Zeire Hazon (Tender Sheep) of New York City, most of whose members were recent arrivals from Germany, tried to obtain funding to establish a farming colony on the western prairies. But a major crop failure in 1835 and the Panic of 1837 doomed this hope.[33]

In 1837 some New York City German Jews formed a commune based on the popular Owenite plan in the Catskills, the same area that nearly a century later would have the most concentrated settlement of Jewish farmers in the United States. The commune was named Sholom (peace) (and changed to "Sholam" by the census takers of the Ulster and Sullivan counties). Sholam is believed to have been founded when Moses Cohen led thirteen families to individual farms, beginning in 1837. In December 1837, 484 acres, in parcels ranging from 20.7 to 70.5 acres, and eleven lots in the area were sold by Edmund Bruyn to William N. Polak, Marcus Van Gelderen, Elias Rodman, Benedict Cohen, Jonas Solomon, Edward May, Zion Berenstein, Solomon Samelson, Ignatz Newman, Joseph Davies, and Moses Cohen. Polak immediately sold his to Moses Content, and three years later Charles S. Saroni bought 187 acres.

The settlers in Sholam apparently realized the futility of depending solely upon farming. They manufactured goose quill pens and fur caps and became cobblers, peddlers, and tailors. Working in the local tanning factory greatly supplemented their incomes, and the tannery's closing around 1842 contributed significantly to the economic failure of nine of Sholam's families by 1842. The 1840 census shows as heads of households only Elias Rodman (with a total of eight people in his household), Joseph Davies (by himself), Moses Cohen (with a household of seven), and Charles Saroni (with a household of eight). Four other apparently Jewish households were in the immediate area.[34]

A communal character for Sholam has been inferred from a pattern of stone piers remaining on the site that indicates construction of a hall more than sufficient for housing and feeding the families. It is supposed that when the building burned, the families were left with no other housing and departed. At least one of its members appears to have settled by 1855 in the largest community then nearby, the busy canal town of Ellenville, which several decades later would become an important center of Jewish farming.[35] Records indicate that after the Sholam fire most nineteenth-century Jews in and around Ellenville did not farm. Like most of their kin who began to arrive in upstate New York in the mid-1800s from Germany, England, and later Russia, they peddled and cobbled throughout the Catskill area, even in spots as remote as Sholam.[36]

As the last few remaining Jews struggled in Sholam, in 1843 a group of New York Jews started a farm settlement in Cook County, Illinois. But because they were so close to rapidly expanding Chicago, they soon melted into the nonfarming community. Also in 1843, Rabbi Isaac Leeser began publishing the first Jewish monthly magazine in the United States, *The Occident,* and in it he encouraged Jewish agricultural colonization. He published an article by a Philadelphia businessman suggesting a grandiose plan to settle Jews in a western territory in such numbers that a state might even be formed, enabling these Jewish farmers to have their own legislature. Other Jewish publications also encouraged Jewish farm colonization, and in 1855 the American Hebrew Agricultural and Horticultural Association was formed in New York. These inducements did not lead to any settlements; "all the meetings and calls and pronouncements were paper talk and paper plans, and no actual farm settlement resulted."[37] There were too few Jews in the United States to support a mass agricultural colonization, and the masses had not yet begun to come from Eastern Europe.[38]

Jewish Farming in Eastern Europe

Although most of the Eastern European Jewish immigrants who came to the United States during the Great Migration were not farmers, they came from areas that had a history of Jewish farming. In 1799 Russia began to consider legislation to get interested Jews into farming colonies to help alleviate the famine in White Russia. In 1802, Alexander I appointed a commission, and in 1804 the czar announced an "Enactment Concerning the Jews" that grouped Jews into five occupational groups, including agriculturists. As a result of this enactment, two years later the first seven Jewish agricultural colonies were founded in southern Russia. The land was more suited to cattle breeding than to small-scale farming, the settlers did not have enough money, tools, and supplies to farm properly, and the government did not give sufficient up-to-date training and funds. Despite these problems, 1,690 Jewish families had been settled in the colonies by 1810, and in 1819 a government inspector reported favorably on the colonies.

Governmental support continued to be uneven and unpredictable in the following decades, but by 1865 there were thirty-seven Jewish farming colonies in Russia, totaling 32,943 people. The May Laws of 1882 sent at least 50,000 Jews from villages into towns and slowed the development of Jewish agriculture, but the colonies were exempted from the May Laws. Natural growth and some changes in policies continued to increase the number of Jewish farmers. According to Herman Rosenthal, a major writer on Jewish farming in Eastern Europe who also led an Am Olam settlement in Sicily Island, Louisiana, in 1882, by 1901 there were more than 100,000 Jewish agriculturists in Russia. Leonard Robinson observed in 1912 that the 1897 census of Russia cited "the number of Jews engaged in agricultural pursuits as 40,611, and the number of souls dependent upon them for support as over 150,000, making the Jewish farming population in Russia approximately 200,000."[39] About 60,000 of the Jewish farmers were settled in 170 colonies, and the others cultivated their own farms.

In addition to the farming colonies in Russia, there were Jewish farmers, including some who managed farms for absentee Christian landlords.[40] In southern Russia many Jews worked on Christian estates, and there were "hundreds of flourishing farms which [were] owned and worked by Jews, although, owing to their legal disabilities, the titles [were] fictitiously held by Christians."[41] Jews also managed large farm operations, leased from Christians or operated for them, that were actually worked by Christian peasants. These large farm operations demonstrated the Eastern European Jew's ability to manage serious farm enterprises, a talent the Christian West might have admired but for the delicate issue of the identity of the exploiters and the exploited. Since the Middle Ages, Christian Europe had not found fault with Christians exploiting Christian peasants, but it recoiled from Jews exploiting Christian peasants. Despite the fact that many Jews farmed, most Russians and Poles still accepted the popular belief that Jews were parasites unwilling and unable to wrest their living from the land with their own hands. (In fact if they had cared to look they would have seen those Jewish hands also working in basic city and shtetl trades, including carpentry and blacksmithing, in addition to farming.)

Rosenthal further concluded that Jewish farms in Russia were just as productive as Christian farms and would have succeeded better if the government had not failed to provide support, as they did for Christian farmers.[42] The noted writer Moses Rischin vividly described the czar's plans to colonize Jewish farmers, noting that the plans "proved unrealistic and went unsustained. Eager Jews, cherishing visions of the redemptive fig tree and vine, were induced to apply antiquated methods to land situated amid desolate steppes, remote from main roads and rivers. Freshly fashioned Jewish peasants lacking marketing facilities, and proper tutelage, faced malnutrition, ruin, and death. Those who survived were without the promised seed corn, cattle, implements, or dwellings, while the land remained unallotted and unsurveyed."[43]

Russia did have considerable numbers of Jews who, prior to the 1881 assassination of Czar Alexander II, had studied secular subjects in Russian universities, taken Russian names, and considered themselves assimilated Russians in all matters but faith. This assimilation was the result of the policy of Nicholas I, emperor from 1825 to 1855, which induced Jews to adopt the westernized Russian lifestyle in the hope of converting them to Russian Christian Orthodoxy, or at least of making those Jews secularized in words and deeds in the style of the Enlightenment German Jew Moses Mendelsohn. A Russian Jewish upper class, or at least a professional class, had developed fairly quickly then, prospering in Alexander II's more liberal reign from 1855 to 1881. While Jews were first forced to take Russian first names, they continued that naming practice quite willingly, especially those with any pretensions of enlightenment. They accepted the empirical sciences, practiced the arts and professions as did Christians, and wore the clothes Christians wore, but they retained their religion.[44] Although the schools and universities were centers of radicalism, their radicalism coexisted with an identity with Jewish culture.[45]

Russia might have seen a major success of Jewish agricultural colonizing if Alexander II had lived. After he was assassinated in 1881, his son, Alexander III, ascended the throne, ruling in absolutism from 1881 to 1894. Because a few Jews had been involved in his father's assassination, he severely persecuted the Jews. If the colonies had been successful, there might have been no need for relief from the hard life and Western anti-Semitism, the two major impulses for Jewish leaders' encouragement of Jewish emigration. On the other hand, if the colonies had been successful in their socialism, Western propriety might have seen Jewish communists in anything but white shirts and ties. But thanks to Alexander III, the Jews in the farming colonies, like other Jews in Russia, began to consider other alternatives. Many educated Russian Jews did oppose emigration, believing that Jews could and should acculturate into the Russian society.[46]

Particularly after the pogroms of the early 1880s, however, two major movements—Bilu and Am Olam—developed in Russia to encourage emigration. Both included agricultural activities as part of their programs, Bilu to a small degree and Am Olam to a major degree. Bilu was founded to encourage emigration to Palestine, where Jews would establish a society with Jews in all occupations, including farming.

Am Olam was founded in Odessa in 1881 by two utopian idealists, Mania Bakl and Moses Herder. It called for the settling of Jews on socialist communal farms in the United States.[47] A member of the movement stated its goal: "Our motto is a return to agriculture, and our aim the physical and spiritual rehabilitation of our people. In free America, where many people live closely in peace and amity, we Jews, too, shall find a place to lay our heads; we shall demonstrate to the world that we are capable of manual labor."[48] In November 1881, Am Olam sent a first small contingent to the United States.

But even if Alexander III's pogroms had not occurred, efforts and funds to resettle Jews outside of Russia might have come to pass nonetheless because even during good times the majority of Russian Jews remained poor and unassimilated to Russian secularism. They were unappealing emigrants. No matter how they farmed, those Eastern European farming Jews still spoke strangely, dressed strangely, and acted strangely as far as the West was concerned. Farming usually prevailed over traditional clothing because caftans and felt hats seldom survived behind moldboards or under hay-laden pitchforks. But even farmers and Russo-Polish Jewish socialists who abandoned "Jewish" clothing and daily religious rituals did not adopt Western dress or Christianity; they adopted Russian-Polish working-class Christians' manner of dress and still spoke Yiddish with gestures.[49]

As one response to the bad conditions of Jews in Eastern Europe, the Alliance Israelite Universelle (formed by French Jews in 1860 to improve the conditions of Jews throughout the world) had as one of its goals the removal of Eastern Europe's impoverished shtetl and ghetto Jews to farms all over the world. Adolphe Crémieux, one of the founders of the Alliance, was primarily in charge. He wrote in December 1869 that "it appears that the destitution of the Jews arises from ancient and deep rooted causes . . . a complete code of restrictive laws has reduced to nothing all means of existence."[50] In effect, the Alliance and Crémieux addressed genteel Europe's "Jewish problem," realizing that much of the problem resulted from the anti-Semitic stereotypes about Eastern European Jews. Crémieux and other nineteenth-century Jewish leaders had a vision of an Emersonian Jew, self-reliant thanks to his own versatile hands. They increasingly recognized that the anti-Semitism of Eastern Europe was too strong to be changed easily, and they did not see Bilu or Am Olam as the answer for the masses of Eastern European Jews.

Organized Jewish Farm Settlements in the United States

When Am Olam was founded in 1881 with the specific goal of establishing Jewish farming communes in the United States, it received an immediate positive response in a number of Russian cities. A first contingent of seventy craftsmen, artisans, and students left for the United States in the spring of 1881. Parts of the Jewish community in the United States also encouraged the communes. The *American Israelite* wrote in 1882: "Send us funds and you will be astonished how fast we will settle on government land every able bodied Russian immigrant. We think that the long deferred project of teaching our people agricultural pursuits can now be speedily realized and the problem [of] what to do with the Russian Jew can at once be solved."[51]

Additional Am Olam groups brought the total idealists to several hundred people, but many of the immigrants never got beyond New York City. Only four colonies were eventually established, and all four lasted only a short time. Sicily Island, Louisiana, was founded in 1882 by thirty-two families but was soon abandoned because of flooding by the Mississippi River. Two communes, Crimea and Bethlehem Judea, were established in South Dakota in 1882, but both ended in 1885 because of debt and other difficulties. New Odessa, near Portland, Oregon, was founded in 1882 by seventy people. It was the most successful but lasted only until 1887.[52]

These potential Jewish farmers worked hard, but larger forces were too strong. Most of the settlers had no experience in farming and missed aspects of organized Jewish life. Stephen M. Burke noted that "their spirits were undermined because many of the farmers were urban people who missed the hustle and bustle and the intellectual vitality of large cities. For the religious among them, there was the additional problem of being deprived of the friendship and services that could only be provided by the religious institutions of a large Jewish community."[53] The fervency of their ideology, which had been a motivation for their settlements, also led to ideological battles and an unwillingness to compromise. But the major reason for failure was bad locations of the farms, far from markets.

Even a major founder of the Am Olam movement in the United States, Alexander Harkavy, did not last long in farming. His experience was typical of many others. After becoming tired of waiting in New York City for his Am Olam group to settle on its own commune, he decided to work on a farm in Pawling, New York, on the opposite side of the Hudson River from the Catskills. His problems began as soon as he arrived in Pawling:

> At the railroad station, where Harkavy met his employer, he was promptly taken to lunch at the station cafeteria. Not desiring to eat any pork, Harkavy, exercising his almost nonexistent English, pointed to the word on the menu that he believed was for an egg. When the waiter returned, it was with eggnog. . . . Harkavy soon found his strength ebbing and the work becoming loathsome. The beautiful vision of farm life that had so ex-

cited him in New York and Russia, and which had sustained him for two weeks on the farm in Pawling, New York, soon evaporated. He left the farm a month after he arrived; because he did not have much money—the farmer only paid him half his twelve-dollar monthly salary—he walked the whole eighty miles to New York City.[54]

Other Jewish farming settlements were started, such as the Montefiore Agricultural Society, which was established in 1882 by Michael Heilprin and encouraged Jewish farming settlements. In addition to the Am Olam farming communes, organized Jewish farming settlements were established at Cremieux, South Dakota; Cotopaxi, Colorado; Painted Woods, Dakota Territory; Beersheba Colony, Kansas; and three locations in New Jersey—Alliance, Carmel, and Rosenhayn. Except for the New Jersey areas, all of these settlements also failed, primarily because of isolated locations and forces of nature. Alliance was founded in honor of the Alliance Israelite, Rosenhayn was supported by the Hebrew Emigrant Aid Society, and Carmel was supported by Michael Heilprin. Because of their location and support, these colonies were able to last until 1891 when the Baron de Hirsch Fund started helping Jewish farm settlements in the United States.[55]

While some of these settlements were part of the Am Olam movements and others received organizational support, stronger support—for settlements and for individuals—would be received from the philanthropy of Baron Maurice de Hirsch. Hirsch, born in 1831 in Munich, scion of an old and prominent German-Jewish family, was one of the greatest philanthropists of his time. In the words of Judith Elkin, he believed that "what was needed was to wean Jews away from urban occupations and intellectual preoccupations and get them back on the land."[56] Not really a Rousseauistic romantic, Hirsch, like those around him, nourished a preindustrial vision of property. To them, working one's own land was certain freedom, something analogous to the freedom of a German *landgraff*, a barony in miniature, ownership conferring self-respect, an occupation generative of health and hospitable to virtue. Given the sights of Lodz and later of Orchard Street, the idea made sense despite its having originated from a kind of patronization and despite the fact that the Jewish farmers in Hirsch colonies did not always own their own land.

Beginning in the 1870s, Hirsch began giving large sums of money to the Alliance for its work in European Turkey. But, recognizing that Jews were even worse off in Eastern Europe, in 1885 Hirsch turned his primary attention to Russia. At first, Hirsch helped to improve condi-

Baron Maurice de Hirsch, ca. 1880.

tions for Jews in Russia, but recognizing a general abuse of the Jews by the Russian government, he became convinced that emigration was the only answer.[57] He believed that agriculture presented the best hope for Jews, and, accordingly, in 1891 he founded the Jewish Colonization Association. Hirsch wrote that "in the lands where Jews have been permitted to acquire landed property, where they have found opportunity to devote themselves to agriculture, they have proved themselves excellent farmers."[58]

Hirsch continued the work Crémieux could not afford, becoming more active as Crémieux became less so. Between 1890 and 1917,

Hirsch funded most Jewish settlement on farms. Hirsch sent agents to investigate the farming situation in various American countries and concluded that Argentina was the best place to establish farming colonies. He purchased 62,000 acres (97 square miles) in Argentina. Jews sent there fared badly for the same reasons that plagued both Jews and Christians homesteading in North Dakota: they had no cash, no credit, no way to pay the high freight charges to and from the depots, and no decent wagons, horses, implements, or barns to bring down unit costs.

The settlement in Argentina also fared badly because of conflict between the Jewish Colonization Association and the settlers. The settlers argued that they should become legal owners of their homesteads after they had paid the cost of the farms. The Jewish Colonization Association feared that private property would frustrate the colonization plan and that independent colonists would be alienated from a communal perspective. The battle was bitter and raged for years.[59] In Argentina, the colonization pattern combined the U.S. homestead system with Europe's village system.[60] Palestine, of course, was the other site settled by idealistic Eastern European Jews bent on farming. Colonies there evolved quickly as kibbutzim, similar both to the collective living characterizing the south Russian colonies and to social organization in Birobidzhan. Bilu had been encouraging settlement in Palestine since the early 1880s and was part of the foundation of modern Zionism. Large numbers of Jews would begin returning to Israel in the following decades, and Hirsch also supported settlements in Palestine, but the concept of modern Zionism had not become strong at the time Hirsch became active in Argentina.[61]

Hirsch, recognizing the large number of Russian Jews emigrating to the United States, also developed a benevolent interest in their welfare. In 1889 he offered a plan for the Baron de Hirsch Fund. Hirsch undoubtedly knew, from his investigations in different countries, about the distressed condition of late nineteenth-century U.S. agriculture. Overproduction, poor roads, high tariffs, marketing swings, credit shortages, and unregulated railroad transport fees so pressed American farmers that they formed societies to present Congress with their demands for reform. Congress acted with little alacrity on their behalf; the bankruptcy of ruined farmers was the only speedy result of farm policies prior to 1913, when Congress established an Office of Markets.[62] But, despite these problems, Hirsch proceeded with his settlement program, perhaps aware of the presence of some successful individual Jewish farmers in the Americas since the seventeenth century. He bought the promised land doctrine appealing to all of Europe, enamored, as were the countless other European settlers here, of the endless frontier, of apparently endless virgin soil. Yet in a *New York Times* article in 1890 the Baron de Hirsch Fund was quoted as saying that it was not encouraging immigration, and that it was to be distinctly understood "that the immigrants must work, and work is the American way. They will be required to give up their foreign dress and habits and to adapt themselves to surroundings which are radically different from those of their native villages."[63]

Despite these caveats, Hirsch's resettlement idea caught fire among some of the impoverished, persecuted Eastern European Jews for whom his plan was intended, and his group easily recruited a few thousand untrained Russo-Polish volunteers for farming colonies. The Industrial Removal Office, sponsored by the Baron de Hirsch Fund and B'nai B'rith, dispersed 100,000 Jews throughout the United States between 1901 and 1916. Many eventually moved to Chicago or back to eastern cities having Jewish populations.

Aggravating the difficulties of settling Jews on farms was an uncanny propensity for Jewish farmers, at least in the United States, to begin operations just prior to a significant national financial panic. In one matter, poor, immigrant Scandinavians and first-generation Americans homesteading the Dakotas had an advantage: they came from farming families. They knew what to do with the land even if fate kept them from doing it, but only a few of the Jewish homesteading families had farmed. A number of Jewish agricultural utopias were attempted from 1880 to 1910, during the years of mass migration from Eastern Europe. Numerous small colonies such as South Carolina's unfulfilled Happyville lasted only briefly, but even Long Island's relatively durable Jewish farming settlements were affected, the smaller of them being abandoned early as "God-forsaken."[64]

During the same years that these various colonies were struggling, the Galveston Movement also was active, for the seven years from 1907 to 1914. Jacob H. Schiff, Israel Zangwill, and a group of their followers abroad arranged for Jews to sail from Bremen, Germany, to Galveston, Texas, and then to settle the Midwest and West. About ten thousand Russian Jews made it to the United States under the Galveston Movement, leaving roots in more than a hundred midwestern towns (especially in Texas, Missouri, Iowa, and Minnesota).

Few of the Jews served by the Industrial Removal Office or the Galveston Movement entered farming. Even those who remained in rural areas and small towns usually went into small businesses. They lacked agricultural skills and money to invest in farms, and they did not want to be separated from Jewish communal life. The few who did try farming usually did not last. The majority were craftsmen and others were peddlers, similar to many other poor immigrants from the unindustrialized small towns in Eastern Europe, Southern Europe, and the Near East. Within a generation, most had graduated from crafts and peddling to proprietorships,[65] the common form of which was some kind of retail food or clothing store.

The Jewish farmers in those first waves went back to town, most of them bankrupt. Prepared for living off the land about as well as were the helpless London gentry settling Jamestown, Virginia, centuries earlier, the Jewish settlers were lucky to escape with their lives. They were of course significantly better off in America than in Russia, for here losers could try again without fear of being lynched in a pogrom; at the time the United States saved lynchings for others. If they had not been victims of financial panics, natural catastrophes, undercapitalization, gouging railroads, and other plagues of pioneering, the severance from their culture, especially from religious ceremony, would have caused them to quit the outland.[66] In towns and cities, Jews at least could be Jews, banding together to pray, to obtain kosher foods, and to ready their sons for Bar Mitzvah, which, under the terms of their faith, required extensive training in reading Hebrew.

On the prairie it was practically impossible for Jews to pray. Not only did they usually lack the artifacts for the holy days (scrolled Torahs, for example), but rarely could they get the requisite ten adult males to constitute a *minyan*, that is, the minimal number to enable prayer to take place in traditional Judaism. In colonies, minyans were possible, a fact that encouraged their growth. Yet whether in colonies or alone on the prairies, Jews attempting to farm in twenty states essentially failed, the ability to form minyans notwithstanding. Writing of Clarion, Utah, for example, and making a distinction between intentional communities, which were planned, and evolutionary communities such as the Catskills, which were not planned, Dubrovsky notes that "the broad outlines of the Clarion story are the same as those of the more than forty intentional farm communities attempted by Jewish immigrants across the whole of the United States in the late nineteenth and early twentieth centuries. The intentional communities all started with high hopes, went through a difficult birth, and were in trouble almost immediately."[67]

In 1900, nine years after its New York incorporation, the Baron de Hirsch Fund, like the Galveston Movement, reviewed the results of its efforts at settlement. As a result the fund reorganized as the Jewish Agricultural and Industrial Aid Society, which had the same objectives as its predecessor but which was prepared to achieve them more practically. That practicality primarily involved teaching the immigrants how to farm.

The society's plan coincided with the reform of labor conditions sweeping New York City at the time. Theodore Roosevelt's reform measures for the city took aim at the notorious needle-trade sweatshops then being worked by immigrant hands, mostly Russian Jews. The miseries of the coal mine and rank exploitation in the dark Satanic mills of Lowell and Providence certainly merited as much notice as that of New York City sweatshops, but the latter were the ones targeted by polite society. Whatever the cause for this selectivity, the Industrial Aid Society joined in the trend and tried to do some good. The propertied individuals around Hirsch were not about to endorse trade unionism or social revolution, movements consuming the energies of most Jews of the New York slum whom the society proposed to aid.

Aid as the society then saw it was both the introduction to the United States of the credit union, and the establishment of Jewish trade schools (excluding the needle trades of the sweatshops). The society also voiced approval of Rochdale cooperatives as another mutual aid device already popular among other nationalities farming the Midwest. Philanthropy of this sort did not quarrel with the basic institutions from which its wealth came; rather, it proposed making those institutions work to benefit more people. The greatest concern of the Industrial Aid Society then was training. Like many well-intentioned men who had risen economically, the prime movers of the society felt that the difference between success and failure was skill. They seem not to have been overly concerned with the grim relationship between mortgage payments and profits from the farms' production and the three deadly plagues of American farming from the post–Civil War period to World War I: monopoly pricing of supplies, monopoly control of marketing access, and radical market price swings.[68]

The Jewish Agricultural and Industrial Aid Society remained committed primarily to planting Jewish farming colonies in the United States, filling them with hundreds of sweatshop volunteers speaking a little English and ready to get along with America. The plans were not accepted positively by all segments of the country. The *New York Times* praised the extent to which the Jewish community took care of its own poor but objected to Jewish agricultural colonies. Referring to other ethnic groups that had established ethnically cohesive farming colonies, the newspaper believed that Jewish colonies "would raise up separate and segregated communities, differing from their neighbors not only in religion but in manners and customs, and presenting peculiar difficulties to the process of Americanization."[69] But to the Baron de Hirsch Fund the rescue was not only from Russia and Poland but also from the American ghetto. The fund began to plant sites closer to large cities and to create larger colonies. Thus, visiting rabbis could attend them and, at least in theory, musicians and actors could visit and thus help to develop a cultural life in the colonies sufficient to keep settlers there.

The society was not alone in its encouragement of Jewish farming. After its establishment in the United States, the Yiddish press, a strong influence in Jewish life in America, continued for several decades to urge "the Jew to become a tiller of the soil, emphasizing the fact that none of the difficulties are insurmountable and can be overcome by persistent united effort."[70] In 1909, "Bintel Brief," a "Dear Abby" type of advice column in Abraham Cahan's *Jewish Daily Forward,* answered a twenty-seven-year-old man who said that most of his friends called him an idiot for becoming a farmer. The editor responded that the debate over the relative merits of country life and city life was not new, but that "there is certainly nothing to be ashamed of in living in the lap of nature. Many people dream of becoming farmers. The cities are full of many diseases that are unheard of on farms. Tuberculosis, for instance, is a disease of the big cities. People in urban areas grow old and gray at forty, but most of the farmers are healthy and strong and live to be eighty and ninety."[71] As this example shows, "Bintel Brief" tended to exaggerate the merits of the farming life.

By the turn of the century, Jewish farmers had settled on Long Island, around Farmingdale, with New York City as a hub, and in and around Hightstown, Freehold, Farmingdale, and Toms River, all in central New Jersey, with Philadelphia as a hub.[72] With some society mortgage support, and with their cultural needs presumably met, the colonies had some chance of surviving. Accounts of the time, however, note a large turnover of colonists owing to fragile economies and lack of sufficient preparation. They tried general farming, potatoes and corn, and livestock, including milk production and poultry raising. Ducks were raised on Long Island and egg-producing chickens in New Jersey. But profit from farming generally was not high in the United States except during wartime, and the idealistic expectations of colonists and their sponsors in the society mostly were not to be fulfilled.

At the side of a cow stricken with mastitis and on which he owed the cattle dealer money, a cow that probably would "dry up" (that is, stop giving milk because her udder would be ruined by the disease), a Jewish farmer, even one making some profit, would have seen life differently than would have a society officer who had led him to the farm originally. The farmer knew that if he could land a decent job in a unionized sweatshop, he stood a better chance of accumulating some New World amenities than he did on the farm. City life was improving, the significance of which was not lost upon women in the colonies. Similar to farm women everywhere, the Jewish farm women milked cows and fed fowls by day, along with their husbands, and boiled diapers and darned socks in heavily mortgaged, ill-heated, dimly lit houses by night. Especially to the women, steam heat, a weekly paycheck, and a predictable monthly rent, emblems of life in a Brooklyn flat, looked good from Hightstown.

Histories of the New Jersey colonies agree on its hardships. Jewish farming in central New Jersey survived in part thanks to the society, but it never attracted the thousands the society had hoped it would. Neither did the Jews who tried farming there even in later years, in the postcolonizing, idealistic period, persist as long as did Jews farming equally good or worse land a few hundred miles north.[73] Jews growing potatoes and raising ducks on Long Island in the first third of the twentieth century appear to have held on to their farms longer than Jerseyites. Unlike the New Jersey Jewish farmers early in the century, Long Island Jewish farmers began as individualists out to make money in farming. They were more like the Russian Jewish farmers not connected with colonies. They expected no steam heat, music, weekly paycheck, or Yiddish theater. They knew that farming profits did not match those of, say, dressmaking, but they would risk less capital in farming than one would in a dress factory and were willing to make a lower profit accordingly.

Being near the society's Farmingdale, Long Island, farmer training school supplied skill and labor not so available to the New Jersey colonies, giving the Long Islanders another advantage. The Farmingdale training facility was a new idea among Jews. There young men from sweatshops discovered tractors, horses, silage machines, bookkeeping—in short, they discovered technology. For the immigrant needle-worker, this was a college, replete with introductions even to such arcane subjects as bacteriology. Such training fit nicely with the hopes of those coming off the boats eager to meet the twentieth century on scholarly terms, and could have substituted for the lack of Yiddish culture to be found, for example, in New York's Delancy Street and Second Avenue. The school was a kind of social presence, offering the surrounding farms its trainees and providing those farms also with knowledge when they required it. As in New Jersey, however, the ratio of those Jews farming in Long Island compared to the number of Jews in cities was small; there were several hundred households farming in both Long Island and New Jersey. Of those hundreds, about half hung on into the 1920s, supplemented by newcomers, mostly graduates of the Farmingdale and Doylestown schools, and prepared to operate businesslike farming. Long Island property development later closed the history of many of those farms; those holding out until then made capital gains from the sale of their farms.

Near Moodus and Willimantic, in central Connecticut, the society similarly settled another group of New York immigrants, initially without sufficient training. As in New Jersey and Long Island, a core stayed and actually farmed successfully, establishing institutions on which the larger settlement in the New York Catskills would depend later.[74]

The Catskills would pass all these other communities in having the largest population of Jewish farmers in the United States. The Jewish Agricultural and Industrial Aid Society, recognizing the importance of this farming community, established in late 1919 a regional office in Ellenville, in southern Ulster county near the Sullivan county line. At the time of the opening, this was its third regional office. The first had opened in Chicago in 1912; it was initially called the Western Office and later was renamed the Midwestern Office. A second had opened in Philadelphia in 1917 and closed in 1935. As the Ellenville office closed in 1945, another regional office opened in Los Angeles, and as the Chicago office closed in 1952, a new office opened briefly in Vineland, New Jersey. Altogether there were five regional offices, and the national office was in New York City.

The Ellenville office, however, was not only the center of the largest concentration of Jewish farmers in the United States. It also was located in the heart of the "Jewish Catskills," the area with the largest rural and small-town Jewish population in the United States, a result of a combination of Jewish farming and resort keeping. The Jewish farming community in the Catskills was so active that the Jewish Agricultural Society would be eclipsed by other organizations founded in the area by Jewish farmers.

Chapter 2

Settling in "The Mountains"

Jews had settled in New York state, outside of New York City, in significant numbers by the mid-1800s. In Syracuse, for example, the first Jewish congregation was started in 1839 when twelve newcomers joined the few Jewish families already there. By 1850, Utica, then a sixty-four-year-old settlement, had 140 Jews. In the same year, Rochester had almost sixty Jewish residents. But these upstate Jews were much more likely to be peddlers, merchants, or clothing "manufacturers" (who sewed in the rear of a store) than farmers. On the edge of the Catskills, in Newburgh, a Lewis Moses Gomez and his sons built a stone house around 1720 to use for trading with Indians. Around 1755, Emanuel Gonsaulus was buried in Wurtsboro in the Catskills; apparently he had died while visiting his son, a trader, there. In 1773 there was a reference to "Jacob the Jew" leasing some land, apparently in Woodstock in northern Ulster County. And in 1851, a Jewish pack-peddler named Aaron Liebenfreund was robbed and killed in Sullivan County. But these were all individuals without an organized Jewish community, and they are not documented as farmers.[1]

Definitions of the Catskills vary, and we need to define them and the "Jewish Catskills" before proceeding. The broadest definition of the Catskills, by the Temporary State Commission to Study the Catskills and by the Catskill Center for Conservation and Development, includes not only Sullivan, Ulster, Greene, and Delaware counties but also Otsego, Schoharie, and half of Albany counties. This definition is advantageous as a basis for forming a comprehensive plan for conservation and preservation, but it is so large that it distorts the physiographic boundaries of the Catskills. Scheller observed that nowadays "people

use the term [Catskills] loosely to cover virtually all the territory between the Delaware and the Hudson rivers, from the Jersey line north
nearly to Albany." Another "common consent" definition, according to
Evers, includes most of Ulster County, all of Sullivan County, except a
vaguely described southern part, and the southeastern half of Delaware
County. Clearly, people are confused about what constitutes the
boundaries. As Mitchell said, "Ask a random stranger on the streets of
Manhattan to locate the Catskills and chances are he or she will
promptly direct you to the resort nexus of Sullivan County, New York."
He noted that a flower child might think of the Catskills as being Woodstock, a cartographer might think of the Catskill Park, an uninformed
tourist might think of the Catskill Forest Preserve, and a mountain
climber might use the Temporary State Commission's broad definition.[2]

It was not until the late 1800s and early 1900s, when Sullivan
County in the lower Catskills developed an important summer resort
trade, that it was accepted as part of the legendary resort Catskills, and
it was in the mountains of Sullivan County and the southern part of
Ulster County that the largest and most successful Jewish farm settlements developed. The lower Catskills were relatively close to New York
City, an important factor in the survival of the Jewish farmers. Orange
County to the south, Greene County to the north, and Delaware
County to the west also had a smaller number of Jewish farmers. But
Sullivan and Ulster counties comprised the area that later would be referred to by some as "the Jewish Catskills." In fact by the 1920s Jewish resort owners in Green County were accusing Sullivan County of
having stolen "the Catskill Mountains" trademark.[3] It was mostly in
southern Ulster and Sullivan counties that "Jewish shop workers and
small store keepers from the city wended their way for a whiff of fresh
air, and in the meantime began transforming a poor, run-down agricultural area into flourishing, prosperous Jewish resort and farming
communities."[4]

When they started coming, the Catskill area already had many
Christian farmers, and the upper Catskills had a number of resorts.
Farming had been a major activity from the earliest days of settlement
by the Dutch, expanding on a base developed by local Native Americans. Christian summer resorts in the upper Catskills had begun in the
early 1800s, when the first major resort hotel was built in 1823 in
Haines Falls.[5] Greene County, the northern part of Ulster County, and
a northeastern tip of Delaware County had developed fame as the

Catskill resort area by the 1840s. These resorts served New York City Christians who came up by boat to Kingston and then went by stage-coach to their destinations, mostly in Ulster County. The more presti-gious older resorts in Greene and northern Ulster counties catered pri-marily to the Protestant aristocracy, and immigrants—mostly German or Irish in the earlier years—were unwelcome.

Both farming and operating resorts profited from and expanded with the building of railroads in the upper and lower Catskills in the robber baron era.[6] In the lower Catskills, the railroad began as the Midland, planned five years after the Civil War to compete with the New York Central's New York to Chicago line. By 1870, the Midland ran its track from downtown New York City to the Catskill foothills, in Summitville, near a juncture of Sullivan and Ulster counties. It then branched into two lines, one from Summitville to Ellenville, paralleling the old and then-functioning Delaware and Hudson Canal. The other line, open-ing a little later, snaked through Sullivan County's high passes and ravines—what really amounted to a wilderness, a kind of frontier—breaking out into New York's central plateau and the Finger Lakes. This line was planned by its promoters to terminate in Chicago.[7]

Although the Midland never got out of New York State and never ri-valed the New York Central, it was significant both as the world's first milk line and as a developer and mainstay of summer resorts. It opened a frontier that, after less than a quarter of a century of development, would become the most populous and the most successful of the Jew-ish farming efforts in the country. With an eye on the benefits to its fu-ture fares and freight revenues, the Midland offered almost from its be-ginning free freight for building materials from the city to any station on its line where one wished to build a summer resort or a farm.[8] The El-lenville branch went through an area long built up because of its prox-imity to the old colonial highway (now U.S. Highway 209) and the canal and thus had less need for promotional offers.[9] Some resorts, several quite posh and frequented by New York society, had operated in the El-lenville area before the railroad, but none served Jews. Wood was the predominant building material, and nearly all at one time or another were damaged by fire before being rebuilt and later bought by Jews.

The branch of the train route through Sullivan County led through rural areas that until then had been populated thinly by tanners who were stripping hemlock for the only known source of tannin and were building a leather trade connected by stagecoach and a turnpike to the outer world.[10] Centreville (later renamed Woodridge), Sandburg (later renamed Mountaindale), Liberty, Liberty Falls (later renamed Ferndale), Luzon Station (later renamed Hurleyville), Pleasant Lake (later renamed Kiamesha Lake), Loch Sheldrake, Livingston Manor, and Parksville were the Midland Railroad's principal Sullivan County stops, and near them the presence of the railroad led to growth in these locations.

Those farmhouses benefited that offered summer board for New York City guests arriving and departing by Midland (and subsequently by Midland's successor, the Ontario and Western). The development of the summer boarding business on a large scale would not have been possible without the railroad. Farmers and boardinghouse keepers encouraged the railroad to provide even more transportation. Speaking of Woodridge, for example, Erna Elliott noted that "the railroad was cooperative. It offered weekend round-trip specials. Often the service was inadequate and the village board repeatedly petitioned for additional trains."[11]

The fully fledged resort hotel, offering board and some entertainment, also benefited. Fishing and hunting were major features at the farmhouses, and parasoled lawn parties were held at the best of the hotels. Wakefield's old photographs tell their stories in the splendid ladies and gentlemen pictured on a Centreville train platform. Those catered to at these resort hotels were largely Wall Street's and Tammany Hall's most powerful men, and at the farmhouses those operatives' subordinates.[12] The latter must have fished for pleasure, because the period's boardinghouse advertisements feature fishing for recreation. As early as the 1830s, Sullivan County was famous for the fishing in its streams and lakes, and fishing would remain its major attraction for decades.[13]

New York's Christian (primarily Protestant) semiaristocracy, which had vacationed in the Catskills for decades before the advent of railroads, engaged in recreations other than fishing. They watered at the great resorts of the period such as Lackawack House, Yama Farms Inn, and Mt. Meenahga, all near Ellenville, and all of which could be traced to the stagecoach and Delaware and Hudson Canal eras. These remained Christian resorts well into the twentieth century but, like Bloomingburg's Sha-Wanga Lodge which came with the Midland, they were sold to Jews and became Jewish resorts in the 1920s. It was poetic justice that the Dan family, Jewish purchasers of the Sha-Wanga, had brochures printed that were identical to those their Christian predecessors had used except that they replaced "No Hebrews Accommodated" with "Kosher Cuisine Featured."[14] Victorian elegance characterized hotel pleasures: cigars, bustles, parasols, oysters, and, of course, the ubiquitous local staples feeding both social classes: dairy products, produce, and, in some cases, game. In addition to fishing, hayrides entertained the boarders. And, to the extent that the Midland's and the Ontario and Western's "Summer Homes" listings of churches actually represent that their boarders participated in religious events, some went by buggy to Sunday church services in a nearby town.[15] Midland's publication, "Summer Homes," appeared first in 1878 as part of its effort to promote the resort business it subsidized through free transport of building material and free stocking of trout streams. Photos and snippets from local newspapers, added to extracts from "Summer Homes," chronicle customs and dimensions of that Catskill resort business.

Jews entered this Christian world of farms and summer resorts as early as 1892 in the person of Yana "John" Gerson, recognized by the society as the first Jewish farmer in the area.[16] He was born in a village near Vilna, Lithuania (then Russia), in 1854. In 1873, he married Annie Griff. He migrated to the United States in 1888 when he was thirty-four years old, leaving behind his wife, their two sons, Elias, about thirteen, and Benjamin, nine, and their two daughters, Esther, four, and Rebecca, one. Two years later, in 1890, the two sons joined their father. Annie and the two daughters migrated a year later. According to the family's oral history, the Gerson family lived on Ludlow Street on the Lower East Side and for a while had a farm on Pitkin Avenue in Brooklyn. In the United States, Yana became "John" and Elias became "Alex."[17]

By 1892, the Gerson family was in Glen Wild, near Woodridge, in Sullivan County. They began with an abandoned farm and built a boardinghouse and a successful dairying operation. Abe Jaffe, with his father and later with his brother, farmed property across the road from what he describes as the old Gerson place. According to Jaffe, the Gerson boardinghouse of tiny rooms and two porches burned in 1925. Today, a small section of a dam walling and a few concrete steps remain, next to a small stream. Like their Christian neighbors, the Gersons produced the area's specialty, iced fresh milk for New York City. The Midland was the first railroad to move bulk milk, drawing it initially from old, established farms along its Bloomingburg to Middletown run, where a farmer in 1871 put ice in a can of milk, shipping it on a pas-

Site of the John Gerson farm, Glen Wild, 1990. The dammed-up stream offered swimming for boarders.

senger train. Shortly thereafter the Midland built a business of shipping iced milk, moving 900 cans (presumably of 20 gallons each) a day from Liberty to Middletown and then to New York City. Soon afterwards, the Midland built creameries to buy, pasteurize, and separate milk at most stations along its main tracks on both the Ellenville and Oswego branches. Gerson probably dealt with the Liberty creamery on the Oswego branch. Bankrupted by the Panic of 1873, the Midland curtailed the milk operation, but the dairy farms and their Catskill towns were so dependent upon the milk operation that one town, Ellenville, in 1877 raised a significant tax of $1,000 to give to the railroad in an effort to restore their service and hence their milk deliveries. The milk operation resumed and was flourishing by 1892.[18]

Not only was Gerson considered the first Jewish farmer in the area, but in 1899 he published one of the first advertisements for a "Jewish Boarding House." His advertisement, which appeared in "Summer Homes" in 1899, said: "J. GERSON—Rock Hill Jewish Boarding House. 5 miles; accommodate 40; adults $6, children $3; transients $1; discount to season guests; transportation free; new house, newly furnished; prepare our own meats; raise our own vegetables; scenery unsurpassed. Jewish faith and customs throughout; 1/4 mile from Post Office; good road to station; fine shade; good airy rooms."[19]

The Gerson household history illustrates a typical Jewish Catskill family combining farming and boarding. When the 1900 census was taken, John was forty-six years old; his wife, Annie, was forty-five; their two sons, Alex and Benjamin, were twenty-three and twenty-one, respectively; and their two daughters, Esther and Rebecca, were sixteen and thirteen, respectively. Alex was listed as having been married three years. Also in the household was Emma Gerson, aged twenty-eight, listed as John's sister-in-law. John's four nieces—Ettie, eight, Celia, six, Sarah, three, and Fannie, one—and a nephew, Nathan, three, also were in the household, although the census indicated that no more than three of the five children were children of Emma the younger. Bringing the household to a total of fourteen were Ida and Abram Block, listed as "servants." Emma the younger and the Blocks were born in Russia, and the five children were born in New York. Emma came to the United States in 1892, and the Blocks had come only the year before, in 1899. With fourteen people in the household, at least John and Annie Gerson had help on the farm and in the boardinghouse. John Gerson later moved to Fallsburg, and in partnership with family members operated a boardinghouse, the "New Prospect." John later lost his fortune when he signed a note for a bakery that went bankrupt. He died in 1935 at age eighty-one, leaving a legacy of having been a very religious person.[20]

Contemporary with Gerson, immigrant Jews by the hundreds yearly had bought or built boardinghouses and farmhouses in "the mountains" (as the clientele of their Christian predecessors in the resort business had spoken of the area), settling independently of the Hirsch philanthropies. Legal records, local newspaper accounts of property sales to "Hebrews," and the increase of listings of "Strictly Kosher" and "Hebrews Only" in the Ontario and Western's "Summer Homes" boarding advertisements show the transfers of Catskills farms and boardinghouses from Christians to Jews around the turn of the century.[21]

Many of these new residents had come to the mountains first as summer guests and returned later to settle.[22] Unlike the New Jersey settlements, the Catskill Jewish farm settlement was unplanned. Paradoxically, the Catskill settlements were on rocky land harder to till and

Jewish guests from the city enjoying the summer in a Catskill Jewish boardinghouse in the 1920s.

less fertile than that of the New Jersey colonies or of the settlements in Connecticut, Ohio, and the western states. Some of the Catskill land had been cleared, farmed, and then partly abandoned to reforestation in the course of the nineteenth century before Jews bought it. Jews bought some of the farms at exorbitant prices, setting themselves up for failure. As Herman Levine stated, "They started out behind the eight ball. They started out with a neglected farm, overpriced and on terms that doomed them."[23] "Let us bear in mind," he wrote, "that even most of the natives, with no mortgages to worry them, hardened by the rugged lives they led, and with generations of farm experience behind them, also found it difficult to eke out a living from farming alone. They, too, kept boarders and worked off the farm to earn a livelihood. The climate and soil were unfavorable to agriculture; poor transportation and marketing facilities made farming very unprofitable."[24]

When German-speaking visitors had begun going to the upper Catskills in the 1870s when the railroad had expanded in that area, religion generally was not important to them. Most were Protestants, many were Catholics, and some were Jews, but all stayed in the same boardinghouses. By the end of the 1880s, however, successful Eastern European Jews were frequent guests in the upper Catskills, and boardinghouses began to be segregated into Christian or Jewish houses. Some of the segregation was voluntary, as many visitors preferred to stay with others of similar backgrounds. This seemed to be particularly true of less-educated visitors.[25] The visitors separated not only by religion but also within religious groups by national origins. Russian Jewish, Polish Jewish, and Hungarian Jewish boardinghouses developed.[26] Even some Jews—especially German Jews—criticized the behavior and lack of sophistication of some of the Eastern European Jews.

In the late 1880s many boardinghouses began to post signs and print advertisements saying that they did not accommodate Jews, regardless of their values or economic or social status. The exclusion was mainly due to prejudice against Jews, and in 1889 the *New York Times* referred to "the anti-Hebrew crusade" in the Catskills.[27] The *Times* concluded that most newspapers in the Catskills spoke out against discrimination and that the discrimination was not as extensive as reported. By 1889, the anti-Hebrew crusade had failed for economic reasons, but most small boardinghouses remained segregated by religion.[28]

As the Jewish farms and boardinghouses increased in Sullivan County and in southern Ulster County around Ellenville, the northern Catskill boardinghouses became less attractive to Jews. The southern Ulster–Sullivan area was closer to New York City, was blessed with the O&W railroad, and offered largely Jewish resort areas in which prejudice was less likely to be encountered on a daily basis. The mountains in Sullivan County and southern Ulster County were not as high as those in the upper Catskills, but to Jews who knew no mountains in Russia or Poland, they were high enough to have scenic beauty and cool breezes. There were also more lakes and streams, and less pollution from tanning, in the lower Catskills.

One Jewish writer described the beauty of the lower Catskills area: "Embraced between the Shawangunk and the Catskill Mountain ranges is a sketch of land which nature in her pleasant moments graced and beautified—an area that is a succession of sunkissed hills and verdant dales. Here countless streams rush from the hillsides and ripple along through vale and meadow. Here are lakes of entracing beauty dotting the landscape like jewels in a golden setting. Here, indeed, is a countryside, the charm and beauty of which have inspired the brush of an Inness and the pen of a Burroughs. And, adding bounty to bounty, nature has also blessed this region with an air that is invigorating and a climate that is health-giving. It was natural for such richly endowed regions to become attractive spots for the seeker after health and recreation."[29]

For the Jewish visitors, compared to the Christian visitors, socialization was more important and communing with nature less important, a fact that also decreased the appeal of high mountains. Esterita Blumberg's descriptions, although written of a later time, also apply to this time period. She acknowledged that they used "high flown" names for their hotel accommodations, that "our 'Pine Lodge' was formerly a chicken coop, 'Deluxe' described nothing at our hotel, and we called any two spaces 'A Suite.' " She noted that they countered these conditions with the sales spiel that little time was spent in the rooms anyway because of all the activities offered the guests. Blumberg concluded that "the funny thing was that we were right. We were giving wonderful value at affordable prices—the rooms were the least of it. Summer in the Catskills became a way of life, with a population that returned year after year."[30]

Around the turn of the century, sizeable numbers of Jews began to farm in the Catskills. Some farmed for only a short time, then gave it up for other callings. Others farmed for decades, frequently combining it with summer boarding. Most were born in Eastern Europe and spent some years in New York City before going to the Catskills, but patterns varied. The Weinberger brothers and their father, for example, arrived in Leurenkill in 1900 and began to farm. They were all shoemakers by trade, however, and one year of farming persuaded them to switch back to their first vocation. Samuel H. Berger settled in Ellenville in 1900, later moved to a farm in Kerhonkson, and during World War I moved back to Ellenville to operate the Fountain Hill House. Samuel Jacobwitz went to the Catskills in 1901 and became a farmer. He then turned to peddling meat and in 1907 opened a butcher shop in Ellenville.

Kalman Goldman became a farmer in Greenfield in 1902, after immigrating to the United States from Russia when he was sixteen and living in New York City for fourteen years. He spent two years in Greenfield, building and operating the Grand Hotel as well as farming, and in 1904 moved to Ellenville. Max Rosenberg came from New York City in 1903, and became a farmer and owner-operator of the West Orchard House. He continued a combination of farming and hotel-keeping at the West Orchard House and at the Echo House for many years, finally switching to hotel operating only. Benjamin Cherney began work as a farm laborer in Pataukunk in 1903. His European fiancée soon joined him and they married, but she was "unprepared to meet the hardships or manage the chores of a farm-hand's wife," and they moved to Ellenville where he became a grocer.

Hyman Levine had a peddler's route between Ellenville and Kingston from 1880 to 1895, lived in Ellenville from 1895 to 1903, and in 1903 purchased a farm on Cape Avenue. The Morris Kinberg family bought a dairy farm and boardinghouse in Leurenkill in 1905, raised ten children there, and moved to Ellenville in 1920. Israel Rosen farmed in Mountaindale and Spring Glen before settling on a farm near Ellenville in 1905, but later he became a builder of bakers' ovens. Jacob Benenson was a bookkeeper, but, after arriving from the Ukraine in 1906, he spent only one month in New York City before deciding that he wanted a farm. He was the first Jewish settler in Honk Hill, and for years he operated a farm with summer boarders there. In addition to these examples, there were numerous other Catskill Jewish farmers too numerous to discuss. As these examples show, some gave up farming and moved into towns, but many others stayed on the farm.[31]

By 1907, when the founding of the Ellenville Hebrew Aid Society marked a milestone in Catskill Jewish settlements, the increase in the number of Jewish farmers and nonfarmers was "shifting into high gear." The Jewish Agricultural and Industrial Aid Society found that by 1908 there were 684 Jewish farms in New York state, 500 of them in Sullivan and Ulster counties.[32] That count was based on second mortgages the society issued. Not all Jews on farms in New York state took those mortgages, however. Financing was in most cases arranged privately, usually through a personal lender, and not recorded. Another estimate was higher. A triangular area with sides of about twenty miles each, with route 209's Wurtsboro through Ellenville and Kerhonkson on the east and Woodbourne through Woodridge (Centreville) and Mountaindale on the west, was said to have supported one thousand Jewish farm households. With easily five hundred more to the northwest, around Monticello, Liberty, Hurleyville, Loch Sheldrake, and Parksville, on the O&W main line, Sullivan and Ulster counties had three tenths or more of all the Jewish farmer households in the United States around 1911.[33]

They inherited from Christian predecessors the general farm, with some field crops and some poultry raised for meat and eggs. The major farm income for these Jewish farmers came from dairying, selling to outlets serving the New York City milk market, and shipping on the O&W. If they did not buy such a farm, they built one like it simply because there was a ready milk market in New York City, because crops and poultry could be sold locally to the summer trade, and because the farmer could (at least in theory) eat off his own land.

Nearly all of the Jews who moved into the area were part of the largest migration in U.S. history, which began in the early 1880s and basically ended with the advent of World War I. As noted, the majority of these immigrants settled in New York City.[34] A small percentage of these Eastern European Jews, but a large number, as well as many Eastern European Christians and Italian Catholics, went up the Hudson River and fanned out into surrounding areas. In Ulster County in 1900, 10.5 percent of the people were foreign born, increasing to 15.5 percent in 1910. In Sullivan County, the figures were 9.4 percent in 1900 and 13.3 percent in 1910.[35] Based on an analysis of given names and surnames, it appears that most of the residents born in Russia or Poland were Jewish and that nearly all of the Jewish immigrants were from Russia or Poland.[36] But most of the 1900 foreign-born in Ulster and Sullivan were not from Russia or Poland and were not Jewish.

The years 1900–1910 were the first period of great growth in numbers of Jewish immigrants. For example, in the Ellenville area (Wawarsing township) in 1900 there were only three heads-of-household born in Russia with apparently Jewish names. One reported that he was a farmer, another that he had a boardinghouse on a farm, and the third that he had a store and tin shop. By 1910, this same area had 166 apparently Jewish families of Russian or Polish background (plus a small number from other areas of Eastern Europe). Of the heads-of-household, 110 were farmers and 56 were not. The farmers averaged 4.9

people to the family, the nonfarmers 4.8. The Jewish immigrant heads-of-household overall were young or middle-aged, most still in the years for having children: two were under twenty; nineteen were in their twenties; seventy-five in their thirties; forty-eight in their forties; seventeen in their fifties; three in their sixties; and two in their seventies. Of the 153 who indicated when they came to the United States, seventy-three had come since the beginning of 1900, fifty-six had come in the 1890s, twenty-one in the 1880s, and three in the 1870s. The farmers did tend to have been in the United States fewer years. Whereas 40 percent of the nonfarmers had come since 1900, 51 percent of the farmers had come in that period. Of the nonfarmers, 25 percent had been in the United States for at least twenty years, but only 11 percent of the farmers had been.[37]

Few of these Jews came with the skills needed to farm successfully. In the century before the mass migration began, there was great movement in Eastern Europe from villages to towns to cities, in a desperate and unsuccessful attempt to escape persecution and poverty. In 1793, for example, Lodz had 11 Jews; it had 98,677 in 1897 and 166,628 in 1910. Warsaw had 3,532 Jews in 1781 and 219,141 in 1891. Many Jews changed their occupations in an attempt to survive. Fewer than 5 percent of Eastern European Jews were farmers, although, for those who remained in villages or small towns, agriculture frequently was a supplementary source of income. One writer noted that "in the villages almost every Jewish family owned a cow or goat, often the sole dependable source of income, as well as some fowl. Jews cultivated their own gardens; they raised the 'Jewish fruits'—beets, carrots, cabbage, onions, cucumbers, garlic, and horseradish; and, despite restrictions, many rented orchards on a seasonal basis from neighboring peasants and gentry."[38]

Some of the new Jewish Catskill farmers probably could harness a horse and milk a cow, but those skills alone were no guarantee of profitable farming. The society noted in this time period that one of its problems was that the vast majority of Jewish immigrants, who comprised nearly all of the Jewish farming community, had little or no farming experience. A random survey of Jewish farmers in the United States taken years later indicated that 63 percent had chosen farming because they liked it, 20 percent because they were dissatisfied with city life, 7 percent because they had to for health reasons, and only 10 percent because they had had previous experience as farmers in Eu-

rope.[39] Noting that these new farmers came from a great variety of occupational backgrounds, having been "tailors, merchants, carpenters,
butchers, vegetable and fruit store operators, workers in shops and factories, peddlers, and odd-job laborers,"[40] the society concluded that
"most of our applicants, therefore, are of necessity obliged to establish
themselves upon their farms first and acquire their agricultural experience afterwards—a process not only tedious and expensive, but in-
volving considerable risk."[41]

As U.S. census entries for 1910 indicate, many of the Catskill Jewish
farmers spoke and read only Yiddish and so could not read English-language books about farming techniques and New York State Experiment
Station bulletins or, a decade later, gain instruction from English-speak-
ing county agricultural extension agents. Catskill Jewish settlers who
knew how to read English, however, could gain such technical knowledge from encyclopedias and handbooks on farming.

The society's Long Island Test Farm, the 500-acre King's Point training school operating from 1904 through 1911, placed its first group of
immigrants on the farm in the spring of 1905. But by the fall of 1908
the society had decided that the results did not justify the expense and
discontinued the experiment. Under private management, test farmers
were placed on the farm for several more years. Of the total of fifty-
eight potential farmers placed on farms by the test farm, twenty-nine
were graduated and provided with farms. Of these twenty-nine, nine
gave up after "a more or less protracted struggle." Even in the cases in
which it was successful, however, the test farm focused on preparing
young urban Jews for work and subsequent settlement on the New
Jersey colonies or Long Island, not on training those who had already
settled and certainly not on training the Catskill Jewish farmers who
could easily slip from a farmhouse to a boarding economy.[42] The society was interested in proving that Jews could farm, not run resorts. It
realized, however, that in order to survive many Jewish farmers also
had to have summer boarders.

While the process of converting a farm into a boardinghouse sometimes was necessary for survival, it was not easy. As Jonas Nass remembered, "We had to build a mile of our own utility poles for electric light and power, and install plumbing to make it habitable for city
folk."[43] But, once converted, the rural setting of the boardinghouse se-
duced the city people. A typical advertisement for a hotel, which, although not a farm boardinghouse, gave city vistors a taste of their farm,

read: "The proprietor keeps a dairy of Guernsey cows, noted for rich milk, butter, eggs, poultry, maple sugar and vegetables."[44]

Some of the farmers who started boardinghouses in this period were to become famous success stories. The immigrant Kutsher brothers came to Sullivan County from New York City in 1907 and purchased a farm because one of the brothers was frail and thought country living would be healthy.[45] Like many other Jewish farmers, they took in summer boarders in order to help meet their expenses. Kutsher's Country Club would later become one of the Catskills' major resorts. Selig and Malke Grossinger were restauranteurs in New York City but, encouraged by the society, moved to a farm in Ferndale in 1913. The Grossinger farmhouse, opened in 1914, would grow into the famous Grossinger's Hotel and Country Club.[46]

Charles Slutsky bought a farm in Leurenkill in 1901. His wife and three sons were still in Europe, and for two years Charles tended the farm without any family help. His daughters and another son worked "in New York City to supplement the farm income and make possible the immigration of the other members of the family in 1903." Morris Slutsky, brother of Charles, settled in the area in 1904, and other relatives followed. The Slutsky family in Ellenville would see their Nevele Falls Farm House grow into the Nevele Hotel and Country Club.[47] Other hotels associated with the Slutsky family included the Fallsview, Arrowhead Lodge, Evergreen Manor, and Breeze Lawn.

Max Levinson came to the United States in 1891, and bought his farm, later the Tamarack Lodge, in 1903. Mrs. Ben Miller and Daniel Roher described its beginnings: "Today's well-known summer resort was then only a small, down-at-the-heels farm, stocked with a small herd of cows and a horse past retirement age. Mr. Levinson played the plural role of farmer, hotelman, and tailor to his children in those early days, and like many other farmers of the period, left for New York City each fall, after the departure of the last guest, to help meet the mortgage payments and taxes, while Mrs. Levinson and the family remained to carry on the farm chores through the Winter months."[48]

And so a kind of spontaneous colonizing developed in the Catskills, aided but not initiated by the society. The rural colonies were like a series of shells around small established operating towns whose economies included Jewish artisans, craftsmen, merchants, food vendors, farm suppliers, farm produce buyers, barbers, tailors, glazers, mechanics, and physicians. Jews lived with their rural Christian counterparts as in the

Russo-Polish shtetls. In 1908, the society stated that "some of the bustling villages, such as Centreville and Parksville, have an almost exclusively Jewish population. Nearly every one of them has its physician, dentist, druggist, and all that goes to make up a typical Jewish rural settlement in the Old Country, but so unlike the native American village."[49]

The Catskill settlements differed from the beginnings of the planned Jersey and midwestern colonies and from self-segregated religious communities like the Amish, Mennonites, or Shakers. The little Catskill towns possessed the social amenities such as synagogues and Jewish businesses that the society found it had to bring to the New Jersey colonies to keep people there. For example, in Ellenville, in addition to the Hebrew Aid Society, which had been founded in 1907, a synagogue was dedicated in 1910, and a Workmen's Circle was founded in 1911.[50] Comparing the New York settlements to other areas, as early as 1906 the society could state that "in New York, however, there is a large number of Jewish farmers of whom we never hear except by chance as our investigators run across them. They do not need our aid and do not ask for it."[51]

By 1906 there were forty-five Jewish farmers' associations in the United States, eleven of them in the lower Catskills. The Livingston Manor Jewish Farmers' Association had sixteen members, the Parksville Jewish Farmers Association sixty-six, the Hebrew Farmers' Association of Ferndale and Stevensville seventy-eight, the Hebrew Farmers' Association of Fallsburg and Hurleyville one-hundred-forty, the Monticello Jewish Farmers' Association fifty-seven, the Jewish Farmers' Association of Centreville Station ninety-nine, the Jewish Farmers' Association of Mountaindale eighty-six, the Hebrew Farmers' Association of Ellenville ninety, the Hebrew Aid Society of Briggs Street sixty-eight, the Hebrew Farmers' Association of Kerhonkson and Accord fifty-seven, and the Spring Glen Hebrew Aid Society eighteen.[52]

Moreover ten Jewish farmers in Leurenkill established a Hebrew school for their children in 1913. The children could not walk to the Hebrew school in Ellenville, and so their farmer parents put an advertisement for a Hebrew teacher in a New York City newspaper. Ephraim Yaffe, who had arrived in the United States from Europe only a few days earlier, saw the advertisement and immediately traveled to Leurenkill to apply for the position. Yaffe fell in love with the area, was hired, and first lived in the Slutsky family's Nevele Falls Farm House. Yaffe noted that "the farmers had no automobiles, their horses were needed on the farms, the roads were muddy after a rain, covered with snow during the winter, and it was impossible for the children to walk after school hours to the Ellenville Hebrew school and back home, in the dark, a distance of three miles or more."[53] Several years later Yaffe became a farmer, but he also taught two classes at the Ellenville Hebrew school "from 4 to 6 P.M., five days a week for $10 per week. This was much more than I could make per hour on the farm in those 'good old days'."[54]

By the eve of World War I, there was a Jewish village network in southern Ulster County, Sullivan County, and, to a lesser extent, in Orange County (around Port Jervis). Nearly all of these inhabitants were Eastern European immigrants speaking Yiddish and heavily accented English; nearly all were transplanted there after some years in New York City and were living in a kind of uneasy symbiosis with indigenous Christians. They did not have anywhere near the capital and experience to begin such businesses as banks, insurance agencies, creameries, lumber yards, blacksmith and harnessmaking establishments, hardware stores, plumbing supply stores, and machinery dealerships, businesses that remained out of their reach for several decades.

Farming Jews in the early years tried establishing credit with the Christians operating these businesses and in some cases succeeded. One interviewee noted that "before the depression, banks would finance farm Jews buying used and new cars. That was in the 1920s. A Mr. Anderson of a local bank approved a $200 loan for me around 1927. Jews were accepted here by then."[55]

In most cases, however, getting credit was difficult, partly because would-be creditors suspected that the newcomers were poor risks, given their inexperience in farming and in resort keeping. Throughout this period the society was aware of the difficulty Jewish farmers had in obtaining loans and concluded that the problem was worst in Sullivan County.[56] In light of the failures of farms and farmhouses the newcomers bought, perhaps the creditors' tight fists were justified.

Yet Christian owners of resort and farm properties in the mountains could obtain credit, although they were overcharged both for it and for the commodities it bought. They got their fire insurance too, overpaying for it also, although it is noted in Wakefield's book, for example, that at least two-thirds of the photographs of houses, particularly of the eminent, are of structures that either had been erected on foundations of burned antecedents or that later burned.[57] Certainly, in light of the remarkable number of fires leveling Christian-owned boardinghouses and hotels, fire insurance for such dwellings ought to have been hard to obtain, let alone finance, for any owner, Christian or Jewish.

As a result only the most successful of the businesses, generally those with high profit or low operating costs, could survive the local price and credit environment. Only the old, established places fell into this category because they were usually "paid out," that is, they enjoyed the luxury of having no mortgage payments to meet. The considerable number of farms and farmhouses available for Jews to buy cheaply in the Catskills showed that all was not well among the Christian operators there, even among those who had gotten started with the help of the railroad several decades earlier.

The Jews starting up in the mountains began as had their confreres out west a couple of decades earlier, facing credit problems and not exactly loved for being Jewish. They shared the lot of all farmers afflicted by the difficulty of obtaining credit then, and like many who were not Jewish, they resorted to mutual aid remedies, then thought somewhat alien and vaguely unpatriotic. Cooperative societies were comprised almost totally of foreign-born individuals, both non-Jews and Jews. Efforts "to interest any large section of American born people in Consumers' Co-operation seemed an almost hopeless task."[58]

The producer cooperative was a mutual aid remedy that U.S. farmers had sought since the nineteenth century. These cooperatives were sought to buy supplies, to market products, or to mill feed collectively in order to eliminate dealer profits and in turn reduce operating costs and the need for credit.[59] Farmers had attempted to form cooperatives under the leadership of the National Grange movement founded in 1867, but the movement had failed for two reasons: it had attempted to do business on the basis of charging cost plus a handling expense, which was unpopular and expensive, and it had permitted members to vote on the basis of the number of shares owned, which had unevenly distributed the power of the cooperative.[60]

Farm cooperatives based on the Rochdale principles were introduced among Scandinavians in the Midwest and other places about the time Jews trying homesteading there went bankrupt. The Rochdale model, which had originated in England in 1844, specified democratic control, with each member having one vote regardless of how many shares he owned, and distribution of co-op earnings to all members with each member's share being based on his proportion of patronage. It sought to provide a fair profit for all the members. Large numbers of immigrants arriving from Finland and Bohemia around 1910 led to the immediate establishment of successful consumers' cooperatives based on these guidelines; the cooperatives were most numerous in Wisconsin, Minnesota, Michigan, Ohio, and Massachusetts.[61]

The Jewish farmers who followed the Rochdale model thus were rejecting the communal property aspects of the Am Olam movement, but they were identifying with the same Lodz socialist ideals followed by Jewish workers in factories. The Rochdale model encouraged a fair profit for the farmers' work, just as the labor movement sought fair pay for the factory workers, but both were far removed from the individualist-oriented aspect of capitalism in the United States.

In Russia, Jews were excluded from the co-ops founded by Christians, but the Jewish culture nevertheless maintained a strong cooperative spirit.[62] Although Jews did not invent farm cooperatives in the United States, they took up their cause quite early, encouraged by the society to do so. While the society encouraged Jewish farmers to begin co-ops, however, it still kept a fiscal distance from them, with no interest in funding co-ops or, until 1920, even in providing first mortgages.

In 1910, there were thirty-five Jewish Farmers' Associations in the United States, of which seven were in Sullivan and Ulster counties. By the following year there were forty-five associations, of which ten were in Sullivan and Ulster counties. The associations were joined together as the Federation of Jewish Farmers of America. The society viewed the local associations as the cohesive force that drew and held the farmers together. The society's 1910 annual report suggests how strong and effective such associations were for the Jewish farmers: "The meetings of the associations are made occasions for picnics, festivals and other social gatherings for the wives and children of the farmers. In some places the young people have also organized literary societies. Religious life among the Jewish farmers has likewise taken on an entirely new aspect. . . . In the political status of the Jewish farmer, the Federation has evidenced a lively interest. It has steadfastly advocated naturalization. . . . The Federation is further bringing about a better understanding between the Jewish farmers and their Gentile neighbors. . . . The local associations are also being looked upon as models by the non-Jewish residents. In some instances they sought and were admitted to membership in these associations."[63]

Jewish-run co-op creameries were established for the Catskills along railroad stops in a number of towns. These co-ops reduced the farmers' fees for cooling, pasteurizing, milk can sterilization, milk storage, and transfer and extended them credit until they sold enough milk to pay those fees. Because the co-ops were nonprofit, extending that credit to the farmers did not threaten the finances of the operation, at least in the short run. An example was the Cooperative Jewish Creamery of Hurleyville, in Sullivan County. It opened in the spring of 1914 with an "excellently equipped plant with all modern machinery" highly recommended by Cornell University. The creamery made butter and cheese, and demand was so great that it had to buy milk from many farmers who were not members of the co-op.[64]

Another example was the Jewish Farmers' Creamery Association of Ulster County which opened in 1916. The *Ellenville Journal* described the building as "28 × 110, with engine house 28 × 40 and an ice house adjacent. The building as well as the machinery is up to date in every respect."[65] It noted that the creamery could handle 500 cans of milk a day and that this capacity would provide local farmers with a convenient and reliable outlet for milk and encourage local Jews to raise cows and dairy farm.

None of these co-ops, however, helped Jews obtain fire insurance, an almost impossible feat for Jewish farmers and especially Jewish resort keepers or those wanting to rent a few rooms to summer boarders. Jews were accused of setting their buildings on fire, and jokes were common about "Jewish lightning." In fact, while the buildings of the Jewish farmers and resort keepers were no less wooden than they were when Christians owned them, they appear to have been hit by Jewish lightning much less than private insurers calculated they would be.

Despite the jokes, fires in the country were (and still are) a problem for all, regardless of religion. The seriousness of country fires is captured in Oriana Atkinson's *Big Eyes,* a novel about the Catskills, in which a farmer accurately says, "When a building catches fire in the country, there's little you can do except let it burn. Sometimes it is possible to save the other buildings near it, if the neighbors get there quickly enough and pour water on the grass around and beat out the traveling fire with wet brooms and evergreen branches. But if there's a high wind and there is no water except a well or a spring, there's no help for it. . . . A spark is all that's needed to start one hell of a fire . . . [or] lightning storms and careless hunters and picnickers in the woods, and fools throwing lighted cigarette butts out onto the dry roadside."[66]

In 1913, the Catskill Jewish farmers joined together to form America's first fire insurance cooperative. Decades prior, the Society for Equity, a large national farmers' organization, had included economical fire insurance protection in its cradle-to-grave program of demands placed before public officials, but it did not spell out the means for establishing the fire insurance.[67] The Jewish farmers simply applied their vision of cooperation to fire insurance as they did to other areas. The founders of the fire cooperative were filled with idealism: "In the beginning the enterprise was a group of immigrants . . . pushed out of the old countries . . . sweated out of the cities. They knew little of farming . . . less of the resort business . . . nothing about insurance. They knew a lot about brotherhood."[68]

Samuel Shindler made the motion to form an insurance cooperative at a convention of the Federation of Jewish Farmers. He was an active socialist, a leader of the Waist Makers Dress Union when it went on strike, and an organizer and leader of the Trade Union League. Elmer Rosenberg, another union activist later industrious in the fire cooperative, was the first vice president of the International Ladies Garment Workers Union (ILGWU) and one of ten people first elected to the New York State Assembly by the Socialist Party of America in 1917.[69] Abe

The Associated Co-Operative Fire Insurance Companies Building, Woodridge, 1985.

Jaffe, whose father went directly to Glen Wild from Lithuania in 1904, was a child when the fire co-op was founded in 1913, but he noted that "there was no insurance for Jewish farmers and resort owners in Sullivan County. So, lots of Russian socialists with Jewish accents living in overt anti-Semitism went to Albany and got a charter. The first policies were published in Jewish [Yiddish] and English."[70]

The co-op was chartered and supervised by the New York State Insurance Department, which, fortunately for these struggling Jewish farmers, did not object to the concept of a cooperative. For those expanding their summer resort business, fire insurance was critical because owners of a property would not take a mortgage for that property if the mortgagee lacked fire insurance. The problem was even worse for keepers of boardinghouses than for farmers. The rate charged by stock companies for farm properties was fifty cents per one hundred dollars coverage, but even one boarder caused the charge to increase to the hotel rate of $3.50 per one hundred dollars coverage.[71]

Christian mortgagors and insurers were either hostile to or indifferent to the Yiddish-speaking Jewish mortgagees. With the state behind the co-op insurance, however, mortgagors could not resist the opportunity for a mortgage even to Jews, especially when no other buyers seemed forthcoming. Unsold property frequently produced little or no income, but Jewish buyers, even when they were the only potential buyers, frequently paid more than the farm was worth because they were not familiar with farming. For those buyers who paid too much, more problems resulted, but for informed buyers the fire insurance was a major *mitzvah*.[72] With the state charter, economic aid from the co-op and moral support from the society, success was slow but steady. Nine months after its founding the fire co-op had 296 members.[73]

The co-op cut out profits and kept operating costs down to a "secretary," who was really the managing underwriter, actuary, and office bookkeeper. The fire co-op thus not only reduced the cost of insurance dramatically but also made it available on credit to hundreds of those lacking it who faced disaster if fire-harmed summer guests were to sue them. The fire co-op followed its policy of a low overhead in all areas: Goodwin and Levine reported that "the office was a one room affair up a flight of rickety steps above an old drug store building in Woodridge. It was heated by a coal stove, furnished with a kitchen table and wooden chairs and staffed by one woman . . . Rose Hecht."[74] Mrs. Hecht, who served the co-op for forty-nine years until 1962, was at first the office manager, the janitor, and the interpreter for non-English speakers.

Being plain, practical men, the fire co-op's charter members named it plainly: the Co-Operative Fire Insurance Association of Sullivan and Ulster Counties. As resorts and farmhouses in Orange County and Greene County became involved, the co-op's name subsequently was changed to the Associated Co-Operative Insurance Companies of Sullivan and Adjoining Counties. With the same sense of practicality they set its office in Woodridge on the O&W's main line of frequent trains, which serviced most of the milkstops. From these stops, the co-op members could go by buggy to Woodridge to meet Hecht. Sometimes they could go to Woodridge to see the appraiser if the appraiser was unable or unwilling to drive a Model T through the rutted, stony, muddy, stream-cut trails on which most of the properties were situated. The farmer could even go by train to Ellenville, Kerhonkson, and Accord via the Summitville junction. That shoestring fire insurance operation did not mark its growth in glossy pamphlets trumpeting the corporations, but it did provide members with two practical public relations items: large calendars blazoning over each page top the millions of dollars of insurance in force in its prior calendar year and large outdoor thermometers which, after the "home office" was completed in Woodridge in 1937, carried the office's photograph.[75] The insurance cooperative was the first cooperative assessment company in New York state to declare a dividend.[76]

The farmers also benefited from their credit unions, institutions originating in the German Social-Democratic Party's worker's banks. These credit unions had been brought to the New York City Jewish ghetto by the Jewish Agricultural and Industrial Aid Society, and from there they were taken by the society to "the mountains" at about the time of the founding of the fire insurance cooperative.[77] By 1913, the New York State Department of Agriculture had created a special bureau to encourage cooperative organizations, largely inspired by the society.[78] The credit unions set up in the network of small towns which were becoming heavily populated by Jews, making several-hundred-dollar loans to almost all applying. Those who applied were practically all farmers and boardinghouse keepers. Their fire insurance co-op and credit unions gave the Catskill Jewish farmers an advantage over their Christian farmhouse predecessors.

The Jewish farmers had a third innovation to help them: the free loan society, a Jewish institution brought along from their Russo-Polish era. A free loan society was basically a group of people who knew and trusted each other and who simply pooled some money, lending at no interest some or all of it to anyone in or out of the group trustworthy and in serious need. The amounts were not large, but they could make the difference between survival or disaster for the borrower. Like the Jewish immigrants in New York City and other urban areas, Jewish farmers and Jewish townspeople in the Catskills formed these clubs, making interest-free loans not only to Jews but also to Christians.[79]

The Jewish resort operations profited from the ever-increasing number of Jewish ghetto workers craving relief for their families from the New York summer tenement infernos, workers who could pay for board with increasingly larger weekly paychecks thanks to the combination of World War I's stimulus to employment and the success of labor unions. The resort business was further helped by another factor that caused mixed feelings among the residents. Ghetto workers sometimes went to the mountains seeking relief from tuberculosis, the "white plague" which was the leading cause of death in the early twentieth century. Some New York City businesses such as Macy's sent some of their employees to the Catskills for short paid vacations in an effort to ward off the disease. Believing that the pine-scented fresh air would defeat the disease, these vacationers slept on open porches and on pillows filled with pine needles. Liberty, in Sullivan County, even had a tuberculosis sanatorium that was a kind of mecca for the famous seeking treatment.

It was not only those seeking cures who came, however, for "fresh air" was emphasized by all the resorts and boardinghouses as preventive medicine all the year. Howard Simons noted that "the phrase 'fresh air' became a fugue," and Alvin Fertel remembered that his family went to the mountains "primarily . . . because, the reasoning was, the children had to get out of the city and get fresh air. All sorts of healthful things were attributed to fresh air. We would be taken out in the coldest weather, bundled up. I recall my younger brother in a carriage, bundled, with his nose sticking out in the winter to get fresh air. Somebody once told my mother, 'Fresh air!' " Some of the resort and boardinghouse owners were afraid that those with tuberculosis would discourage healthy tourists from coming and downplayed this aspect of the boarding business while emphasizing the "fresh air is good for you" approach.[80]

To take advantage of this market Jewish farmers tried to buy farmhouses with extra rooms that could be rented out. But when times were unusually difficult, a few families even rented out their own rooms and slept in sheds, barns, or tents. Joyce Wadler, for example, remembered that "when things really got crazy, the family or parts of the family would move into a tent. If business was really cooking, they would do this number. I think sometimes even guests would end up in tents or they would double up."[81] It was welcome income to the struggling farmers. As the manager of the society's office in Ellenville, Herman J. Levine, described it, in the 1920s, "The owners [of farms] in those days couldn't afford to put in a pane of window glass if the glass was broken. . . . They would plaster it up with cardboard. That's how poor they were. And in the winter they would take a lot of the manure and put it against the foundation in order to make it warmer, in order to provide more heat for the house."[82] Atkinson accurately mused in her novel of early 1900s Catskill life that "seeing the district for the first time in June, no city dweller would ever guess the hardship and misery that the mountain climate imposed on the shivering inhabitants in winter."[83]

In fact some of the men who had farmhouses had to live in New York City for the winter to practice other trades, leaving their families to mind the cows and chickens. Levine recalled more than half a century later that "at the end of the summer when they found they couldn't meet the mortgage, the taxes, and the interest, the husband would leave for the city to go to work, whatever work he could get to do, and the wife and the children and perhaps a laborer of the area would remain on the farm and operate the farm."[84]

The Kaminsky family of Greenfield Park was one of many families that did just this. David Kaminsky and his family moved from the Lower East Side to Greenfield Park in 1916, buying an eight-room farmhouse and sixty-eight acres. For many years after settling at Greenfield Park, David Kaminsky returned to New York City in the winter. There, he made money as a presser from the end of October to February or March. He would return to Greenfield Park some weekends during the winter. A Polish Christian man helped the mother and children on the farm. Nearly seventy-five years later, Ann Macin, David Kaminsky's daughter, remembered that in general the Polish helpers were good workers and got along well with the Jews. Joyce Wadler remembers that her grandfather—who was killed on his farm when he went to get the cows during a thunderstorm and was hit by a tree—started as a tailor and became a farmer, but "never completely gave up tailoring, from what I can see. He was always back and forth to the city."[85] Into the 1930s, hotel association meetings were held in the winter in New York City for mountain hotelkeepers who were working in the city in the winter and hence could not attend meetings in the mountains.[86] Jewish men also worked in cities closer to their homes. Al Cohen's father went to Poughkeepsie, about forty miles away, to work in the clothing industry during the winter.[87]

The Jewish farm wife also endured great hardships, prompting Gertrude Badner to say, "I got [to Ulster Heights] in 1923, and women were slaves in the mountains."[88] The Catskill farmhouse women willingly cooked for boarders in the financially tight summers and, in the winter, snowbound, their wells iced, their eggs frozen to unmarketable worthlessness fifteen minutes after being laid, their grocery bills gathering interest, they anguished with their husbands about how they would pay for chicken feed even if they were able to get over the snowdrifts to get it.[89] Sara Cohen described the Jewish farm women, idealized as the strong Yiddish Mama,[90] and her very human labors:

> Without any improvements and without any sanitation, this brave pioneer woman struggled. In her low-ceiled, kerosene-lit little house she tolled from early in the morning until sundown at the arduous tasks. In the summer time her new duties kept her so occupied that she neither had time nor energy to think of anything, least of all herself. . . . She can tell you of having to melt snow in order to get enough water for her daily needs. She can tell of being snowed in for several days at a stretch without any food in the house and without being able to communicate with anyone. She can also tell you of going through the agonies of childbirth, alone, and with a doctor twelve or more miles away.[91]

Further handicapped by their imperfect or nonexistent English-language skills, and lonesome in "sparsely settled sections where neighbors—especially of their own class—[were] few and far between," it is no wonder that Catskill farmhouse women found appealing the city workers' urban comforts—steam-heated flats, nine-hour workdays, female companionship, steady paychecks. To help ease the burden of farm life on these women the Council of Jewish Women sent representatives, beginning in 1918 in the Sullivan-Ulster area, to improve sanitation and to instruct them in home economics, domestic science, and personal hygiene.[92]

Yet even with outside help and the help of his wife and children some of the Jewish farmers found survival too difficult and returned to the city permanently. But most stayed, remaining solvent because they were willing to accept substandard housing, to build less than show-piece farm buildings, and to work summers as both boardinghouse keepers and farmers. Like all farmers, the Jewish farmers gambled on a good price for whatever it was they grew, but they had an advantage over their counterparts in other regions in America since they were as-sured at least of a good local summer market.

Immediately following U.S. declaration of war in 1917, the Jewish farmers of the Catskills, under the leadership of the society, began a special war program to increase food production. The society cooper-ated with the Patriotic Farmers' Fund in making emergency loans to Jewish farmers, increasing the placement of farmhands on farms, and offering several municipalities the free use of vacant farms owned by the society, as well as other activities.[93] About 250,000 Jews served in World War I, the majority of them immigrants and many not yet citi-zens.[94] But, like Christians, there were some Jewish individuals who wanted to avoid military service. Because farmers were deferred from military service, a number of wealthy New York Jewish needlecraft fac-tory owners found in the Catskills places both near enough and far enough away to hide their sons. These "farmers" abandoned their farms in 1919 at the end of the war. Athough those facade farms were the exception, they distort the overall statistics of legitimate Jewish farming in the Catskills.

It was not unusual for a farm to go from Christian to Jewish tenure in the late nineteenth or early twentieth century and then to go to one or two more Jewish owners by 1930. Most of these potential farmers approached the farms with the hardheaded hope of making more money on them than they could as sweatshop workers. Some came with a bit of a Rousseauian nostalgia for the pure life, the heritage of Am Olam and of the Baron de Hirsch Fund's encouragement of late nineteenth-century Jewish colonizing. A shifting of Jewish farm settlers to town businesses and some back from the businesses to farms contin-ued, however, testifying to a practicality in the Catskills overriding any initial idealism in the settlers.[95] These people searched for situations at least as compensating as wage work but without its disadvantages. If farming suited that objective, many stayed with farming. War-driven agricultural market prices made all farming in the United States appear profitable, Catskill farming included. Jews were not blind to that cir-cumstance, and being able to live among other Jews was also attractive.

The war brought a new institution, the kochalein ("cook by your-self") resort. These were farmhouses and boardinghouses converted to rental operations where the summer guests rather than the housewife or hired cooks prepared their own meals in the former cook's kitchen, cooking on gas hot plates or coal- or wood-burning stoves and sharing iceboxes. Usually the visitors brought their own kitchen utensils, as well as their own bed linens and towels, and shared the kitchen with others in the boardinghouse. Levine described the kochalein: "The farm owner would rent every room in the house to people who sought a cheap vacation. The vacationers would come, the family and all, and sleep in one room. In addition to that they would have kitchen privi-leges whereby they had a one burner gas stove or they could cook on a part of the stove. They would also get a section in a closet in which they could keep their provisions, and they would have a section in one of the refrigerators that they would share with other roomers. They would do their own eating in a common dining room . . . they would buy from the farmer whatever he produced, vegetables, eggs, milk, and the farmer also would do the shopping for them."[96]

The kochalein "required both sociability and a certain competitive-ness: the first to get along with those who shared your kitchen, the sec-ond to get to the stove before they did."[97] Crowding in the kitchen and chaos in the dining facility notwithstanding, the farmer-owner was able to retain a summer income. This new arrangement provided the owner almost the same income he obtained from serving meals or "boarding." Some farmers retained the institution after the war be-cause of its lower operating cost, a circumstance more significant after the onset of the Great Depression in 1929.[98] In most cases, the wife and children would spend the summer at the kochalein, and the husband, who had to continue working in the city, would come up on weekends. So many men came up to the Catskills on the weekend train that it was referred to as the "bull train."

Despite the fall in produce prices following the war, and to some ex-tent because that fall lowered prices of farm property, Jews continued buying mountain properties. They benefited significantly because of the co-op insurance on mortgages and through the other mutual help agen-cies they had developed. For a while they continued to buy a couple of hundred properties a year, with most of the new owners raising and growing several types of produce and livestock using the equipment that frequently was included in the purchase price. Gradually, after World

War II, they moved from dairying to more profitable poultry-raising. Swelled by immigration, employment, and a good birthrate, the number of New York City Jews increased; since they were generally orthodox, they bought only kosher meat and poultry. Kosher poultry, at that time, meant that kosher butchers had to buy live fowl. Thus a burgeoning live poultry market in New York City defied the postwar farm price drop and created the shift from dairying. (This same shift occurred in New Jersey and in Petaluma, California, for the same reason.) Furthermore, the slogan "fresh from nearby farms" practically guaranteed city sales of farm products in prerefrigeration days. This slogan had a special application to the kosher fowl trade, but Jews were not alone in seeking live poultry for city slaughter. Christian farmers also raised for that trade.

With the advent of reliable large flatbed trucks, the poultry business expanded from what it had been when a farmer sometimes sent a few crates of eggs to a New York City destination by the O&W Railroad. Previously the farmer had had to take his crates by horse and buggy (rarely could he get enough credit to buy a Model T Ford) to the railroad station siding in town. The distributors' flatbeds, however, came up to the farm, catchers, crates, and all, and took whole flocks directly into the city central market for resale within hours. The gamble was whether all the birds would survive the trip and gain the market health inspector's approval before the final full truck weighing. Dealers attempted to pay on the final weight they delivered, not on the weight they loaded. And, to know what that dealer delivered, a poultryman would have had to accompany the truck to delivery, something he could not manage often.

The poultry business had other risks, such as diseases against which technology had no remedies. Coccidiosis, a kind of dysentery, could wipe out young birds in a week, leaving a farmer with nothing but their aching memory as payment for feed, chicks, and fuel. Moreover the chicken business was held in disfavor by banks and agricultural establishments such as the Grange League Federation (GLF), which milled and sold feed through local cooperatives serving chiefly dairy farmers in this traditionally dairying area. Poultrymen rarely could qualify for Federal Land Bank mortgages, initiated by the federal government after the Jewish Agricultural and Industrial Aid Society began its mortgage program in 1920. The federal mortgages would either finance a new purchase or refinance an old one, and they were issued when private banks would not take a risk at an affordable interest rate. Some

Jewish dairymen qualified for these new mortgages.[99] Poultrymen often could not qualify, however, because the Federal Land Bank's local board members, who passed on initial applications, were successful Christian dairymen, often with fully paid farms. The members were aware of the negative risks of poultry farming but were unlikely to grasp the positive potential of the New York kosher poultry market.[100] But even the society was hesitant to lend money to develop poultry business then, leaving the Catskill Jewish farmers in a bind. Some poultry farmers obtained short-term notes from local banks to carry them over the winter and fund their summer farming and resort programs, provided that they could repay the notes.[101]

Although the Jewish Agricultural and Industrial Aid Society originally was not limited to agriculture, by the early 1920s it was. The Industrial Removal Office of the Society, which moved immigrants from congested cities to small towns, had become a separate organization by 1907. In 1922, the name of the society was changed to the Jewish Agricultural Society, and the society expanded into extension work.[102] It began to field more farm agents, a move paralleling the U.S. Department of Agriculture's development of a county agent extension system. The theory behind the agent system was that better farming techniques could rescue farmers from unprofitability and that the best way to teach better techniques was to demonstrate them to the farmers on their own farms. Seaman Knapp, a secretary of agriculture before World War I, promoted the concept, and it became an official federally sponsored program in 1917. This was just in time to augment agricultural productivity for the brief war period, and, ironically, the new efficiency and productivity would ultimately generate the surpluses that would aggravate the farm crisis in the 1920s.

For over a decade prior to the county agent system's inception in 1922 the Jewish Agricultural Society had recognized the need to train people to farm and so sponsored agents of its own to train the Jewish farmers. Aware that even more help was needed, it opened a field office in Ellenville at the end of 1919, and the office began functioning at the beginning of 1920. David B. Alcott was placed in charge of the office and served for a short period. Ellenville was chosen because it was right in the heart of the Jewish farming districts of Sullivan and Ulster counties, and because this area had by far the greatest growth, especially in recent years. The society noted that soil and weather conditions in Ellenville were not altogether favorable for farming, but the region was a favorite spot for Jews seeking to begin farming because of its proximity to New York City and because its large Jewish population made for a better social and religious life.

The same features that brought Jewish farmers also attracted corrupt farm agents and dishonest land speculators to the Catskills, and their actions helped lead to some grossly inflated land values. It was one of the major problems the Ellenville office had to fight for many years. The office also would serve as the headquarters for the society's educational work, which was conducted in conjunction with the New York State College of Agriculture, and the headquarters of the society's sanitation department. As population increased, sanitation became an increasingly significant problem.[103]

The Ellenville office served Jewish farmers in all of upstate New York, the majority of whom were in the Catskills. Alcott became head of the loan investigation work at the society's headquarters in New York City in April 1922, and Herman J. Levine, who had been an extension agent, became the manager in Ellenville. For all of its remaining twenty-three years, Levine headed the office with the assistance of his "loyal and devoted" secretary, Bertye Lefkowitz, and by a succession of Yiddish-speaking extension agents who brought farm knowledge to the Jewish farmer's door.[104] The technical help meant much to the solvent or near-solvent farmer, but it meant little to those who had bought farms at war-inflated prices and had to pay off the mortgages with postwar low-priced milk and vegetables. Overindebtedness could preclude such people from switching to poultry because they could not borrow enough to make the switch.

Special circumstances—expanding resort business summer markets and proximity to the urban kosher market—separated the economy of postwar Catskill Jewish farmers from farmers nationally, however, and increased productivity resulting from knowledge taught by the society's agents improved their conditions. But they still needed what most farmers needed and did not get from the private sector or the government, and what the Jewish farmer could not get from the society—financing for conducting and expanding operations. The society endorsed the credit union idea in an effort to stem bankruptcies, and Ellenville's and Woodridge's credit unions did what they could. Credit unions, however, dealt in hundreds, not thousands, of dollars, and to expand or refinance operations a farmer needed thousands for feed, buildings, stock, and machinery. Commercial banks continued to lend large amounts only for short-term notes in certain cases, and the Federal Land Bank was not chartered to make production loans.

The society usually loaned only a couple of hundred dollars in short-term loans for operating capital. As Al Cohen noted, "The JAS had limited funds for [mortgages], and had no funds for capital expenditures. So, the loans they made were basically to buy a flock of chicken and raise them, to buy a couple of cows or a couple of horses, or to provide seed money for planting your fields in the spring."[105]

Although some Jewish farmers' first-generation sons were willing to farm and already had agricultural college backgrounds by the mid- and late 1920s, they lacked the operating capital to expand.[106] By then, the economic situation of Jewish farming in the Catskills was similar to that of U.S. farming in general: their common denominator was a credit shortage.

This shortage opened opportunities for those able to marshal private capital elsewhere. They could begin economies of scale by buying out the bankrupt and marginal producers, producing more for less, and making profit for fewer people, but this business contraction had limits. Automatic poultry feeders and waterers, antibiotics, and milking machines and coolers had not been invented. This lack of appropriate technology to make large-scale economies feasible was the real impediment to poultry and dairy farming, in the Catskills and everywhere else. Not all of the Jewish farmers had capital crises, however, and many of those who did not used the credit they obtained based on their successful farming to build hotels.[107]

Production credit shortages were not the only problems facing Catskill farmers in the 1920s. By 1920, the local cooperative creameries had failed, and the problem of how to market milk profitably arose again. In a few years, the statewide New York Dairyman's League, a milk-marketing cooperative accepting milk from Jewish-owned farms, solved the mechanical problems of milk marketing but could not raise the low prices of raw milk. Catskill Jews became members of the League. Their summer resort businesses, which the society looked upon as at best a necessary evil, produced much of the cash they could count on. The milk market was augmented by a significant local hotel summer market for other farm products.

Jewish hotels grew, accommodating thousands of guests drawn by reduced price round-trip O&W tickets. Jewish farmers supplied these hotels with baskets of live fowl, crates of eggs, veal calves, daily twenty-gallon cans of raw milk (raw milk was served on tables in some resorts), and bushel baskets of string beans, cabbages, summer squash, sweet corn, and potatoes. All were weighed or counted carefully on beam scales at the hotels, scales that sometimes were discovered to have been rigged to weigh light. The rooming business used farm products also but not much more than would have been used in the boarding-house.[108] This trade could not always fend off debt, nor could it fund farm expansion, especially into large-scale poultry raising. When a herd or flock was stricken by disease, as often happened, debt was as devastating as it had been for midwestern homesteaders a generation or more before.

The number of Jews striking out for Catskill farming continued to rise despite this adverse fiscal situation. This lure was complex; it resulted from a combination of the newcomer's unrealistic appraisal of the potential profitability of the situation, the zeal for an alternative to sweatshops, and the example of other Jews who had already become established and successful. For a few Eastern European Ashkenazi immigrants who came after the war, the love of the idea of farming also resulted from Am Olam–inspired idealism. Whatever the reason, they came to the Catskills. The sizes of their farms did not increase much past the sizes they bought. Dairy farms needed considerable land, including enough to utilize all the manure or to put the manure far enough away from the farmhouse to minimize odors.[109] But poultry farms did not need much land, and poultry expansion usually was feasible on the land available. Moreover, the increase in the numbers of Jewish farmers meant an increase in the prominence of Jewish institutions, making the area even more attractive to Jews who considered settling there.

The towns also provided two other mutual aid institutions relatively unique to the Jews. Health and personal insurance associations, *far-banden,* were old socialist institutions transferred to the United States cities by Eastern European Jewish workers. Most familiar was the Arbeiter Ring, or Workmen's Circle, with thousands of city members, mostly in the needle trades. The Arbeiter Ring, strongly socialist, would later be "a decisive factor in defeating Communist Party ambitions in the Jewish Community."[110]

Branches of the Arbeiter Ring opened in towns in the Catskills, having their own halls for meetings and socializing. Many of their members were farmers. Included in the nominal insurance fee was burial coverage and, far more vital, complete hospital-surgical coverage at Workmen's Circle facilities or at contract institutions. In other words, a member could go to a major New York City hospital on Workmen's Circle insurance. Social Security would offer nothing like those benefits, and nowhere else in the United States did farmers enjoy that kind of security. Thus, a city worker belonging to an insurance branch in Brooklyn could consider trying a farm in the Catskills, knowing that he and his family had a health safety net. As in the case of the fire insurance cooperative, the farmer owed a debt nominally to the New York State Insurance Department for granting charters and tolerating this remarkably thorough, inexpensive, practical, somewhat socialistic poor man's medicine. The real debt was to New York City's unions which guided the politics to which the Insurance Department answered.

Another farband was the International Worker's Order, also chartered by New York state and primarily a city worker's health and burial society. The IWO (its popular title) was created by the Communist Party to serve the leftist unions whose politics differed from those under the umbrella of the Workmen's Circle. The split arose from an issue dividing socialist doctrine internationally since 1913: some workers supported World War I, and subsequently the workers were divided on whether the Russian Revolution was consistent with the interests of U.S. workers and whether the USSR was legitimate. The IWO had no branches of any duration in the mountains, but it did have individual members there benefiting from its insurance policies, a few of them Jewish farmers.

Beginning in the late 1920s and continuing through about two more decades, the health benefit organizations secured life for their Jewish subscribers, who thus had less reason to go back to the city. The Workmen's Circle meeting halls were in fact a kind of secular shul, resembling what in the city was the gathering place for secular Yiddish culture based on Jewish history and the Yiddish language as distinct from Hebrew. But, unlike the city branches, the country branches hardly schooled children. The buildings' uses resembled those of union halls in that all types of argument on issues cultural and political could be heard there on meeting nights.

The farmers enrolled in the circle reflected in their politics a kind of factionalism similar to that of the varieties of seventeenth-century English dissenters. They reflected a mélange of doctrinal differences in an already dissenting movement. The cleavages in this case mirrored their advocates' pasts in other lands where, against worse adversities, they sided with either Kerensky or Lenin on a definition of proper governance. For the more acclimatized and generally better heeled, the arguments were not over Kerensky or Lenin, but Wilson or Coolidge and Hoover. Among the Workmen's Circle the majority sympathized with Kerensky and so with the Russian bourgeois democracy eclipsed by Lenin, Trotsky, and subsequently Stalin.[111] But a few Bolshevik sympathizers joining the circle for its social atmosphere and medical benefits quarreled many long nights with the Mensheviks, all in the kind of doctrinal differentiation one could find in the four Yiddish papers they received by daily mail from New York.

Socialists, roughly followers of Samuel Gompers then, read the *Daily Forward*. Bolsheviks, sympathizers with or members of the new U.S. Communist Party, read *Die Freiheit* (Freedom). Those who were ideologically neutral with secular interests read *Der Tag* (The Day), a paper with a scope analogous to the *New York Times*. Like the *Times*, it covered national and international events, medicine, and art, obviously appealing to the analytically and intellectually inclined. The few religious Jews in the circle read *Morgen Zhournal* (Morning Journal), a paper focusing on rabbinical events that would have been essentially urban issues here or abroad and not of daily concern to the Catskill farmers.

That the newspaper was so significant in their lives indicated the extent of the Jewishness of their lives—and Jewish farm lives—in the Catskills. Pained as they were for cash, Jewish farmers who were not even members of farbands subscribed to the daily Yiddish New York newspapers, which came on the mail trains on their day of publication. Sometimes when they drove buggies into the towns to shop for their boarders or roomers or to pick up feed, they bought the papers at local newsstands. These Jewish farmers maintained the European habit of keeping informed on international issues and thus were able to exercise a European pastime, that of discussing the news with other Jews if they had the time to do so.

In addition to the newspaper, the society's remarkable journal, *The Jewish Farmer*, was available to the farmers in both Yiddish and English. *The Jewish Farmer* was first published in 1908 and lasted until 1959. There was a lack of Yiddish writers familiar with farming and farm problems and a lack of terminology in Yiddish for some modern farming terms, but the unique bilingual farming magazine was warmly welcomed.[112] It was affectionately referred to by some as "The Yiddish Farmer."[113]

The Jewish Farmer was a morale booster for the whole of Jewish farming in North America, read in almost every Jewish farm home and conferring an esprit de corps to these efforts. It featured articles on farm management and Jewish farm achievements. Most of its issues praised achievements in farming by individuals, complimenting them with photographs of them at work. It was a kind of very nice backslapping similar to that of a company newspaper designed to make those getting their pictures or names in print feel good about what they did. *The Jewish Farmer* also kept farmers apprised of the latest information.[114] The society encouraged good farming as well as good citizenship through other means. It sponsored prizes for crop diversification and work against poultry diseases, for boys', girls', and women's work on the home farm, for sanitary conditions, and for community welfare.[115]

The Jewish Farmer, as the official publication of the Society, did vary over time in its approach to the issue of boardinghouses. In the case of the Catskill and Central Connecticut operations, the magazine at first mentioned practically nothing about the boarding business on which some of the Connecticut farmers also began depending. Again, while the society preferred that Jews only farm and rejoiced when they did so, it also recognized the economic necessity of boardinghouses.

Although much of their Jewishness was experienced through cultural, political, and social activities, religious activities also continued to be important to Jewish farmers. Before 1907, when the Hebrew Aid synagogue was built in Ellenville, religious Jews held minyans in each others' homes or in the house of one member of the minyan. They subsequently prayed in hotels on the significant Jewish holidays such as Rosh Hashanah and Yom Kippur because many hotels stayed open through September for those holidays. But the town Jews and the farmhouse year-round operators had other religious obligations, chiefly the preparation of adolescent males for Bar Mitzvah. They met these obligations by building talmud torahs, that is, shuls or schools where youths could be instructed in Hebrew for prayer and where the instructed prayed with the initiated.

Like the first New York Ashkenazi shuls, these Catskill shuls copied their Russo-Polish counterparts, often built as two-storied stucco on frame. The lower floor was sparsely decorated for use by what was basically a congregation lacking a rabbi. The buildings were about twenty feet by thirty feet, usually with a Mosaic tablet pressed into the stucco of the streetside gable, or a leaded or painted Star of David window in lieu of the more costly tablet. The entrance door usually was of two panels and painted white, and sometimes it had a small stained glass semi-circle in the upper quarter. Almost invariably simple four-inch framed wooden double-hung windows, the trim generally painted green, flanked the doors and puncuated the long walls. The rear short wall usually remained blank, a receptable for the ark, or the Torah scrolls. The second floor was reserved for the stark schoolroom presided over by an unpaid or underpaid even more stark elder.

The society funded several of these small synagogues. A 1923 letter from Levine, by this time manager of the society's three-year-old Ellenville branch office, addressed the problem of the absence of Talmud Torahs in a number of localities where the society had planted farmers: "In the city, financial difficulties are overcome by the free Talmud torahs. In the country, the poor farmer, who cannot pay, finds that without his contribution no Melamed can be engaged. The poor farmer finds that his next door neighbor, and his next door neighbor are no richer and he dare not broach the subject, because of his inability to contribute as he might be expected to, or as he would like to, or his pride urges him to. It remains as like an open wound growing more painful as this problem continues unsolved."[116]

Levine also mentioned that towns like Ellenville and Woodridge provided Talmud Torah instruction, thanks to some sort of "public spirited" individuals there, and that farmers living near those villages sent their children there for Talmud Torah. But he also noted the tendency of those frustrated by bad luck and hard times to blame the lack of religious facilities for their return to the city.

In 1924, two itinerant religious teachers went to the Ellenville area. The United Synagogue of America and local farmers each paid half of their salaries, the Jewish Agricultural Society office in Ellenville supervised the program, local farmers served on a board of education, and the United Synagogue provided curriculum advisement. The teachers met with children at several central locations, each serving several communities, and the program continued until better transportation and better facilities became available locally.[117] The shortage of Jewish personnel led to problems. In discussing Hebrew schools in Ulster Heights and Phillipsport in 1927, Levine wrote that "it was physically impossible for [the Hebrew teacher] to take care of the classes during the summer months because of his position as schochet [ritual slaughterer]."[118]

Dairyland's pre-1920 small stucco shul, still standing on the corner of New York State Route 52 and what is now Synagogue Street, was

Congregation Knesset Israel, Ulster Heights, 1987; main unit built 1924.

Congregation Anshei, Glen Wild, 1987; built before 1924.

Congregation Anschei, Hurleyville, 1991.

built with collections from farmers and boardinghouse keepers and a society loan. David Levitz remembered that the Ulster Heights synagogue, Knesset Israel, was built in 1924 and that "each farmer and hotelman around chipped in $25 to get it started. We got a part-time Hebrew teacher to teach the kids. They came from Woodridge and Fallsburg."[119] Although the Dairyland shul and its nearby Ulster Heights shul were more farmers' shuls than the others, they were rather typical of others built shortly afterwards in Glen Wild, Mountaindale, Kerhonkson, Loch Sheldrake, Woodridge, Bethel, Kiamesha Lake, Swan Lake, Parksville, Livingston Manor, and other Catskill hamlets. As Levine recalled, synagogues then "were built all over creation."[120]

As in most shuls in the Russo-Polish shtetl, the small Catskill shuls functioned in a kind of democratic, spontaneous anarchy kindred to the orthodox service itself, wherein there is no rabbi and each man takes on equal responsibility in reading and praying, using only prayerbooks and, occasionally, the Torah. There is no separation of altars and pews. Bar Mitzvah itself in those shuls was as it had been for centuries, featuring a reading of Torah in Hebrew by the initiate before the initiated and only a modest celebration. One interviewee remembered that "the family would bring some herring, cake, and schnapps for after the service. There were no Bar-Mitzvah parties."[121]

Synagogues also provided much of the social life for Jewish farmers, especially on Jewish holidays. One interviewee, for example, noted that "Simchas Torah was the big good time when we'd bring stuff down to the shul. That's after Rosh Hashanah. We used to bake eleven-pound challas and honey cakes whipped by hand. We had a 'pitchak' [pickled cow's feet] scooped on the side and we dipped chunks of challah in the hot stuff. We made 'kishke' [cow intestine stuffed with flour or potatoes]; meat was expensive and we had to go for it to Woodridge, several miles over a bad road. We got the kishke from Mr. Schoeman who butchered cows in Dairyland for others."[122]

Many Catskill farming Jews sent their children to the Talmud Torahs doubling as shuls in all of the small towns, and the parents themselves sometimes came to Friday night services. Most of the children who went were boys preparing for Bar Mitzvah. Among the orthodox, girls received no equivalent of that initiation. The orthodox generally wore full shawls and yarmulkes but neither phylacteries nor tzitzis (the tasseled ritual undershirt). Their core of orthodoxy was less form and more function. They took turns reading Torah on the Holy Days; they

Congregation Ahavath Sholom, Jeffersonville, 1991.

Temple Beth El, Kauneonga Lake, 1991.

*Kerhonkson
Jewish Center,
Kerhonkson, ca.
1940.*

were as little concerned with who prayed best as they were about who farmed best. The point to them was getting the job done. The search for perfection in ritual was no more conceivable to those farmers than it was to the nonorthodox.[123] Pilpulism was impractical, even if it had been desired.

Other Jewish farmers, however, attended no shul. They prayed, if they prayed at all, at Rosh Hashanah–Yom Kippur services held at the local hotels—at the invitation of the hotelkeeper, free of charge. For some Jewish farmers, September's relief from haying, harvesting, and boardinghouse obligations conferred an almost scripturally pastoral ambience to the services, an ambience graced less by zeal for prayer than by the absence of work.

Even some of those farm Jews considering themselves communists or sophisticated socialists occasionally attended a holiday service at a nearby resort hotel, drawn as if by habit (after World War II, they would go with more deliberation). The majority of Catskill Jewish farmers, regardless of their own level of observance, could not reconcile themselves to the idea of permitting their chidren to grow up ignorant of their religion or at least of Jewish culture. As the society's 1924 annual report put it, "For two thousand years they have been ready to sacrifice all for their faith and now in the land of religious freedom, they are not prepared to surrender their ancient ideals."[124]

The small town high schools indicated the extent to which the generation and a half of Jewish Catskill settlements had become established. By 1927, Ellenville, Kerhonkson, Liberty, Woodridge, Mountaindale, and Monticello high school graduating classes featured many Jewish names on honor rolls, as valedictorians and salutatorians, on basketball rosters, and in plays. Some were the violinists at local village theater productions of transliterated Yiddish plays, where the stagework was in Yiddish but where the playbills were transliterated Yiddish sounds from Hebrew to the Anglo-Latin alphabet. The majority of the Jewish farmers could not buy their children violins, but the presence of violinists shows that a violin teacher, as well as a piano teacher, was probably available locally.

The cultural situation in the Catskill towns underwent a revolution of the same kind Jews had brought to New York City. Until then, with the exception of mid-nineteenth-century Germans and some Italians, scholarship and instruction in classical music in the United States belonged primarily to upper classes. In small towns like Ellenville, Liberty,

Congregation Agudas Achim, Livingston Manor, 1991.

Hebrew Congregation of Loch Sheldrake, 1991.

Hebrew Congregation and Talmud Torah, Mountaindale, 1985.

and Monticello, the upper class consisted of bankers, insurers, physicians, attorneys, and some well-off merchants and farmers. Among the Catskill Jews, children of cobblers, plumbers, small storekeepers, and small farmers not only made the honor rolls in college preparatory courses, but they also went to college. Some went to the State College of Agriculture at Cornell, some to state vocational agricultural colleges like Delhi, New York, and some to universities to learn professions. As early as 1920, the Jewish immigrants in New York City had begun the transition from proletariats to members of the middle class,[125] and the rural Jews were no exception to this desire for upward mobility.

While a few of the Jewish farm children merely learned the local version of nonstandard English and held the low academic expectations such language embodies, it would seem from the high ranking of most of the Jewish high school students that only a few followed that route, something a city Jew considering farming would have appreciated. The studious Jewish farmer student could have been beaten up as a "know-it-all" except for the fact that in those Catskill schools he had a little safety in numbers. The rough stuff would come after school, if it came at all, as in the Bronx—as he walked home alone, attacked as much for being a scholar as for being a Jew.[126]

By the late 1920s, the dozen or so Catskill towns and environs were microcosms of Jewish life both in New York and in the Russo-Polish shtetls. In these Catskill towns and on their peripheral Jewish farms, Christians and Jews lived close to each other, generally learning fairly quickly to appreciate their interdependence. Jewish farm life did not provide the proximity to universities and concert halls enjoyed by cosmopolitan Jewish Muscovites and Odessans. But as in the shtetls, prayer, music, and hard work produced a life quite tolerable as long as it was free from pogroms. A Jewish immigrant from a shtetl probably would have been at home in those Catskill towns, with the added advantages that he would not have to worry about pogroms and that some of those with whom he would trade in the surrounding countryside would share his cultural interests. In addition he would have more room in which to live and would eat more and drink cleaner water.

Basic businesses such as hardware, lumber, heavy machinery, coal, oil, banking, and business insurance generally were not Jewish owned or operated in the Catskill towns through the 1920s. The Jewish farmers and resort operators had solved their fire insurance problem through

Hebrew Congregation of Spring Glen, 1991.

Congregation Ahavath Achim, Swan Lake, 1991.

their 1913 cooperative, but they had not established a cooperative that would address basic business issues other than milk marketing. The Jewish farms, mostly in the horse and buggy stage, did not have a great need for machinery. Multiplication of Jewish hotels, however, provided an opportunity for Jews to enter the building supply and lumber businesses by the mid and late 1920s, enterprises from which the local Jewish farmers also could benefit.

As the decade ended, a local Jewish businessman had started a Chevrolet dealership, providing lenient credit not only for cars but more importantly, for trucks. Ladenheim's Chevrolet car and truck dealership shocked the local Ford dealership, rooted in Ellenville almost since the beginning of the Model T. And Rosenthal's Ellenville Lumber Yard was the most successful lumber dealer in the Catskills for several years. Jews from the area patronized these places not so much because they were Jewish owned, although the Yiddish spoken there was an attraction, but because they offered good terms. Rosenthal's and Ladenheim's success rested in extending significant credit to those Jews who could pay only with anticipated profits. Like the other Jewish businessmen in these towns, they extended liberal credit not only to Jews but also to Christians.

By the end of the 1920s, thousands of Catskill Jews had established a fairly stable mixed economy of farmhouses, rooming houses, dairying, poultry raising, and vegetable crops, the chief farming component being dairying. Their farms duplicated the acreages of their Christian predecessors (most were between thirty and one hundred acres) and generally were unaffected by the economic phenomenon of consolidation whereby one farmer bought out the land of another. Many of the Jewish farmers had become members of the Dairyman's League, a fact that attested to their acceptance by that body of Christians.[127]

In all these institutions, Jewish farmers had enough of a net to hold them to the Catskills. They had built a kind of economic symbiosis with the predominantly Jewish townspeople and with the Christians who still ran the basic businesses such as banks, hardware stores, and electric power, coal, and fuel oil supplies. Despite these networks, Jewish organizational help also was still important.[128]

Marking its success in propagating Jewish farming, the society sponsored a state fair of farming Jews at the Ellenville Fair Grounds on Columbus Day in 1928.[129] The event was symbolic both because it was a Jewish harvest fair held on a secular holiday instead of on Succoth,

Congregation Bnai Israel, Woodbourne, 1991.

Ohave Sholem, Woodridge, 1985.

the scriptual harvest fair which the religious and irreligious farm Jews had occasionally honored, and because it was held at a site normally used for Christian farmers, firemen, traveling circuses, and the like. Farmers, boardinghouse keepers, business people, village Jews, and non-Jews were brought together by the Columbus Day event.[130] This event symbolized better Jewish-Christian relations, and indeed things overall were better.[131]

Two Jewish celebrities, Dr. Jacob Lipman, dean of the New Jersey State College of Agriculture, Rutgers, and Louis Marshall, a prominent constitutional lawyer, addressed the Columbus Day crowd of over 10,000. An attendee called it "the greatest gathering of its kind in the history of New York State."[132] Lipman's presence underscored an unstated proposition that New York State's College of Agriculture at Cornell University had not yet noted but would later—that Jewish farming in New Jersey was reflected in a Jewish dean at Rutgers. Cornell Ag, as it was called, simply Cornell to the farmers, did not have a Jewish professor in the agricultural area, let alone a dean. Not only was

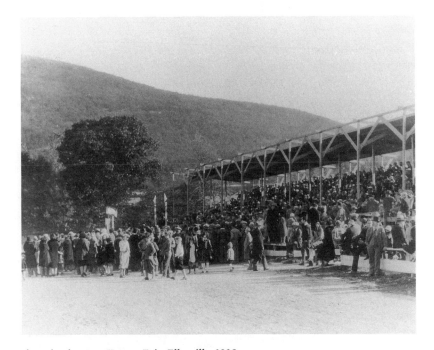

The Columbus Day Harvest Fair, Ellenville, 1928.

Talmud Torah, Woodridge, 1985.

Wurtsboro Hebrew Congregation, Wurtsboro, 1991.

Lipman a dean, a prestigious position especially to the people of the book, but he also was an immigrant, a fact that made the immigrant farmers even more proud. The Columbus Day event told those participating and those noticing that Catskill farming Jews had arrived as an economic and social entity.

But Catskill Jews knew well that arriving economically through hard work did not mean the end of prejudice. Much bigotry existed in

Examining chickens at the Ellenville Fair, 1928.

Congregation Tifereth Yehuda Veyisroel, Kerhonkson, 1991.

Synagogue in Parksville, 1991.

the United States in the 1920s, and some of it had been manifest near the Sullivan-Ulster area. In 1924 the Ku Klux Klan had signed up members in Woodstock in northern Ulster County, burned a cross, issued robes, and then vanished with the initiation fees. In the same area, Windham, Stamford, Onteora, Elka, and Twilights Park actually tried to exclude Jews.

Some isolated instances of overt anti-Semitism occurred in the lower Catskills. For example, when land was bought around 1927 to build a synagogue in Kerhonkson, a cross was burned on a lot next to the synagogue land.[133] But despite some visible opposition in 1899 in Sullivan County to the increasing number of boardinghouses catering to Jewish immigrants, bigotry in Sullivan County and southern Ulster County in the 1920s did not reach the level of the anti-Hebrew crusade of the late 1880s and early 1890s in Greene and northern Ulster counties or the level of exclusion that persisted in those areas for several more decades.[134] However, Jews still felt a need to prove themselves. As late as 1927, in reporting on the Jewish Agricultural Society's night school, the *New York Times* emphasized Gabriel Davidson's statement that "the strong trend of Jews toward the farm is evidence of the falsity of the popular conception that the Jew has neither desire nor aptitude for life on the farm."[135]

The reception to Jewish farmers, and to Jews in general, varied according to community and time period. Bigotry as exemplified by the Ku Klux Klan and the restrictive communities was worst in the northern Catskills. But despite some anti-Catholic feeling that surfaced in the area during Al Smith's Democratic candidacy for president in 1928, the four Catskill counties of Delaware, Greene, Sullivan, and Ulster, unlike the southern United States, did not decrease the percentage of their vote given to the Democratic Party because of his candidacy. The Catskill Democratic vote was 30.9 percent in 1920, 28.9 percent in 1924, and 31.6 percent in 1928. The Democratic vote, combined with other small party votes, stayed about the same in these three elections.[136]

Jewish farmers owned land adjoining that of indigenous Christian farmers, and the neighbors often would meet at fences or property lines. Friendly interactions developed, if not friendships. Frequently a Jewish farmer, breeding his scrub cows that often came with the farm he bought, paid for stud service of his Christian neighbor's pedigreed bull. Jews and Christians often crossed paths at the hardware store, bank,

Synagogue in Dairyland, ca. 1940.

Rural synagogue at intersection of road between Kauneonga Lake and Swan Lake, 1991.

Synagogue in Swan Lake, ca. 1940.

lumberyard, creamery, railroad station, post office, and, of course, public school. They also met in special situations. One interviewee recalled that "we had a Christian doctor, Dr. Orr, in Grahamsville, who charged fifty cents a visit. He came on a horse and buggy to the farm, and he charged five dollars a confinement. He got rich in the lumber business, not doctoring. He was a fair guy, treating Christian and Jew alike."[137]

With Jews in these towns gradually running their basic businesses, and with some of the Jewish farmers beginning to prosper, there was some envy from those Christians who thought of themselves as being displaced. But these towns helped the Catskill Jewish farmers by lessening bigotry. For example, the Jewish townspeople employed at reasonable wages Christians who had made less in Christian-owned businesses. The burgeoning resort construction business employed local carpenters and other building craftsmen. In effect, Jewish resort expansion and Jewish farming brought cash and relatively full employment to the Catskill area despite the indigenous population's unenthusiastic welcome to the newcomers with the strange tongues and religion.

Mutual understanding did progress. In the Woodridge summer resort, at the produce supply firm of Stapleton and Penchansky, John Stapleton, the Christian partner, spoke Yiddish to his customers, as did William Penchansky, the Jewish partner.[138] After Stapleton and Penchansky joined with James R. Elliott in business, Erna W. Elliott wrote that "Stapleton (Catholic), Penchansky (Jewish) and Elliott (Protestant), congenial partners for many years, were alluded to as the 'League of Nations'."[139] The Christian owner of the *Ellenville Press*, Irving McNally, learned Yiddish from Ephraim Yaffe and set type in Yiddish for notices and advertisements in his local newspaper. Robert Stapleton, an attorney in Ellenville, and son of John Stapleton of Woodridge, learned Yiddish while growing up in Woodridge by going to shul with his friends Mitchell and Morris Penchansky, the sons of William Penchansky.[140]

Chanukah plays were performed in halls owned by Christians. When a Yiddish play, *Dus Emese Glick (Lebensbild)* (True Luck [Picture of Life]), was performed at Shadowland Theatre in 1930, the playbill showed advertisements by twenty-one local firms: DeWitt Clinton's Tires, etc., the Brodsky Brothers' Ellenville Post Garage, Mr. and Mrs. A. Rothkopf's General Dry Goods, Mr. and Mrs. W. E. Nathan's Choice Groceries, Ab. Masors' Ellenville Paint Store, Soloman and Radosh's Sanitary Barbers, Mitchell House Garage, Kaplan's Millinery, Campbell's Drug Store, Irving Ostrander's Furniture and Undertaking, William D. Cunningham's

Stapleton and Penchansky's store, Woodridge, 1987. The sign dates to the 1930s.

Law Offices, Bueltmann Brothers' Jewelry and Gift Shop, Thos. J. Mc-Mullen's Pianos, etc., Rose and Douglas Plumbing, Mr. and Mrs. J. Tanenblatt, Dr. and Mrs. Jack Blumberg, H. Weinbrot's Wholesale and Retail Fruit and Vegetables, John Dunlop's Insurance, the Terwilliger Agency (insurance and real estate), Cleon B. Murray (attorney at law), and Homer C. Kuhlmann's Cars. In other words, the advertisments included a mixture of Jewish and old established Christian firms. Anti-Semitism appeared to have diminished by then.[141]

Economic envy and Christian teachings did occasionally manifest themselves as convenient anti-Semitism. Jewish schoolchildren sometimes experienced verbal and, occasionally, physical abuses. Larry Batinkoff's father and grandfather had managed farms in southern Russia, and after living with dissatisfaction in New York City for about ten years, his father moved the family to Ferndale in 1919, when Larry was three years old. Larry was the only Jewish student in his class. Despite his family's relatively easy adjustment to farming because of its farming background, he remembered his fellow students as being initially unkind to him but eventually leaving him alone and accepting him.[142] Al Cohen remembers that when he was a young child in the middle 1920s, "one of the kids with whom I was friendly, I had an argument with him one day, and he said, 'You dirty Jew, you killed our Christ.' I didn't know what that meant. I came home and asked my folks what the kid meant by that, and they didn't give me a good explanation. They just said 'Oh, he's an anti-Semite'."[143] Ruth Levine Frankenstein, Herman Levine's daughter, remembered that expressions of anti-Semitism were not uncommon and that "Jews were strangers to many Christians in the 1920s and 1930s, even into the 1940s."[144] Abe Jaffe remembers a mixed pattern in Glen Wild: "Anti-Semitism in grammar school [in Glen Wild] was overt, but gradually, by the end of the 1920s, it was not so overt. It was still around, but covert."[145]

On the other hand, another interviewee remembers that "when I went to school in [the area] I felt no anti-Semitism even though at one time I

Ruth Levine on the steps of the Jewish Agricultural Society office, Ellenville, late 1930s.

was the only Jewish kid in the school."[146] Esterita R. Blumberg, daughter of the activist Elmer Rosenberg, says that she suspects that her father—who probably believed that living in conflict and being victorious over adversity built character—"didn't give a lot of thought as to what it was like for his children to grow up in the chilly atmosphere of an area steeped in anti-Semitism and reaction" in western Sullivan County. But after they moved to heavily Jewish Woodridge when she was a child, "it was a little like entering heaven. . . . Our gentile neighbors learned our language, knew our customs, observed our holidays!"[147]

Acceptance did not come quickly, nor did it come as quickly as the Christian advertising in the Ellenville Jewish playbill might suggest. But with very few exceptions adult Christians in the area seem to have refrained from harassing Jews. As in other times and with other groups, though, it took only a few bigots to make life miserable for a number of people.

In turn the Jewish immigrants, while maintaining their Jewish values, were also eager to learn English and to become citizens. For example, about 1920 the Workmen's Circle in Ellenville organized a Yiddish school to teach the children Yiddish. But there was little interest, and the school did not last long because "the Jewish people, by that time, became more Americanized. Even the older generation, who immigrated from Yiddish-speaking countries, started to speak English."[148]

The society and the Council of Jewish Women jointly sponsored mass meetings to encourage and help immigrants to become naturalized. In April 1926, for example, meetings were held in Monticello, High Falls, Ferndale, Accord, Liberty, Woodridge, Ellenville, and Hurleyville. The council was strong in Ellenville. These meetings sometimes featured prominent Jewish and non-Jewish speakers, and at others the members could get help in filling out applications and enrolling for citizenship classes.[149]

Jewish women participated in many activities other than naturalization. Pearl Trotsky Levine, Herman Levine's wife, taught Jewish classes and was active in the Council of Jewish Women and the naturalization drive. Although not a farm wife herself, she exemplified strong Jewish womanhood. She had attended the Hebrew Technical High School in New York at night and graduated from the Teachers' Institute of the Jewish Theological Seminary, where she was a student of Rabbi Mordecai Kaplan. Ruth Frankenstein, the Levines' daughter, remembered her mother: "My mother was a powerful force in my father's life and influenced greatly whom he became. My father admired his Pearl and looked to her for many things. . . . Upon their arrival in Ellenville, in the early 1920s, it was my mother who initially moved out into the community and coaxed my father to join in. . . . She nominated the first woman—Helen Potter—to be elected to the Board of Education and she [Potter] went on to become president. . . . Probably frustrated herself, she [Pearl Levine] wanted her four daughters to have careers and eventually they did—a legislator, a psychotherapist, a teacher, and a pediatrician."[150]

Women were important to success for the Jews in the Catskills. The society's manager in Ellenville "saw settling on a farm as a family affair. He interviewed wives as well as husbands. He used to say he looked at the woman's hands to see if they would be good for milking and her nails to see if they had to be manicured. He believed that a woman's attitude, her readiness to work hard, endure hardships, and live far away from family in new surroundings greatly influenced the family's success on the farm."[151]

The Baron de Hirsch Fund had hoped Jewish farming would reduce anti-Semitism by proving to Christians that Jews were productive. With the help of the whole family significant progress toward that goal had occurred on the lower Catskill farms and in the towns as the 1920s ended.

Chapter 3

Surviving the Depression

In October 1929, the stock market in New York City crashed, leading to the Great Depression. But even before the 1929 crash, farmers had major financial problems stemming from deflated prices and gutted markets. The farmers' share of U.S. national income dropped from 15 percent in 1920 to 9 percent in 1928, a 40 percent drop.[1] Farmers received some help from the Federal Land Bank and from the Capper-Volstead Act allowing cooperatives to represent farmers, but conservative Republican survival-of-the-fittest politics were riding high, and farmers got little sympathy from the government. At times like this, a 1929 letter from a Jewish farmer to the Jewish Agricultural Society in Ellenville was especially poignant: "I have today received a note from the Jewish Agricultural Society and a letter telling me that I was granted the short term loan. That letter and note brought tears in my eyes. Picture a man, for no reason of his own, put into a condition without the least bit of credit, all the people look at me as though I have committed an awful crime. Yet I don't feel guilty of any and here, me not being able to even pay the interest to you. And here you showing me your kindness and lending me yet money for seeds, and things for the garden necessary and chicks. How could I thank you enough. . . . As long as I live, I shall never forget you and the Society, as you give me courage to struggle on."[2]

The nation had changed remarkably by 1930, and so had the Catskills. Previously, the farmer who lost out on the farm could go back to the city for a job, but now that route was closed. As the economic hard times continued, the traditional rural to urban migration was reversed as many returned to the farm. The number of Jews seeking farms was the second-highest ever (after the boom year of 1920). The *Mountain Hotelman* described the desperation of the situation: "Many city folks are trekking to the farm to avoid starvation and destitution. Children are returning to the parental farmsteads. Parents are finding refuge with their children. Brother is going to brother. Friend is going to friend. Here on the farm they can find, if nothing more, at least food and shelter." The newspaper also recognized the farm as a last resort, as a place where "at least the farmer can protect his family and himself."[3]

Facing the most difficult year of its history in 1932, the society concluded that "probably not since the hectic colonization period which accompanied the Jewish mass immigration of the 1880 decade has there been so keen an interest in farming by Jews as there exists today. . . . We do not subscribe to the grandiose plans that are put forth to turn Jews en masse to the land. But we firmly believe that there is room for more Jews on farms and that this is an opportune time to place them there."[4] The nation was used to frequent depressions, and at first most did not realize how severe and long-lasting the effects of the crash would be. It was not until the fall of 1931 and the early winter of 1932 that most people began to realize its severity and to start using the political arena to effect change.[5]

Meanwhile, those Jews already farming in the Catskills had to survive as best they could. Urban unemployment obviously decreased milk, egg, and poultry consumption and in turn adversely affected them. By the early 1930s, for example, eggs sold at their lowest price since 1907.[6] The society was caught in a dilemma between helping city people who desperately needed loans to settle on farms and helping established farmers who desperately needed loans to enable them to continue farming. Furthermore, its loan funds were low because of low repayment of outstanding debt, and the attempt to balance the requests of the needy farmers and hopeful farmers "called for painful decisions."[7]

The resort business also was seriously affected. Most employed Jewish city workers no longer could afford to board wives and children in resorts in the summer as they had in the past, much less scrape together the train fare for about eight round trips to see them. But for families with any kind of income, summer in the mountains for the wives and children was still almost a necessity. A superheated East Side tenement was made hotter by nightly cooking, was unrelieved by the luxury of electric fans, and had as its only local recourse sleeping outside on the fire escape. The advent of summer polio epidemics added more pressure. Some of those who had enjoyed the pleasures of summer mountain boarding before the crash and could afford humble lodging were willing to go to the mountains in reduced circumstances.

Deprived of boarders who could pay the rates to which they had become accustomed, farmhouse operators found themselves mired in credit problems with local grocery and meat suppliers who pressured them for payment. All this combined to expand the kochalein or "cook by yourself" rooming business. Crowding whole families into single rooms already was commonplace, but in hard times it was even more frequent and acceptable to the crowded. Kanfer refers to the kochalein as being a step below the bungalow in status and as being "considered the slums of the Catskills" where the poorest lower east siders could get fresh food and air. It is poetically true that "in the old days, people went to mountain hotels and slept happily in a broom closet because it was more spacious and more country than what they normally had at home." It is also true that looking backward, with the advantage of more modernity and comforts, things can look comparatively bleak. One summer visitor, speaking of a later time and looking back about thirty years, said, "They [my children] couldn't get over the smallness of it, I mean the actual tininess of it. The entire bungalow wouldn't fit into a normal-size living room. The bedrooms were just big enough to accommodate two double beds with a space for one person to stand between them. The living room—there was no living room. There was

Bess Meyers and children at a picnic, Woodridge, late 1920s; in the background, a typical kochalein farmhouse.

just a very tiny kitchen, a three-burner stove, a wooden icebox, cold water." But despite the plainness and smallness of the kochaleins, Kanfer's description of them as "slums" is too severe, especially in the years after the crash.[8]

The kochalein rooming business had special attractions for farmhouse wives. In boardinghouses they almost always were the cooks, at least until the businesses evolved into hotels. Freed of life over the stove of a summer kitchen, of cooking on a coal- or wood-burning stove three meals a day for two months for twenty to forty boarders, the wife of the farmer who ran a roominghouse instead had less work. She only had to stoke that stove at 6 a.m. daily and twice later in the day for the roomers who might have used it, at least until she could afford the propane gas hot plates. The amount of wood she chopped and carried, or the number of full coal and ash pails she carried, remained the same as when she was the only cook. She plucked chickens for her own use now; the roomers plucked those she sold them, unless they would pay extra for plucking. The kosher slaughterer (schochet) came through on his route in the early morning to slaughter the chickens left in wooden-dowled crates at the roadside, as he did for the boarding business.

The farmer would charge the slaughtering fee of a few cents to the roomer, a benefit to the farmer's cash balance especially if he had to lay out cash or obtain credit until the boarding bill was paid. In some cases, farmers themselves slaughtered chickens without charge for the roomers not concerned with kashruth. Becasue the chickens were cheaper this way, the roomers were encouraged to consume more. If the farm had vegetables, raw milk, and the much sought-after sweet corn, these could be sold to the boarders. Freed from the boardinghouse kitchen, the wife could make a few more pennies by taking the horse and buggy to the nearby village and get groceries and meat to re-sell to the roomers (or to buy for them for a small fee).

As the kochalein expanded during the depresssion, the farm wife could put in even more time on animals and crops.[9] Her husband and children no longer had to be waiters, busboys, and chambermaids, so the whole family had much more time for farmwork. The society recognized and encouraged this shift in responsibilities, noting that farmers "are casting their eyes more and more back on the farm. This is the time to take advantage of their receptive mood."[10] But, as throughout its history in the Catskills, the society's help was mostly in such areas as education, community service, and small second mortgages, with lit-

A Jewish family digging potatoes near Oak Ridge, ca. 1930.

tle real financial help.[11] Although the society still was not able to give much financial help, many farmers did put more emphasis on the farm, enlarging their dairy herds, expanding their barns, raising more chickens, building more chicken coops, and working more land. But, as was the case for all farmers in the United States, farm product prices during the depression returned little reward for their labors.

Unlike the rest of suffering rural America, which depended on urban markets fairly exclusively, the Catskill Jewish farmers continued having their summer local markets and hence were able to get a better return on their labor and investments than farmers elsewhere.[12] In the mid-1930s, during the bad times, the society came to appreciate the combination of farming and resort business as "not only providing farmers with additional income, but also in bringing a ready market for their product to their very doors."[13] Gabriel Davidson, manager of the national society, attributed the survival of these farmers during this period to "being close to markets, having the opportunity to retail their products, and (even with hard times) being able to find some city work."[14]

The Jewish farmers continued to supply the slightly more lucrative summer resort markets with as much of their produce and livestock as they could. The *Mountain Hotelman* called for more cooperation between farmers and resort keepers.[15] With the depression, and with the shift of guests to less expensive options like the kochalein, some resorts

Dr. Gabriel Davidson visiting Jewish farmers, 1940s.

were having difficult times financially. It is debatable—and was debated—whether the problems were all because of the depression and
competition from kochaleins, or whether the resort businesses had
overexpanded and would have run into financial problems anyway.
Gabriel Davidson, manager of the Jewish Agricultural Society, thought
the problem was a combination of overexpansion and high interest rate
loans—a time-bomb.[16] The *Mountain Hotelman* editorialized against hotel
owners trying to outdo each other, but expansion continued.[17]

Chicken, a mainstay of Ashkenazi cuisine, remained in high demand among the summer guests of the resorts that were succeeding.

When sold live to hotels, chickens brought a few cents (10–15 percent) more per pound than in the New York City wholesale live poultry market. Retailed to the roomers, it sold for a little more. A farmer could make several hundred dollars more during the summer on broilers and eggs alone, which, in the depths of the depression, was an incentive to pursue the poultry business. Most Jewish consumers still had European tastes because most were immigrants and Europeans expected mature fowl. In fact, much of the United States shared a taste for mature hens and cocks, and the Catskill farmers sometimes would sell their yearling hens to summer boarders even if the birds had a few good months of egg-laying left in them. Generally the birds were boiled for soup, with the unripe yolks left in the bird appearing as a delicacy in that soup.

About 1933, however, a new taste became cultivated—a taste for broilers, a taste developing chiefly among first and second generation Jews who would try new foods their parents did not cook. Broilers were the males that were "sexed" when they were one-day-old by a

Peter Kaplan and his poultry breeding house in Kerhonkson, ca. 1937.

new visual method invented by the Japanese for differentiating the chick genders. They were raised to a three-pound market weight. It took at least fourteen weeks to bring a male bird to market weight then, which meant a considerable investment in "mash" (milled feed) and cracked dry corn used for fattening. The farmers aiming at that market started broiler chicks (which cost two or three cents rather than the five or six cents for the more desired females raised for egg laying) in late March and early April for local kosher slaughter in July and August. Females, loosely termed pullets after the name for the nearly mature hen, had to be started earlier because it took six months before they would lay eggs large enough to be marketable. Moreover, because the poultry farmer had to start the egg-laying earlier in the season than was usual, there were fewer eggs produced more slowly (egg production increases with the lengthening of the day).

Buying sexed chicks from hatcheries, high egg cost, the need for insulated brooder houses, large fuel bills, and buying feed on almost six months of credit all added to the costs of raising broilers. Except for established farmers, everyone had to pay for chicks with cash, and the Jewish farmers interested in expanding poultry operations had not yet established enough of a credit history to obtain loans or credit. Thanks to the resort business, the Catskill Jewish farmers were more nearly solvent than most farmers in America. But even for them cash was scarce in the early spring when roomer rents had long since been used to pay the prior year's bills and when collectors wanted payment on the winter's coal and grocery bills. Because of the unavailability of ready cash at the beginning of the broiler season, neither the egg business nor the broiler business boomed despite the expanding interest in broilers for summer use.

Those who kept cows might have counted on a monthly milk check—the underpinning of the Catskill farmers' income for half a century—but milk prices were far below production costs. In 1931, a milk war between competing companies had reduced prices farmers received for their milk by 40 percent or more.[18] By 1933, milk prices were so low that these farmers joined the national milk strikes. They protested by spilling their milk outside creameries rather than delivering it inside, thereby hoping to garner the same public notice for their bad circumstances that striking industrial workers got for theirs.

Dairy farmers also tried to cash in on the lucrative resort market. Just as they aimed to have their layers produce market eggs by July,

The Perlman family feeding ducks and geese, 1930s.

Catskill farmers aimed to have no dry or nursing cows in the summer months. They tried to wean calves by the end of June so that they could sell raw milk from their tuberculin-tested herds locally (providing un-pasteurized milk to others outside of one's immediate family was still legal in the Catskill counties). Cows required less feed per unit of market item (milk) than did chickens. Cows were also cheaper to breed because they ate locally grown hay and pasture, while commercially raised chickens ate milled grain and supplement feed plus cracked or whole corn, all bought from sources off the farm.

To raise low prices, dairy farmers, encouraged by state experiment stations, tried to improve their herds by upbreeding the cows with bulls whose genealogy suggested higher yields. It was a new process at the time; stud fees for such bulls were high, and the bulls were hard to find. Results were slow because at best it would take two years for a calf resulting from such a mating to become a milking cow, and half of the offspring would be male anyway. (Artificial insemination was several years in the future.) A dairyman could improve his herd quickly with

Benjamin Miller evaluating a cow, ca. 1940.

pedigreed high-producing cows or calves, but it was an option few Catskill Jewish dairymen could afford in the depression. Given their debt, few could get credit for this kind of production investment. From a lender's viewpoint, such an investment was risky even to those with good credit because mastitis, a ubiquitous and almost incurable teat infection, respected no pedigree. It could ruin any collateral the pedigree might have represented to a prospective lender.

Increasing the number of quality cows was another approach farmers used to produce more milk, but it required more hay and pastureland. More land meant more fencing and liming of soil (if the farmer could even buy adjoining land worth working). More cows also meant enlarging barns—more hay storage and milking stanchions—and buying more horses, or even a tractor. Farmers wanting to expand would also need machinery, including the emergent milking machines, plus better refrigeration facilities than a springhouse provided. All these necessities required more than short-term credit. Some Jewish farmers, like the Kross and Levitz families, took that route, building the barns themselves. They filled their new barns not only with their own hay but also with hay cut on neighbors' idle fields.[19]

Increasing vegetable operations was another possibility for farmers, and some, like the Resnicks, who had some open fields, grew cabbage and other crops for the New York market. Sweet corn, summer squash, and string beans were planted with the same marketing objectives. Even if the farmer had horses or tractor rigs to plant more vegetables, he hardly could do that on the rock piles passing for farms that so many of those places constituted. And vegetable prices yielded no better return per dollar of investment than milk.[20] Unpredictable weather was, of course, always a potential problem. Sometimes a little humor could ease the disappointment. One farmer's wife, noting the stunted potatoes, would joke that her husband "planted potatoes, but got peanuts."[21] They tried all types of undertakings to make a living. For example, the Mirkin family in Stone Ridge raised bees, Arpod Fisher in Montgomery raised silver foxes, and Nathan Weingarten near Kingston raised wood chucks. One Jewish farmer raised guinea pigs and another mice for laboratory research. The Poplock family grew mushrooms in a former icehouse that had been given to a former employee when the icehouse on the Hudson River went out of business.[22]

With a few exceptions, Catskill Jewish farm operations, with or without resort features, already mortgaged, their operators in personal

The Louis Resnick family in a cauliflower field, Oak Ridge, 1920s.

debt for production and personal credit, were not candidates for either short-term or long-term credit. Summer incomes helped rescue them temporarily, but were not enough. As was true of farming generally, the credit crises of the 1920s had gotten even worse for the Catskill Jews in the depression.

The few Jewish farmers who did have credit coming into the depression were those who carried Federal Land Bank mortgages. Herman Levine and Joseph Kooperman, the idealistic Woodridge attorney whom the fire insurance co-op had recruited in the early 1920s from the Brooklyn tenants movement, helped the farmers obtain the mortgages. Joe Kooperman and his bride, Ethel, also an attorney, continued in the 1930s to try to obtain such mortgages. They were successful in a few cases, but even a farmer with a mortgage found it difficult to succeed because of low milk and poultry prices and difficult credit terms.[23]

One farm family typical of those who did get mortgages was the Siegels, dairymen and cauliflower growers on the Irish Cape Road (where Irish farmers had owned dairy farms) between Ulster Heights and Napanoch. Their 1926 Federal Land Bank mortgage and its relatively low interest gave them several years in which to stabilize their herd and buildings, but depression milk prices delayed their mortgage payments.[24] Most first mortgages continued to be held by prior owners, and Federal Land Bank mortgage refinancing was still uncommon for the Jewish farmers. The society continued extending second mortgages but in small amounts

The Shapiro family of Monticello gathering carrots, 1940s.

Arpod Fisher, a former chef from Hungary, on his farm in Mont-
gomery, 1930s.

and with conservative terms. Despite the slight benefits of a summer cash
flow that set them apart from other farmers in the depression, most
Catskill Jewish farmers were ineligible for either federal or conventional
mortgage refinancing because of their unfavorable debt-assets balances.
Some applied for such financing nonetheless but did not obtain it. Local
banks, which had extended some operating credit to small risks, had to
be more conservative in the winter of 1929–30. They had less to lend.

Moreover potential creditors, including federal lenders, doubted Jewish farmers' proficiency in farming technology. The society's extension agent program, hardly a decade old, was not yet perceived by Christian bankers as being effective (except for those like the Siegels who had the proof of a good dairy herd). Al Cohen concluded that the society "had service people who, I believe, were as valuable or more valuable to the Jewish farmers than the extension service would have been. Now, the extension service had no qualms about working with the J.A.S. representative or service men because he was a man of college caliber. So he had free access to that office for pamphlets or literature that he could pick up there and make available to the Jewish farmers when he was visiting. And, he was well-versed in poultry nutrition, poultry husbandry, some dairy."[25]

If times had been better, lenders who wished to take reasonable risks might have seen good collateral in a new development: the agricultural education of these farmers' sons who, on graduating from local high schools, went to Rutgers or took two-year agricultural programs at the New York State agricultural colleges at Delhi and Cornell.[26] Farm

The Poplock mushroom farm, 1930s.

Jack Siegel watching for crows in a cornfield, 1933.

building construction, drainage, herd and flock management, sanitation, and even concrete mixing were taught there.

These sons absorbed new technology from state college of agriculture experiment stations that would have made them more efficient farmers and lowered their unit cost of production. While their parents might have learned good building design and livestock disease control in Yiddish from the society agent, no Christian lender could know how much they knew. Their sons, however, learned "at the source," so to speak, and should have been a better risk, but that made little difference to potential creditors.[27] The depression reduced the chance for

Catskill Jewish farmers to expand production just when they could have with the help of the society agents and their own sons' serious interests in farming.

In contrast to the Jewish farms, the established, well-capitalized, Christian-owned farms remained relatively unaffected by the depression. Their credit was sound, their machinery was unencumbered by debt, their land was ample and arable, and their route to the latest farm technology was already in place. Those farmers continued improving their output, buying machines, and improving their herds.[28] It was impossible for the Jews who knew of those places not to feel that they were centuries and social classes removed from them. Not many Jews had to worry about such awareness, however. Those farms were not numerous in the resort area by that time; several stretched along the valley from Port Jervis to Kingston, some were near Grahamsville, and a few others were scattered around the area. They were chiefly dairying operations, a few with their own creameries and bottling plants. Their owners intersected with the Jewish farmers at the feed store, where the Jews often had to pay cash while the Christians could enjoy credit, a difference the Jews definitely knew.

In 1930, the Jewish Catskill farmers took steps to remedy their distresses. One step was the organizing of a National Conference of Jewish Farmers in New York City in October. Over 300 farmers attended the main session, and Jewish farm women also met under the auspices of the National Council of Jewish Women. An agricultural exposition was held that drew about 14,000 people. Some farmers from the Catskills attended and exchanged ideas on farming techniques and leadership development.[29] An even more significant step for the Catskill Jewish farmers, however, was the formation of an action association, the Federation of Hotelmen and Farmers. Its purpose was grand, if vague, as were other contemporary political attempts to deal with the depression.[30]

Soon after its founding, the federation's newspaper, the *Mountain Hotelman,* on January 16, 1931, praised the establishment of the federation as an instrument to right wrongs. It said in English—not Yiddish—that its uniting of "the various sections of Ulster and Sullivan counties, with their diversity of interests, into a brotherhood, working for the common interests of all, was an accomplishment of itself. To have done as much as it did for its members in the brevity of its existence is really surprising and presages no small measure of success."[31]

Voices of Lodz socialism and unionization echo here; certainly no business association would have complimented itself for serving "brotherhood" in this sense.

Road paving was a major concern of the new federation. Muddy roads, of course, affected everyone, Christian and Jewish, although farmers were more likely to be inconvenienced than people in towns and villages. Helen Hill Aldrich, daughter of a Christian farmer in Grahamsville, said, "in the old days there were certain times of the year the dirt roads were impassable. I remember my father had a team of oxen and in the muddy season, he would keep them hitched up all day, so that when someone went axle deep in the mud he could just lead out the oxen and pull them out. The mud kept the village isolated to some extent."[32]

Articles in the *Mountain Hotelman* on March 14 and April 25, 1930, first urged members to lobby Albany for state assembly passage of a bill funding rural paving and then celebrated passage of the bill. Better roads made it easier for farm children to get to school despite adverse weather conditions. A farmer in Divine Corners wrote to Herman J. Levine on November 27, 1930, to thank him for his help: "I wish to take this opportunity to thank you for your interest and help which have greatly influenced the education of my children, for your fine work has secured transportation facilities for them, thereby making it possible for them to go to high school regardless of weather and road conditions." A farmer's wife also wrote that "our bus started yesterday. . . . Please accept our heartfelt thanks." Roads were also important for economic reasons. Spring thaws and flooded fords in the Catskills, as in the rest of rural America, suspended truck traffic on which farming was increasingly dependent, and summer dusts kicked up by increasing numbers of automobiles annoyed summer resort visitors. While hotels on main roads got their roads asphalted, drained, and fitted with concrete culverts over fords and washout points, roads to farms remained dirt and mud in rainy weather well into the post–World War II era. The condition of the private farm road running from the public road to the farm home and buildings depended on the farmer's own resources, and it rarely got more than shale or stone, if that.[33]

The federation also made its voice heard on Federal Land Bank loans, cooperative insurance, farm labor, and farm taxation.[34] The *Mountain Hotelman* helped improve transportation for schoolchildren. The newspaper criticized school districts that ignored a state law requiring school districts without a high school to provide transportation to a high school in another district. The newspaper noted that "the sons and daughters of our distantly situated farmers and hotel keepers" were also entitled to an education and encouraged farmers and hotel keepers to let the newspaper know if they had problems.[35]

The *Mountain Hotelman* also fought prejudice in general as well as specific instances, such as discrimination against Jewish applicants for teaching positions. It encouraged Jews, Catholics, and Protestants to work together in harmony.[36] As a result of the anti-Catholicism that had appeared in the 1928 presidential election when the Catholic Irish-American Al Smith ran against Herbert Hoover, the newspaper created in Ellenville an interfaith committee, called the "Good-Will Movement" or "Better Understanding Movement," to organize a mass meeting on the bigotry issue.

On March 14, 1930, the *Mountain Hotelman* chronicled the meeting, which had been held on March 4, and reported that "the hall was filled to capacity with visitors from Liberty, Parksville, Monticello, Woodridge, and other sections of Sullivan County."[37] The Sullivan county Good-Will Movement was sponsored by a lodge of B'nai B'rith, the Jewish fraternal organization concerned with antidefamation. The inauguration meeting followed on March 24, and the *Mountain Hotelman* wrote that "about eighteen months ago, the rabid rabble which includes the arch bigots held an anti-Catholic meeting in Norbury Hall, Ellenville, New York, advertising it near and far as a meeting at which the Catholic Church would be exposed. An impostor, representing himself as an ex-Priest, was to tell all he knew—rather all that the mob expected to hear. On Monday evening, March 24th, from the same platform in Norbury Hall in Ellenville, Protestant ministers, Catholic priests and a Jewish Rabbi propounded the brotherhod of man."[38] The newspaper cited months of efforts by Jews, Protestants, and Catholics leading to the meeting. Themes of the March 28 article reveal its writers' nineteenth-century romantic, democratic, and encyclopedic sensibilities: "Monday night, March 24th will long be remembered by those seeking to live in peace and harmony with their fellowmen. . . . It is instinctive for us to be friendly with those whom we know and distrustful with those with whom we are unfamiliar. . . . When we learn to have respect for the customs and beliefs of other groups we will see that we have no monopoly, but rather share goodness, truth, and beauty with them."[39] This Keatsian concern with "goodness, truth, and beauty" echoed the immigrant Second Avenue idealism at odds with the utilitarianism then influencing life in the United States. This idealism surfaced repeatedly in the governance of Inter-County, in the fire insurance co-op, and in civic activities such as the Better Understanding Movement.[40]

Obtaining local school positions was a special problem for Jews, particularly at the start of the depression when all jobs, especially public service jobs, were coveted. The Ellenville school system, for example, had adopted a rule that local teachers and teachers without experience would not be hired, a rule that "hit the Jewish teachers on two scores—because they were local and they were inexperienced."[41] The Catskill Jews were not concerned only about bigotry that they themselves endured. When a Catholic teaching applicant was discriminated against in Harriman, New York, in 1931, it was discussed by the Ellenville-based *Mountain Hotelman*. The newspaper noted that the barring of a schoolteacher from teaching because she was a Catholic is "a severe blow to lovers of fairness and those anxious to preserve the fundamentals of our country." Praising a bill introduced to the New York State Assembly "prohibiting any school authority from inquiring into the religious affiliation of any applicant school teacher," the newspaper, as if remembering its constituency, cautioned that a Jewish applicant still could be discriminated against because of "semitic name or physiognomy."[42] In the early 1930s, Herman Levine spearheaded "get out the vote" drives, at first "to elect a Gentile supervisor who promised to appoint a Jewish teacher to a position in a one-room schoolhouse." Levine was elected to the school board in 1931 and in 1934 was elected president of the board, a position he served in for years. He also successfully fought to eliminate invocations of Christ at school meetings.[43]

By 1933, the Ellenville public school situation had become more tolerant and included more Jews, partly because of the Christians' changing attitudes and partly because of the increased size and activism of the Jewish population in the area. In 1933, twenty-three of the forty-three local high school graduates in Ellenville were Jewish, and a rabbi delivered the baccalaureate sermon. As Levine wrote Davidson on May 23, 1933, "For the first time in the history of Ellenville the Board of Education has decided to have the Baccalaureate Sermon delivered by a Rabbi. Now the problem is to find a Rabbi who would fill the bill. You are acquainted with conditions in Ellenville and appreciate my problem. Can you help me?"[44]

It was a problem that Levine and the Jewish community welcomed, for it signaled equality and acceptance in one more area of life. Similar

One-room school near Ellenville moved by the Slutsky family closer to their resorts and restored, 1991.

changes occurred in other villages. Esterita Blumberg wrote that "during the depression days of the middle '30s a Jewish Board of Education hired many of their own graduates, so that the faculty reflected the population of the village,"[45] and she remembered that she had her first Jewish teacher in Woodridge in the fifth grade.

Frustrations resulting from the depression caused some to blame Jews for economic hardship, but recognition of common problems also led to a sense of joining together for common survival. At the end of 1930, the *Mountain Hotelman* gave thanks that such organizations as the Ku Klux Klan could find no footholds in the area.[46] In view of the Klan's declining strength in the North as contrasted with its strength in other parts of the United States,[47] the situation in the Jewish Catskills seemed capable of being solved. Based on a study it conducted of three hundred Jewish farmers in seventeen states in 1934, the society concluded that Jewish farmers were getting along well with their non-Jewish neighbors.[48]

Like people everywhere, the Jewish farmers and business people of the Catskills had conflicts, petty jealousies, pride, and other traits that led to problems. And just as it tried to bring together Jews and Christians, so did the *Mountain Hotelman* try to heal rifts within the Jewish community. In 1930, for example, it showed the danger of community centers closing because of internal disagreements and pleaded for the Jewish community to prevent this "disgrace."[49]

Despite lobbying for paved roads vital to farm transport and resort operation, for lower utility rates critical to operating resorts more profitably, and for other goals, the federation's tangible achievements were limited. Its intangible achievements were greater. The existence of the organization, and especially its militancy and the fact that its ideas were expressed in fairly good English, if somewhat flowered with terms spoken by French revolutionaries and English political romantics, marked the readiness of its members to move into mainstream political economy. Jews were becoming activists in parties, platforms, policies, and programs that could bring them relief. The *Mountain Hotelman*'s idealistic echoes derived in large part by the fact that it was a one-man weekly, edited and published by Ephraim Yaffe, the Hebrew scholar turned farmer–boardinghouse operator, who had settled at Leurenkill in 1913. Like a mulamed (a wise teacher) turned socialist, or like Moses, Yaffe attempted to lead his people from adversity. For example, he warned those whom he felt were jeopardizing their financial security "by believ[ing] that they can transform their dairy farms into poultry and vegetable farms without much ado that they are playing with fire and possible serious consequences."[50] He recognized that both obtaining and repaying credit were still problems.

Yaffe also cautioned the farmers that if they did not sanitize their dairying operations, they were endangering the health of those who consumed these products and furthermore that these customers might take their business elsewhere. (The resorts were still serving guests raw milk.) Good milk sanitation would "help keep our local milk market for our own farmers," Yaffe concluded, trying to justify to his readers what they perceived as harsh demands by county sanitation departments. In cooperation with the Department of Farms and Markets and the state board of health, the society launched a program to produce cleaner and better milk, and the response of the farmers was "gratifying" to Yaffe.[51]

The common practice of a tenant packing as many sleepers as he might into one room also attracted considerable notice from county health departments. At some boardinghouses, single bathrooms served thirty or forty people, with toilets emptying into single stone cesspools adjoining the dwellings. By this time even many of the small rooming houses did have flush toilets and stationary wash basins, but the hard soil could not always absorb the increased waste. Heavy rains magnified the problem.[52]

The health departments in Sullivan County, and particularly in Ulster County, threatened to close down the resorts for sanitation code violations, codes of which most operators knew nothing. Whether the health departments bore down on the Jewish resort keepers out of a disinterested concern for health or whether they were motivated by prejudice against Jews is unclear. Possibly it was a combination of both factors. At any rate, the society helped the resort keepers improve their sanitation conditions not because it encouraged farmers to enter the resort business but because it realized that without that business the farmers would go bankrupt and default on the society's first mortgages.[53] For some years prior to the crash, the Ellenville office had provided the services of Dr. Edward Goodwin, an "Americanized" Jewish sanitary engineer, who counseled the farmers in sanitation improvements. As Levine described it, "The question of sanitation was a very important one because at one time there was an outbreak of diarrhea, and the State Board of Health was going to close down all the rooming

Rabbi Isaac Landman (left) *and Herman J. Levine examine a sanitation exhibit in Ellenville in 1928.*

houses and all the boarding houses mainly operated by Jews. So, they enlisted the cooperation of the society because of our Jewish approach, the language, etc., and the society engaged Dr. Edward Goodwin."[54]

Dr. Goodwin worked for the society from 1919 until 1950. He was a captain in the U.S. Medical Corps in World War I, where he was in charge of sanitation for a large cantonment, and before that he had been in public health work for many years.[55] Gabriel Davidson, general manager of the society, visited Camp Dix (New Jersey), noticed how "spotless and spic and span" it was, and knew that Dr. Goodwin was "our man."[56] The society established a rural sanitation department in 1918, largely because of the poliomyelitis epidemics of 1916 and 1917, and then hired Goodwin to be in charge of it. He focused his attack on four fronts: sewage disposal, garbage disposal, the water supply, and the fly menace.

The society sought to increase awareness of sanitation through such methods as lectures, classes in New York City to encourage summer guests to cooperate, and the formation of the Sanitation League in Ellenville in 1920. The league had 30 members at its formation in 1920 but increased to 412 members by 1922. It wrote its own code, gave certificates of merit to those who met the code, and cooperated with the society and the state health department.[57] The area of Sullivan and Ulster counties was singled out for primary attention because there were so many farm-boardinghouse combinations there and because the society's sanitation department was headquartered in Ellenville. The society said that the mission of its sanitation department was "to keep those regions so richly endowed by Nature free from pollution and contamination, a healthful refuge for the tired city toiler." By 1923, conditions had improved somewhat in the Sullivan-Ulster area, and the sanitation department spent more time in Connecticut, Massachusetts, New Jersey, and Pennsylvania. But the Sullivan-Ulster area remained the single large, important area of concern, and the treatment of sewage there remained a serious problem.[58]

Goodwin designed relatively inexpensive sewage layouts using cesspools and leaching beds made of native materials, mostly stone and the usual logs. As the county health departments became more adroit in pursuing the rooming houses (they did not police as vehemently the large hotels, with whom the rooming houses were competing), they expanded their concern from cesspools to the issue of the cleanliness of water sources, claiming wells were threatened by farm waste. These were the same wells that for half a century under Christian and then Jewish

boardinghouse operation on the same properties had never been criticized. Just as the Jewish farmers had speculated about the counties' concern with cesspools, they also speculated about whether this new attention to wells was a result of improved sanitation engineering or a result
of increased efforts to persecute them for other reasons.

The anti-fly campaign enforced by county health ordinances caused
the society to demonstrate to the farmers how to erect safe, screened,
and properly limed outdoor toilets (privies) and how to build garbage
incinerators as an alternative to the commonplace garbage heaps located behind barns. The threat of polio, discovered to be carried by flies,
increased the urgency for such alternatives.

In dining rooms, bedrooms, porches, and the milking areas of barns,
farmers and boardinghouse keepers used flypaper, that simple but
sticky streamer about two inches wide and three feet long that at the
day's end demonstrated how many fewer flies there were in the world.
It cost little and, in many of the boarders' and farmers' opinions, ended
any need for further action. Those stretched and hung nickel rolls
(cheaper by the dozen), flecked out by evening, at first were the Jews'
attempt to humor officialdom. After polio was traced to flies, those un-
sightly, sticky decorations testified to one's public-spirited, personal
combat with the disease, a fight that produced the same feeling of sat-
isfying self-righteousness that people had felt when they had subscribed to public sales of "beat the Hun" Liberty Bonds a little over a
decade earlier. (Most did not install screening, which required a cash
outlay not calculable into the costs of board or rent after 1929.)

The problem of maintaining a pure water supply edged out flies as
the most difficult problem to solve, especially by 1935, when the rooming houses began to expand into bungalow colonies. Goodwin advised
on water sanitation to the extent that solutions did not require drilling
wells and modern chlorination of surface water. He was perplexed by
the county health departments' insistence on chlorination even for water that originated from springs in uninhabited sites. Places were shut
down simply because they did not chlorinate, not necessarily because
their water test showed bacterial contamination. But drilling deep wells
and buying their concomitant pipe, casings, and pumps were far beyond
the credit ratings of nearly all the operators. Water chlorinators cost
thousands of dollars and required additional hundreds of dollars to wire
them to the water sources. A farmhouse's or rooming house's gross
summer rental income often amounted to under a thousand dollars.

The chlorination problem was solved ultimately in the mid-1940s by Joseph Garelick, a Jewish plumber of Hurleyville. He invented a simplistic chlorinator, a check valve plastic drip device fed from a wooden barrel by rubber hoses, and appropriately he called it a "Simplex" chlorinator. He mixed the solutions quietly in his yard, using inexpensive and quite available HTH powder and plenty of local water, solutions that the farmers themselves could have made at their barrels for pennies if they had known of the existence of HTH. Each carboy of the solution was five dollars, and at least one carboy was needed per week. Many young farmers lugging carboys of Garelick's calcium hypochlorite solution through woods to oaken dispensing barrels at water sources got ripples in their backs from the weight. But the farmers bore the cost of the Simplex chlorinator to keep their rents coming in. Garelick's chlorination did not remedy the most egregious of the health ordinance violations, the leaching of cow barn cleanings into shallow stone-lined wells. The cost of the ultimate solution to that problem—a drilled, steel-lined deep well equipped with proper pumps and pressure tanks—in some cases caused a farmer to give up the rooming business in favor of farming entirely.

While the sanitation engineering was intended to advance the resort side of his business, the Jewish farmer could apply its techniques to agricultural ends as well. He could learn how to build a form for a concrete cesspool cover reinforced by old bed bars and other steel scrap, learn how to mix concrete to fill them, and then transfer the experiences to farm building foundations. He could learn how to use string and a simple bubble-line level to ditch land for draining, learn how to lay fieldstone taken from old stone walls to line cesspools, and learn how to split the stone and use it as the economical filler in the concrete foundations of farm buildings. This experience in elementary civil engineering prepared him to build barns and, more significantly, chicken coops economically of native materials lying around his property.

The society continued another kind of instruction: its annual fair, which, following the crash, could not match the splendor of the 1928 event in Ellenville. By 1934, however, the society's staff held fall harvest fairs in the Mountaindale and Woodridge high schools. There they introduced the Jewish farmers to the same types of events that Christian farmers had enjoyed for years. At the fairs, Jewish farm wives could see their first home canning demonstration. Or they could exhibit what they had learned to can (or, more accurately, to "jar") a year

The Mountaindale school, 1985.

earlier, a wondrous achievement to these women in light of the total lack of such conservation in Eastern European tradition. Children exhibited their biggest pumpkins, cabbages, squashes, corn ears, chickens, and calves, if they could transport them there. The fair combined, or even replaced, the Jewish harvest festival of Succoth with Christian America's county fair as adopted from England. While some of the attendees perceived the events as a bit of hokum wrapped in certificates and ribbons, they found the camaraderie sufficiently appealing to take the trouble of hitching up a horse or of finding a ride on someone's truck to get there. Also appealing were the pots of boiling kosher hotdogs at an almost affordable nickel a piece, corned beef and pastrami on rye sandwiches sometimes showing up at fifteen cents each, and soda, both celery and cream. These items were not traditional at most county fairs in the United States, but at Woodridge and Mountaindale they were the alpha and omega of good eating. For most Jewish farm families attending in those hungry years, the fairs were almost their only fun.[59]

In 1936, the society formally recognized that "the lack of social life for teenagers and young adults on the farm impelled many farm children to leave." The society tried to improve the social and cultural life for young people, primarily by establishing farm youth associations.[60]

Some Jewish parents also tried to induce their sons and daughters to stay on the farm. Young people took short courses in agriculture in the winter. For young adults, some parents increased farm operations to make room for another income or gave their children farms of their own—either by dividing their farms or buying nearby farms. They hoped, by example, to encourage more city youths to move to the area to bring "youthful, vigorous, and intelligent accretions to the Jewish farm movement."[61]

Despite the society's resort sanitation projects and the sanitary milk program of which Yaffe spoke in the *Mountain Hotelman,* the boarding and rooming cash flow was not enough income to run the farm. The farm itself, without more production and a better level of capitalization, could neither pay its mortgage nor support the farm family. Even when some farmers (and sometimes their wives) resorted to working in the city in the winters, finding work was difficult.[62] Most could not put amenities like central heat and electric refrigerators in their homes, and many did not have telephones. To keep warm they fed their kitchen stoves with wood they chopped and whatever coal they could buy, sleeping in the kitchens or over them. They carried water from wells or streams if their plumbing froze. They conserved whatever cash and credit they had for investment in their businesses.

The farmers knew that either the farming portion of their businesses had to become more profitable or that the resort portion of the businesses would have to replace farming. In many cases the resort operation did replace farming completely. Some hotels, like Yaffe's Breeze Lawn or Joseph Slutsky's Nevele and his brother Charles's Fallsview, milked large dairy herds until the late 1930s when the requirement of pasteurization ended the profitability of that milk. But these were in the minority. Those hotels that had cows and closed during the winter sent their cows to farmers who would take care of them until the hotel reopened for the summer season.[63]

The majority of hotels by the 1930s were built from scratch on unfarmed land, and even most of the hotels built from farmhouses gave up their herds. Both farmers and hotelmen tried to help each other. At the 1931 convention of the Federation of Hotelmen's Associations, a resolution was adopted urging hotelmen to buy from local farmers and to let farmers know which crops the hotelmen needed.[64] The society continued to vacillate on the farming-boardinghouse issue, favoring farming as always, but facing reality. By the mid-1930s, the society rec-

ognized that boarders had been an important factor in helping mountain farmers ride out the storm and in succeeding years recognized the
mutually beneficial interaction of the two.[65]

In some cases, farming, generally poultry raising, replaced or at least
dwarfed the resort operation. The farmers who took this route expanded floor space with buildings framed with locally cut and sawed
lumber and set on concrete that was hand-mixed with locally dug sand
and gravel and often moved by shovel-loaded horse wagons.[66] Those
farmers who had a knowledge of concrete and carpentry from their
work on sanitation engineering had an advantage. Others who could
read blueprints or had gained building experience in other ways also
built farm structures, including dairy barns.[67] Most of the expansions
did not include improved production technology, either in improved
stock or improved nurture of the stock, so the farmer needed to sell
more to cover his added expenses. Summer resort trade continued to
furnish that market for eggs at least for two months a year, but the New
York City wholesale market did not absorb more production because
of high unemployment and consequent underconsumption. So farmers had to install labor-saving devices if cash or credit could be obtained
and to have lower-priced chicks from breeder flocks producing more
eggs per hen on less feed. These were difficult goals to achieve, but the
need to achieve them did not disappear simply because they were
caught in the depression. With mortgages in which they had invested
years of earnings the Jewish farmers, like many other farmers, were in
a vicious cycle. They could not afford to abandon their land and other
investments.

As noted, by 1932 more Jews had gone to the Catskills to farm, desperate to escape from the depths of the depression in urban areas. They
came despite low market prices for milk, eggs, poultry, and vegetables
and the absence of adequate production credit. As the 1930s continued, another kind of newcomer came, also trying to find a way to survive but also bringing more skills. These people were young first- and
second-generation Jews, not interested in the boardinghouse business
and hopeful that money could be made in eggs through proper management. Some, like Abe Jaffe, came to operate land their fathers had
bought and had not developed. After he graduated from college and
could not find employment in the teaching profession for which he
prepared, Jaffe returned with his brother David, also educated as a
teacher, to their family land. Others, like Max and Beatrice Brender,

The Jacobsons, father and son, of Parksville, on their farm, 1930s.

who bought land in Ferndale, came from city life and came educated as well. Brender, a former officer in the U.S. Army Corps of Engineers, bred superior Leghorn laying hens for his own hatchery and supplied chicks to the area's struggling poultry raisers who were buying chicks of dubious strains from great distances. Brender could sell chicks locally at lower prices and still make a profit.[68]

These new Jewish farmers thought that they could make more money in scientific poultry raising than they could in the city at a time when their educations would hardly get them subsistence jobs. The depression had stymied the climb from working class to middle class for thousands of upwardly mobile Jewish immigrants in New York. For most of those who remained in New York City, "the garment industry provided the job of last resort once the depression dashed their chances for mobility out of the working class."[69] The novelist and essayist Irving Howe described how his parents, whose store was wiped out in 1930, became garment workers.[70] But some were not willing to remain in or return to the garment industry. They were adventurous, educated, ready to move if necessary, and ready for new approaches to work. They were ready for scientific farming in all areas and came to the Catskills with their hopes. Entering farming, they inadvertently became guides to the now-indigenous Jewish immigrants, some of whom were free to put more time into farming because the expansion of the rooming business had pushed them out of boarding. The new farmers showed the earlier farmers that money could be made in poultry and so encouraged the established farmers to pursue their own inclinations to raise more chickens.

All of the Jewish farmers shared a need for production credit and a less costly source of the elements of production, a need that inspired them to develop some sort of cooperative to buy feed economically. The feed was primarily for their egg flocks, which by 1933 could average up to one thousand hens—a large number then—but was also for their dairy cows and work horses which were still numerous. Although mostly pasture and silage eaters, cows fed supplements of milled rations high in certain proteins, vitamins, and minerals would produce more milk. Horses fed special supplements were healthier and thus could work harder, increasing the farmers' desire for these rations if they were affordable. As the 1930 Yaffe caveat indicated, the farmhouse and boarding operators were becoming seriously interested in poultry, attracted by the relatively short span from the time one invested in chicks to the time one shipped eggs. For chicks, the lag time was eight months, contrasted to the years it took to raise calves to productive cows. Also attractive was the possibility of getting out of the long cycle necessary to upbreed dairy cows to quality producers. Production for poultry could be on small acreage, in buildings that could be made of local materials. The area's farmers could still ship eggs directly to stores in New York City at slightly above wholesale prices on the O&W as farmers had for half a century.

The indigenous farmers knew how cooperatives should work, because those producing milk belonged to the Dairymen's League, because some remembered the old cooperative creamery, and because the society had a policy of encouraging membership in such organizations (examples of the latter were the cooperative credit unions in Woodridge and Ellenville and the fire insurance co-op). The importance of the fire insurance co-op was kept alive especially because obtaining adequate fire insurance was a major problem following the depression: fires increased during that period and, because valuation of buildings was deflated, a decreased coverage of buildings resulted.[71]

On March 11, 1932, Elmer Rosenberg wrote an article in the *Hotelman* specifically turning Yaffe's generalized "brotherhood" unionist voice to the price-cutting issues then plaguing farm prices and resort incomes. His headline, "Shall We Organize and Exist or Compete and Destroy Ourselves?," expressed disenchantment with the free enterprise competition driving the national economy.[72] Rosenberg's call for the formation of cooperatives to lower production costs and to market products, couched as it was in unionist terminology, showed a militancy unprecedented in farm organizing except among the Scandinavian and Bohemian immigrants. Placed in the context of the fire insurance co-op, the credit unions, and the Dairymen's League and the Accord Farmers cooperatives, it was more than rhetoric. The *Mountain Hotelman* praised the work that the Dairymen's League did for dairymen and told poultrymen they would not be in their deplorable state if they had a poultryman's league.

Rosenberg's column and Yaffe's editorials show that the Jewish farmers were moving toward co-ops as a way of life as the old national "League of Equity" had preached half a century earlier. The Catskill farmers knew in general about other farm cooperatives, chiefly marketing organizations, in the Midwest and South, and they knew even more details about the well-organized Central Jersey Co-operative.[73] Farmers in the area from Kingston in the north to Spring Glen in the south had bought feed from the Accord Farmers' Co-operative Association, affiliated with the Grange League Federation. The Catskill Jewish farmers, however, did not feel comfortable with the Accord. It was not a Rochdale cooperative, and it was not especially warm to the idea of Jews serving on its board of directors even if by some fluke a Jew should be elected. The Grange membership was nearly all Christian and in providing socialization as well as economic help often had a

Christian flavor. In Halcott Corners in the upper Catskills, for example, one Jewish farm daughter noted that they participated in the Grange but that its members "sang songs with Jesus in them which Jewish kids never mentioned."[74] Accord also was hesitant to give credit and did not like dividends. Moreover, it was basically a dairy feed miller and did most of its business in Ulster County, while the new poultry business was expanding in Sullivan and Orange counties. The Accord Farmers' Co-op did not deliver its feed and farm supplies to farms, a serious problem for those unable to afford their own trucks or those who had little time to drive their horses and wagons to the depots for loading.

The Inter-County Farmers' Cooperative Association, Inc., or "Inter-County," as it was more often called, was formed to meet the farmers' needs. Encouraged by the society, Jews about 1934 had formed their own marketing and feed-milling Rochdale-style cooperatives in New Jersey's Hightstown–Tom River–Vineland area among the evolved colonies and in Central Connecticut around Willamantic and Moodus. The society was in close contact with those cooperatives, and the Catskill co-op was similar in organization. Its first president, Harry Kaplowitz (later Kaplow), ranked the founders of Inter-County as the Jewish Agricultural Society first, Joe Kooperman second, and its first general manager, William Berman, third. The society's Benjamin Miller called Kooperman, one of its charter board of directors members, its "godfather."[75]

Precisely how Inter-County began is not reflected in records and varies with the teller. It likely started when a group of fifty-five Jewish

The Inter-County Feed and Farm Store and automated feed mill, 1984.

Ulster County and Sullivan County farmers applied to the society in February 1934 for a $1,000 loan to buy milled feed, fertilizer, and seed in pooled orders. Apparently they obtained the loan. The feed might have been that about which William Berman spoke in his retrospective, where he explained that he and two other farmers traveled to Hightstown's Central Jersey co-op to see how it worked and to arrange for direct purchase of feed from it. According to Berman, it was a truckload of feed; according to Miller, a carload.[76] The $1,000 loan might have been for feed bought elsewhere, because Benjamin Miller cited March 1936 as the first time the new co-op had bought feed and had it delivered to its $15 a month rented warehouse situated on an O&W siding in Mountaindale.[77]

At any rate the March 1936 date agrees with Berman's story that one night in early 1935 some farmers met in the offices of the Woodridge Credit Union (or at the Ellenville Workmen's Circle Hall, according to another account) resolved to organize a feed-milling cooperative.[78] Initially, twenty-five farmers pledged to buy five $5 shares each in the co-op, some pledging without their wives' approval, others with their wives' urging. Years later Berman would remember that the money was a significant amount then and that "it was as painful for a farmer to part with five dollars as to have an eyetooth pulled." Most paid for their five shares on the installment plan. They pooled, confident that "Mr. Roosevelt's marvelous instrument," the newly created Federal Bank for Cooperatives in Springfield, Massachusetts, would lend the balance needed to start milling.[79]

The new bank did not consider the new co-op creditworthy at first, and, in Berman's words, they "found the going tough." But the Jewish farmers kept their faith in economic progress. Counseled by Kooperman and by Miller and Levine from the society, the co-op solicited short-term loans from nonfarmer friends and some advance money from members. Inter-County bought a $475 mixer to begin mixing feed in the Mountaindale warehouse.[80] By July 1936, another New Deal creation, the Rural Resettlement Administration, which dealt with destitute farmers, agreed to lend the new co-op $4,000 and to lend destitute farmers wanting to join the co-op the twenty-five dollars each needed to buy shares.[81] According to Miller, the president's report delivered to the co-op's first annual meeting in December 1936 noted that the co-op had grown to thirty-six members in the first eight months.

The co-op bagged the mixed feed in the same 100-pound jute sacks in which the raw feed ingredients arrived on rail cars and contracted with independent truckers to deliver it to the farmers. The farmer paid a penny or two per bag for this service, a fee easily recouped in the time it saved the farmer, time that in turn could be invested in additional work on the farm. In its first year, 1936, the co-op sold 41,470 bags of feed, for total sales of $67,514.[82] By February 1937 the co-op operated its own trucks and began its own delivery system. In 1937, it sold 57,264 bags of feed, for total sales of $131,155. Net patronage refunds allocated from all operations increased from $1,916 in 1936 to $2,820 in 1937.[83]

Some present at the meetings of Inter-County might have thought about the irony of the government support of co-ops. Money was borrowed for co-ops from the class that was reluctant to lend directly to the Jewish farmers. Those farmers saw the irony especially because of the interest of common men in the popular concept of political economy. Although discussed privately, especially by the more politically conscious and the left-leaning, the point was never discussed publicly. Recognizing the need for the co-op, its members took the Springfield money without asking questions and went to work building the cooperative.

"Godfather" Kooperman handled most of the legalities for Inter-County, such as obtaining the state charter. Like most of the farmers, he was transplanted from the city; an idealist, he also knew about financing risks, charters, by-laws, applications for credit, shares, and property transfers. As the members discovered—sometimes to their bewilderment—he was masterful also in parliamentary procedure and Robert's Rules of Order. His idealism had earned him the communist label. For this reason a few people wanted him to resign from his position as a successful fundraiser for the United Jewish Appeal, but he refused. By the mid-1930s, the majority of Jewish socialists in New York had given up their political theories to support Roosevelt's specific policies, partly upon the urging of the *Jewish Daily Forward*,[84] and were not unduly bothered by criticism for supporting socialism, Social Security, and a national health plan.

Inter-County's tentative first board of directors made by-laws almost immediately upon organizing in March 1936, giving one vote to each member, electing the board of directors for limited and specific terms, setting the periods for meetings, and establishing qualifications for membership. While being a farmer and owning shares in the co-op were required for membership, being Jewish was not, and fairly soon the co-op also had Christian members willing to associate with a predominantly Jewish group.

The first board of directors included some farmers who made a traditional Catskill living by producing milk, poultry, and vegetables and by running a summer resort. It also included some newcomers, such as Abe Jaffe, the Hebrew teacher, and the Brenders, who had been to college, who had known no sweatshops, and who owed the society nothing.[85] The Cohen brothers in Kerhonkson took up farming as an alternative to unstable city work in the shaky 1920s economy; one of the Cohen brothers was later elected to the co-op board. Several dozen other newcomers, most of whom had planned on entering professions but were stopped by the depression, also brought new knowledge to farming. If they had any ideological axes to grind, they kept them to themselves and consequently gained the society's praise.[86] They had come to make money farming, not to pursue an ideal.

Although most of these newcomers rejected the resort trade and focused on scientific poultry raising and breeding, they needed credit as much as the older immigrant farmers. But the credit they needed was far beyond the resources of the cooperative credit unions in Ellenville and Woodridge. They wanted to build and equip new operations, and their credit would have to come from banks, lumberyards, and private lenders. Being more educated, and in some cases tied to families already established in the area, they were somewhat more creditworthy than their predecessors had been when they had started. Some of the new farmers were local residents who had taken two or four years of tuition-free training in agriculture at Cornell. Inter-County, the source of good, economical, deliverable feed available on limited credit, was the common ground of the newcomers and the older farmers. Although the political idealists saw the feed co-op through its beginnings, the less ideological newcomers formed its later character.

Mutual respect between the immigrants, who were not as well educated but who held strong political ideals, and most of the newcomers, better educated but not as idealistic as the immigrants, produced in the Inter-County co-op an institution of mutual aid greater than the fire insurance co-op and more helpful to the farmer's prosperity than the society's services. Within three years of its operations, it was the institution enabling many Catskill Jewish farmers to do what the society had hoped they would do—make all their money farming.

The manager for the second board of directors was a member of the original board, William Berman. Another political idealist, he, although more retiring than Kooperman, like him was said to have been a communist. Willie, as he was called, prematurely bald, nearsighted, of medium build, and a bit bent over from a life of peering, had married into one of the successful, older Ellenville dairying families, the Kleimans, after having been a Cleveland grocer.

Berman oversaw the milling of the open formula, which in 1936 was similar to Accord's. Inter-County also followed Accord's policy of printing the ingredients of the formula on tags sewn with a hand-operated stitcher to each bag of milled feed. Several types of cow feed fitting rations (to increase milk production), horse feed, and chicken feeds, including bags of plain corn and wheat, came from the primitive assembly lines. Initially, members thought that they could not afford the delivery cost of one or two cents per bag. As they did at the Accord Farmers' co-op, they came to pick up the sacks at the mill, some by horse and wagon, some with Model T or Model A trucks. They socialized, or tried to socialize, at the new Inter-County Co-op while waiting for feed, but Berman, bent on business, discouraged socializing.

People like Harry Kaplowitz, whose farm was nearly fifty miles away between Kingston and Saugerties, hardly had time or trucks to pick up feed and instead took advantage of delivery. Because he was the president, his example set the standard for saving money by staying home and working. Other farm co-ops in the country by then had regulations that allowed members with large accounts special benefits, even to the extent of permitting them more voting power. This practice had even been extended into a new federal law, the Agricultural Marketing Agreement Act of 1937. This act was designed to help marketing co-ops sell more of their products by setting base prices by authorizing the establishment of federal farmer-directed programs that would be funded and regulated by the U.S. Department of Agriculture. To pass, a proposed regulation had to be approved by at least two-thirds of the eligible voters or by those growing at least two-thirds of the products grown by those voting.[87] The original Inter-County board, however, had established that co-op members would not receive volume discounts for buying, that board members would serve without salary and with a minimum of expense reimbursements, and that board members would be elected by a policy of one member/one vote.

In its first year, the search for a better formula to gain more eggs for a pound of feed and an hour of work ultimately led the Inter-County Co-op to Cornell. Max Brender, who resembled Clark Gable down to the voice and penciled moustache, who, unlike the immigrant Inter-

County founders and board members, stressed "co-op" on its first syllable, broke the ice with Cornell and helped persuade the college to share its formula for feed. All was made on the premises by hired workers instructed by Willie Berman. Thus practically from the start the product milled there was as good as could be bought anywhere. It also was cheaper, deliverable, and obtainable on more credit than the farmer could get anywhere else.

Inter-County was so successful that in 1937 it moved to larger quarters with a bigger mill, an ancient warehouse on an O&W siding in Woodridge. The building was refitted, thanks to their financially successful Mountaindale year, with the backing of the Springfield Bank, with technology and carpentry ideas borrowed from the central Connecticut and Hightstown cooperatives, and with Brender's and Berman's experiences and imaginations. The building looked like a huge barn, one-third of it attached to the rail embankment (good for emptying carloads), the rest upright for about forty feet, prefaced by an office on a platform, all about twenty feet from the grade. It was roofed with corrugated tin, and sheathed with weathered gray clapboards faintly tinted with red pigments.

To renovate the warehouse for their purposes, the board of directors hired some carpenters they knew, led by Abraham Nosenchuck, a farmer and co-op member with some building experience; they also hired assistants, most of whom were Christian mechanics who until then had doubled between garages and sawmills tending the local machinery. These Catskill mechanics, like many working people in mid-1930s America, had no appetite for unionization or any kind of collective action. To them a cooperative was still un-American, which, during World War I, had meant pro-German. To many in the mid-1930s, cooperatives were associated with Soviet Union. For some of the mechanics, whose lives were tied to the small businesses that employed them, co-ops were unpatriotic, communist, and economically sinful because they were an alternative to capitalist production and marketing. They remembered the letter bombs and the shocking 1919 Palmer raids. The jailing of Eugene Debs and the postwar Palmer raids a decade earlier accurately reflected most of the Catskill mechanics' political ideals.

Some politicians on the right and their followers linked Jews and communism,[88] and many in the Catskills were certain that Inter-County was communist. The political right found support for this charge from apprehensive local businesses, especially feed businesses, who also cried "red." Conveniently ignoring the examples of the Accord Farmers' Co-op and the Dairymen's League, competing busineses defamed Inter-County, encouraging their employees' fears of unemployment and arguing that the co-op smacked of public ownership of capital, which they argued was inefficient and hence threatening to the economy of the commonweal.

For the Jewish farmers, such New Deal policies as co-ops and Social Security were not communistic, or even socialistic, but simply ethical and good business.[89] Non-Jewish mechanics were more eager for employment by Jews than they feared Jewish communists, however. They gradually changed their views of the co-op. They found the wages paid for building the new mill legal tender and higher than they got at the garages and other sawmills. The mechanics and the drivers hired as the co-op began operation put to rest any doubts they might have had about their new employers' integrity when their paychecks came on schedule and their employers paid overtime and installed grain dust controls for workers' health.

Many of the Christian mechanics and drivers continued work at the mill for many years alongside some sons of Jewish farmers. They discovered something relatively unknown during those times: that even Jews carrying the communist label turned out to be decent people and employers. The Christians working with the Jewish farmers finally discovered the spirit of the 1922 Capper-Volstead Act, which legalized the agricultural marketing cooperative and which by extension made legitimate the agricultural manufacturing cooperative.

Worker morale and output were high at the co-op mill, an unusual circumstance in depression manufacturing. In 1936, the co-op directors fit the buildings' insides with stout posts, beams, girders, and flooring as the wood came to them. The wood was all cut from local hemlock, much of it virgin, tough, knotless, and close-grained. They installed new hoppers, grinders, motors, pulleys, and belts. They built home-planed white pine chutes for the burlap bags; they wired and piped and did not paint at all. The result was starkly nonarchitectural, but it was utilitarian, economical, and efficient.

Inter-County members picking up feed in Mountaindale sometimes detoured a bit to admire the growth of the new mill. In a way, to the Inter-County members that building was their release from bondage. Although they did not speak in such analogies then, those looking back on it certainly did. Joe Kooperman expressed his pleasure at having the rare opportunity "of witnessing democracy in action on the industrial field" and wrote that "the members understand and know the difference between being a captive account, actually a serf in captivity, of big private enterprise whose only interest in the farmer is to make huge profits for itself out of his toil, and being a member of a democratic cooperative whose business belongs to the farmer and whose economic power enables the farmer to successfully compete with those huge financial monsters and to retain his economic freedom and independence."[90]

Miller wrote that "the ideal grew into an idea which fired the imagination of a small band of visionaries who believed in a better world through working together."[91] The spirit of the Jewish commandment read on Yom Kippur that "the wages of a laborer shall not remain with you until morning" infused the Jewish farmers' managerial method at their co-op and on their farms.[92] They paid their obligations, surprising some and endearing themselves to local Christian businesses despite any prejudices proprietors or employees might have been nursing.

The society was becoming less central to the Jewish farmers as other co-ops became more successful, as was in line with its objectives. Throughout this period, it continued to give strong support to efforts to begin co-ops. In 1930 the society could say, "Agricultural leaders see in cooperation the best remedy for farm ills. . . . Our society has always been a believer in the cooperative movement." In 1939 it was working with nine purchasing and selling cooperatives in Connecticut, New York, New Jersey, and Michigan, as well as with several credit unions.[93]

With the success of Inter-County assured by the opening of the Woodridge mill, the prospects were improved for those Catskill Jewish farmers who had long hoped to expand their poultry operations. Mash was the major cost of poultry raising, and the chief impediment to poultry raising—lack of a dependable and economical source of mash—was now removed. They were also able now to buy what had been unaffordable basic operating equipment. The co-op sold brooder stoves, watering jars, and semiautomatic water cans below local retail prices. It also sold metal mash hoppers, indispensable for baby chicks but a luxury for hens and for those farmers who nailed hen-sized hoppers together from local planed pine or hemlock. They bought what they could not make and made much, building much of their capital with their own hands.

By 1939, weekly carloads of bagged grain arriving directly from the West and Midwest were being milled on the rough, thick plankings. The grain was contracted on credit both from commercial suppliers like Cargill and from the Farmers' Union cooperative of the Dakotas. The bags were unloaded from boxcars by millworkers who were sometimes helped by the farmers themselves when they were there picking up feed. Practically everything came in hundred-pound burlap sacks, cotton stitched top and bottom, and what didn't came in a variety of wooden barrels or brown bags like those used for packaging cement. The reused cloth bags bore a diversity of logos of the once-indispensable corporate suppliers now being supplanted by the co-ops. Inter-County continued the burlap conservation by charging a nickel (later a dime) for each refilled bag, refundable for all sound bags returned. Content with sheer utility, Inter-County never printed its emblem on anything other than a display bag in the two decades it bagged before the advent of bulk feed delivery.

Business boomed, mostly as a result of expansion of egg production in the area. Trucks delivered feed to those not willing to pick it up at the mill. Farmers with rooming houses, vegetable farms, or dairying operations welcomed late spring and summer delivery, especially if they were over ten or so miles from the mill. Cost of a bag of feed averaged about a dollar, and the delivery fee was about 2 percent or two cents per bag. Even into the World War II period, some farmers figured it was worth their time to save the charge and transported the feed themselves by horse or track-drawn wagons (tractors were rare until the war years), pickup trucks, cars, or station wagons. They unloaded the bags one by one, with help from sons and hired hands. In March and April, the farmer had to go to the mill to fetch the week's feed because Willie Berman stopped delivery service during these months of muddy roads. Filled or even half filled with heavy loads, the co-op's huge Macks and Internationals sank to their axles in dirt lanes dry enough for horses, guaranteeing wasted afternoons spent in unscheduled unloadings, jackings, blockings, and yankings.

Within a few years of Inter-County's inception, many members' lives revolved around it, for in addition to economic aid it also provided social succor. The annual and semiannual meetings, where Willie Berman read his financial reports, were microcosms of union in diversity. Some wore business suits, others plaid, but all were working together to hold on to their farms while others, on their own in depression America, lost theirs. They were people who gathered what enlightenment they could and, cooperating, took control of their destinies.

Two events underscored that control. One was the endless hours of debate on policy by the hundreds attending. Some debated in standard English, others in Russian-accented English, and some fortunate enough to have escaped Nazi Germany spoke English accented by German. All were regulated by Joe Kooperman's firm grasp of Robert's Rules of Order. Because debates were always followed by floor votes binding on the board, the members could control the direction Inter-County would take.

The second event was the public reading of the list of those delinquent in paying back the credit they owed. The very existence of the by-law allowing the reading practically guaranteed a short list. One dreaded being on it. As in any credit organization, the delinquency of any individual burdened the others in the group. But in a nonprofit co-op, where everyone knew everyone else and where everyone struggled to survive, avoidable delinquency of debt practically amounted to ostracism. An ideal of collective responsibility, in addition to the widespread belief held by most Americans then that living off one's neighbors if one could suport oneself was unethical, helped keep the lists short. For those on them, a lawsuit was first; expulsion from the co-op followed. Expulsion meant being turned over to the high prices and short credit of commercial feed dealers, a fate that also helped deter delinquency. Joe and Ethel Kooperman, acting for the board, nonetheless delivered over thirty delinquent notices to members in the first twenty-five years, including some to board members.[94]

By 1940, only four years after starting business, the Inter-County co-op began to replace the society even in teaching farming techniques to the Jewish farmers. Willie Berman prepared medicated feed according to Cornell's latest breakthroughs to fight ruinous poultry infection. While sometimes a veterinarian would come to a sick flock to diagnose it, more commonly farmers brought their diseased fowl to the county laboratory for study. At first a society agent would help farmers contact the lab and would lend experience to the preliminary diagnoses. Subsequently, farmers did these things themselves. The co-op's speedy mixing and delivery, often within a day, of the remedy prescribed, was a great financial boon to farmers. And because drug companies in those days did little research on farm animal medicine, experimental feeding drugs were made available as soon as the colleges released them.

Medicinal feeds were mixed also for horses and cows, and Berman obtained quickly and economically whatever drugs farmers might need to administer to livestock directly. These special services often saved a draft horse, a cow, or a flock of chickens that otherwise might have

Morris Tessler of Kerhonkson with his prize horses, 1930s.

been lost and consequently made the difference between profit and loss. Although such services cost the co-op money, they ultimately encouraged prosperity instead of unproductive costly misery. The bag of specially medicated feed was like a special loan from the Springfield Bank for Cooperatives: it repaid more than its principal many times.

The worst of the depression was over by 1935. The Inter-County Co-op had, more than any other institution, helped pull the Catskill Jewish farmers through the worst years of the it. The combination of farming and rooming houses also helped bring in guest money, and the hotels brought, as even the society had to admit, "a market to the farmer's very door."[95] They also diversified their farming and so increased their potential sources of income.[96] Moreover, throughout the depression years the Jewish farmers gained a modicum of equity in their mortgaged property, learned basic farm management, and, in the resort business, where some of them continued, learned general business management as well. The more intrepid among them learned basic plumbing, carpentry, masonry, and electricity by working along with skilled craftsmen they sometimes employed to build their rental bungalows, improve their rooming houses, or modernize their barns and chicken coops. Some learned how to operate and maintain used trucks and tractors. All these things helped the Jewish farmers in the Catskills see the depression through with fewer bankruptcies and foreclosures than U.S. farmers in general had.

During the depression Jewish farm women generally canned food, fed the men (including the hired men), washed laundry, bore children, and did the basic farm chores. These included working with husbands and children through endless, dusty hours sandpaper-polishing, grading, and candling eggs for the high prices such eggs got from the New York City egg dealers, New York City butter and egg stores, and family groups directly. Chores also included milking and feeding cows by hand, driving horses, and, for some, driving trucks. They worked uncomplainingly, as part of the family, as did most farm families anywhere. But as the economy improved, by the late 1930s they and the rest of their families were beginning to see the benefits of their labors.

There were also simple benefits to country living. Fathers spent many hours with their children, unlike fathers who worked in factories and who had little time to spend with their children after long days of dreary work. Some of the farm children undoubtedly wished for fewer hours with their fathers, since many of those hours were spent working instead of playing. But farm and town children enjoyed the

Jewish farm children on the Relis farm, near Stevensville, ca. 1930.

country. Ruth L. Frankenstein, who grew up in Ellenville, wrote of the pleasures of country living:

> We grew all kinds of vegetables and flowers, enjoyed picking and eating cabbage, fresh sweet corn, asparagus, beans, cucumbers, lettuce, tomatoes, grapes, strawberries in season from our garden, and adorning our house with arrangements of petunias, gladioli, dahlias, peonies, irises, and an assortment of annuals and perennials from our yard. We picked all kinds of berries, including blueberries, blackberries, currants, elderberries, strawberries, and grapes for preserves, jams, and wine. We tapped our maple trees to collect sap for syrup. . . . Growing up in the country afforded us the freedom and peace of going into the woods after school, getting to know the wildflowers—violets, dogwood, milkweed, pussywillows, trilium, mountain laurel, jack-in-the-pulpit, trailing arbutis, rhododendron. Many an afternoon we spent fascinated by little creatures—lizards, toads, frogs, worms, snakes, and bugs. We learned to recognize the birds—orioles, cardinals, sparrows, blackbirds, bluebirds, blue jays, crows, hummingbirds, robins by their colors, their song, the color of their eggs, and the shape of their nests. We identified the trees by their bark and their leaves.[97]

Most of the Jewish farm families still occupied the old houses that had come with their properties, without insulation or central heating. Most still carried water in winter when their pipes froze in the subzero weeks of December through February. But their ledgers had positive balances, major debt notwithstanding. They were getting some local credit and were ready to expand their farms with it.

While the co-ops had taken over more of the economic life and more organized religious life existed, the society still helped local Jews with such matters as widows' pensions, old-age pensions, naturalization, employment placement, placement of orphan children, and domestic relations. It had started the Inter-County Jewish Youth Association, a speakers' bureau, a Jewish Book Week, and library projects. Although the Inter-County Co-op was taking over the teaching of many farming techniques, the society also continued such work. In 1940, for example, it developed a sanitation exhibit on the lawn of its office in Ellenville, more elaborate than the one that had been exhibited in 1928. The exhibit included a protected shallow well, a septic tank, a garbage incinerator, and subsurface absorption lines. An article in the *Kingston Daily Freeman* observed that the exhibit showed the Jewish farmers' desire to be good neighbors as well as good farmers. It noted that the display "has proved invaluable to countless farmers in this area. Inaugurated primarily for Jews, the exhibit has been open to the general public. All creeds are graciously received."[98]

As the pleasant tenor of this article indicated, Jews were becoming more integrated into the general community.[99] Gabriel Davidson of the society concluded in 1935 that Jewish farmers were no longer looked upon with condescension, but there still was some concern about prejudice. Morton Shimm, who had a sixty-acre farm near Liberty around 1940 (and who would later be the society's agent in Ellenville), had to take his milk out to a road a mile and a quarter from his farm in the winter to meet the son of a Christian dairy farmer who had a pickup route. Speaking of the son, Shimm said, "I remember him saying to me one time as I brought the milk up the corner, and I had a little frost on my lips, he said 'You know, you're a white Jew, you work for a living.' I said, 'Well, we all work for a living, it's just that I happen to be a farmer, a Jewish farmer.' So, we understood that all Jewish people had to work. They weren't all bankers, either. We got along all right." Shimm went on to remember that most county government farm agents did not seem prejudiced, with the exception of one who some of the farmers "thought was not very attentive or caring about their needs, who was quite anti-Semitic. It was not open, but you could see by the way he worked, the way he spoke."[100]

Jews still were not hired as government county agents. Al Cohen, the long-time manager of the Inter-County Co-op, states that "the Extension Service was entirely non-Jewish, throughout the country. In fact, as an aside, when I first entered Cornell [in 1930], I indicated an interest in preparing myself for a job with the Extension Service. At the time, my faculty adviser suggested that I try some other field. He didn't explain why, and I didn't realize until years later why he had said that. There were just no openings for Jewish boys in the Extension Service. . . . Years later, in south Jersey, in the Jewish areas, they did have an opening and did employ a Jewish extension agent. To my knowledge, that's the only one who was ever in the extension service."[101]

Although occasionally Jews still encountered isolated moments of prejudice against them, the Catskills nonetheless were a haven when contrasted to the treatment of Jews in Europe in the mid-1930s.[102] In its 1935 report, the society noted that "among our callers this year were German refugees and relatives and friends of Jews in Germany who came to inquire about opportunities in farming." In the following year the Ellenville office reported that German Jewish refugees "claimed

Mr. Shilepsky, a refugee farmer near Monticello, plowing in the 1940s.

quite some" of the branch's attention, and by 1939 there was a small nucleus of refugee farmers in the Catskills. Ten areas in New York state, however, had groups of refugee farmers: Deposit, Bainbridge, Norwich, Windham, Binghamton, Catskill, Albany, Middletown, Glens Falls, and Nassau. By this time, farm land in Sullivan and Ulster counties was generally too expensive for refugees who had lost their savings, and none of those areas was in Sullivan or Ulster counties. Catskill in Greene County to the north and Middletown in Orange County to the south were the only towns in the larger Catskill area.[103] Meanwhile the society was arguing, unfortunately without success, that the United States was capable of absorbing many more Jewish immigrants.[104]

Chapter 4

Prosperity and Its Challenges

In 1940 military preparedness spurred a general economic revival and more cash in more hands. Fortunately for the Jewish farmers of the Catskills, growing numbers in the services had to be fed. Cities once more could pay more for food as the economy improved. New York City's newly funded appetite for eggs, chicken, milk, and produce consumed all that the local farms could produce. People began to eat better and to eat more protein-rich food. The Lend-Lease Act of March 1941 also benefited American farmers, who helped provide food to Great Britain, primarily pork, eggs, cheese, evaporated milk, dried skim milk, dried beans, and some canned vegetables and processed fruits.[1] The need for egg and milk products especially benefited the Catskill Jewish farmers as farm prices rose.

The federal government encouraged farmers everywhere to increase production. Catskill Jewish farmers did so by improving the quality of their milk herds through the statewide program to upbreed using artificial insemination, a recent, tremendously advantageous breakthrough. It developed cows that yielded more milk from the same amount of fodder. The farmers produced cleaner and better milk, but new regulations prevented them from retailing raw milk so they had to move toward cooperative pasteurizing plants.[2] The farmers also increased their vegetable crops.

Above all, the farmers "pushed through" more productive hens in the same amount of space. That meant buying chicks of better pedigree and vigilantly culling out unproductive fowls, which the farm family learned to spot by sight and feel. It meant removing from the chicken coop floor litter soaked with wet manure to prevent coccidia from ru-

ining the fowls. Crowding the chickens overloaded the litter with manure and caused drinking areas to become puddles. Because egg prices
more than doubled, even more farmers with scrub herds or small
acreages for hay and silage corn (both of which were needed for feeding milk-producing cows) quit dairying, and converted their barns into
chicken coops. Changeovers were chiefly on least arable acreage, inefficient since the Delaware and Hudson Canal era.

Since the co-op could supply feed relatively inexpensively and on
some credit, conversions were sufficiently promising to prod some of
the lumberyards to extend credit on lumber and hardware. But any
farmer wishing to protect his equity proceeded with the wisdom guid-
ing Inter-County's mill construction: local pine and hemlock locally
sawed saved half the cost of finished lumber. The only constraints on
expansion came after Pearl Harbor, when building material and labor
became scarce because of war priorities. The nation aimed for a 7 percent rise in milk production and an 11 percent rise in egg production
for 1942.[3] The co-ops and the credit unions helped the farmers to expand to meet the increased demands of wartime America.

The fire insurance co-op covered the fire liabilities of the expanded
farm operations. This was important because chicks were brooded
around coal, propane gas, or kerosene-fired stoves in individual small
frame "brooder houses." Many small houses rather than one large one
minimized potential loss from fire and permitted limited quarantines if
a brood became diseased, but risks remained. The credit unions could
provide small loans to cover exigencies (sometimes including the costs
of repairing farm buildings), and the feed co-op supplied most of the
raw material for production. Local breeders like Max Brender and Larry
Batinkoff, known by then far beyond the co-op, provided the pedigreed
chicks less expensively than the poorer quality stock available elsewhere. Some farmers saved money by buying Brender's and Batinkoff's
roosters for mating with their own hens and could incubate chicks and
improve stock just as one could gain improved heifers by artificial insemination. He could buy a 1,000-egg hatcher from Sears, Roebuck for
a few hundred dollars on time payments if he had any equity at all,
saving hundreds of dollars in chick costs annually. With these innovations, the farmer could have a good chick supply at a time of an acute
shortage of good chicks, a time when the New York City Federation of
Kosher Butchers was working out a plan to buy directly from chicken
farmers in order to divert poultry from black markets.[4] But, for most

Daniel Resnick, Jr., feeding chickens, 1944.

poultry farmers, labor-saving innovations were still limited chiefly to installing winter water supplies in chicken coops so that in winter they would not have to carry water by the bucketful up and around staircases to the thousands of hens.

War production needs shortened the supply of labor-saving milking machines, but even when available the milking machines were costly and less kind to udders than hands were. The cost and shortage of supplies limited the installation of running water to only a few farm build-

Ducks on Sam Yellin's farm near Glen Wild, ca. 1945.

ings such as those housing livestock. Morton Shimm's experiences were typical of many farmers. He recalled that while his wife was in the hospital having their baby, he had to stay home to take care of the livestock: "I had the livestock to take care of and we had a terrible storm, an ice storm, a sleet storm. It was very cold also, and I couldn't let the cows go out of the barn down to the brook where they watered themselves—we had no running water in the barn—because it was just too slippery. They just couldn't make it. I was afraid they would break a leg or something. So, I was carrying water to them from the pump outside the home. The electric wires were down from the storm. I had no running water in the house because the electricity was off. The toilet froze up and cracked. I'll never forget that period."[5]

As in industrial work, longer working days generated increased productivity. In the Catskills, some farmers gained those additional hours by giving up the rooming business. Others hired hands, sometimes from Joseph Blaustein's Jewish Agricultural Society recruitment office in New York, and in practically all cases the hands lodged and ate with the family. As the United States entered the war, however, the availability of hired hands dwindled, and "improvised measures such as weekend and vacation employment, victory corps, teen age hiring, helped fill the gap to some extent but the sum total did not make up for the lack of experienced farm workers."[6]

A typical winter scene in the Catskills, this one at the Steinberg farm, near Ellenville, in the 1940s.

In the summer of 1943, the federal government allowed 3,500 workers from Jamaica to work in the United States under a special program. Because of a serious labor shortage among the sweet corn growers in the Rondout Valley, Ulster County was permitted to have 125 of the Jamaican workers. In addition 250 older girls were also hired who were housed throughout the county (some even in the Girl Scout camp).[7] Both contingents of workers were warmly received; one local newspaper specifically noted that "a distinctly favorable impression was created by the [Jamaican] contingent which is composed of young men many of whom are said to be college graduates."[8]

In the spring of 1944 two farms were picked as sites for the society's Victory Farm Cadet Training Program. The society chose the farms, owned by Joe Brill in Accord and Sam Stein in Pataukunk, because they were efficient and productive, their equipment was extensive, and Brill and Stein were talented teachers. Ninety-two high school students—Jews, Catholics, and Protestants—from New York City, divided into four groups, were sent to the farms for ten-day training periods each. All but

Victory cadets from the city receiving farming instruction on Joe Brill's farm, 1944.

six completed the training, and all of the eighty-six graduates were placed on jobs to help in the war-generated labor shortage. More than a hundred jobs were available when the first group, numbering eighteen, graduated. When an agent from the New York Department of Education visited the Ellenville farms, he praised the attitude and zest of the boys.[9]

The *Jewish Farmer* also lauded the Victory Farm Cadet Training Program's effort to better interethnic understanding. The magazine started an article with the names "Joseph McNamara, Louis DeRossi, Theodore Cohen." After noting that these were some of the boys in the program, the article continued: "Back home, in the boroughs they came from, the McNamara's, the DeRossi's, the Cohen's may have rubbed shoulders and even been pals. But then again, they may have looked askance at each other; they may have come to believe in race distinctions. If any one of them had brought any such ideas to the Ulster county training centers they must have either entirely disappeared or become very much attentuated, as germs invariably do when exposed to air and sun-

Cadets working on Sam Stein's farm in Pataukunk, 1944.

shine."[10] The *Ellenville Press* concluded that the boys learned to respect each other's beliefs and differences, and that the program "was true democracy in action."[11]

While the Victory Cadet program was a social success, it made little progress toward reducing the national labor shortage. To solve that, one simply worked longer and as efficiently as possible despite the constraints on new technology caused by war priorities. Those few farmers who had tractors also decreased use of them to save fuel and in-

Cadets getting planting instructions, in front of the J.A.S. office in Ellenville, 1944.

creased their use of horses, thereby increasing their own work. A Cornell war emergency bulletin concluded that ordinary farm horses were worked only seventy ten-hour days a year and gave suggestions to farmers on how to get twice that much work from their horses.[12]

The war also caused shortages in the materials needed for the long-standing effort to improve sanitation. Screen wire and garbage cans, for example, were scarce. The labor shortage meant that sanitation inspectors were scarce, so enforcement of government regulations was more lax. But the farmers' awareness of the importance of good hygiene and their extra efforts to maintain it kept the sanitation of their farms to safe prewar levels.[13]

During the war years Jewish farmers also raised some victory gardens, prompted chiefly by gentle pressure from the society. It believed that a multitude of small plots supplementing the farms' official maximum productivity would significantly increase the national total of food produced. The government held that victory gardens improved nutrition and thus kept the farm workforce healthy and productive. People with victory gardens were urged to can surplus vegetables within two hours of harvest to save vitamins in the vegetables.[14] Some people criticized the gardens as mere backyard vegetable plots accompanied by

The Goldman family on their farm in Loch Sheldrake, 1940s.

patriotic hoopla. Critics claimed that time spent on the gardens should have been used to produce real income from more hens, eggs, milk, or commercial crops, that it simply was time taken away from commercial production. Actually the victory gardens were mostly activities for the children, many of whom had joined a Jewish chapter of the 4-H Club, guided by the society's local director and his extension agent.

This club awarded blue and red ribbons sometimes complete with testimonials, for heifers, bull calves, fowl (especially pedigreed fowl), particularly large vegetables, superior egg laying, and profitable broiler projects. The society hoped that these rewards would encourage farm youth to stay on the farm. But, although the children appreciated the society's efforts, they also recognized them as hype and were not to be easily persuaded. Most of the Jewish farm youth had seen all the unromantic details of farming firsthand; many had witnessed their parents haggling with livestock dealers, banks, and creditors and had even seen bankruptcy proceedings. They knew that the stakes were high and that the real prizes were co-ops, collective planning, and avoidance of bankruptcy. For adolescents whose relatives were ominously mute in occupied Eastern Europe, the prizes and hoopla seemed even less important in the scheme of things.[15]

Jewish farmers in general were proud of their contributions to the war effort. Of all male Jewish farmers in the age group eighteen to forty-four, 7.5 percent served in the war compared to 6.4 percent for all male farmers in the United States.[16] As the war ended, the Jewish Agricultural Society asked itself if the returning soldier, the discharged war worker, and the disabled tradesman would "cast their eyes toward the farm."[17] The society expected its greatest growth on the west coast and established a branch office there but believed that the Catskills also would grow.[18] Some new farmers moved to the Catskills, and some sons returned from the war and decided to try farming. Within the United States, there was a debate over whether returning soldiers should be encouraged to enter farming, but the prosperity in the Catskills made it unnecessary to discourage any newcomers.[19]

Mel Lesser illustrated this pattern. In 1943, his father moved from Brooklyn to Kerhonkson. "He didn't know much about farming," Lesser recalled, "but he came from Carnarsie in Brooklyn where he and an Italian neighbor couple raised five hundred hens in common. He always wanted to farm." Mel moved his father to the farm and then went into the military, but when he was discharged from the army he too went into farming in the Catskills:

> I returned from the army in '45, spent the summers of '46 and '47 on the farm, and by '48 decided to go into farming on a piece of my father's farm. In '49 I built a house of rough lumber like everybody else, and converted the barn into a three-story chicken coop for layers, and doubled the width of a 20 foot by 20 foot brooder house. Over two decades I built capacity from 1,500 layers to 25,000 layers in cages, with 8,000 starter pullets and some meat birds on range. The meat birds were raised in wire range shelters and let out during the day to eat grass and also receive feed as a supplement, as was the practice then. The meat birds were a sideline. We sold half of our eggs to dealers and half to local hotels, for example, Homowack Lodge, The Granite Hotel, and bakeries. Sometimes we sold to Inter-County. In the winter I sold mostly to dealers.[20]

At the war's end, the constraints associated with it also ended, and new, relatively inexpensive, more efficient technological innovations brought promises of higher profits to the Catskill farmers. Things were looking good for the Catskill farmers. The society concluded that the Jewish farmers of the Catskills had developed their own leaders and built their own community services and that better roads and cars had made the area "almost a suburb of New York City,"[21] where the society's national headquarters was located. Moreover some Jewish farmers, unlike their Christian counterparts, had kept some ties to New York City because of friends and family there and because of its Jewish flavor. The society closed its Ellenville regional office in 1945, although it kept an extension agent there for years longer. Its resettlement work in the Catskills was also essentially completed except for a small number of Holocaust victims. The society settled seventy-five displaced persons on New York farms between 1947 and 1953, when special immigration acts expired, and at least seventy-five more settled independently of the society.[22] But although nearly 10 percent of the post–World War II Jewish displaced persons became farmers, as noted earlier few of these settled in the Catskills because farms there were so expensive.[23] As it closed its Ellenville office, the society reviewed the changes that had occurred with its help and with the help of other individuals and agencies:

> Fraud in farm purchases had virtually been stamped out. Sanitary standards compare favorably with those in well ordered farm communities and are above the level of many. Farming has advanced quanitatively and qualitatively. Herds are tuberculin tested and blood tested against

Herman J. Levine in his New York City office, 1946.

Bang's disease. Registered stock has been brought in. Artificial insemination is being practiced. Modern poultry buildings house flocks of the finest breeds, and Jewish poultrymen are among the leading breeders in the state. . . . In general, the farm economy is better rounded and more diversified. Cooperatives and credit unions have been organized, community centers have been built.[24]

The property transfer from the society to the Hebrew Aid Society, which then became a congregation, was a perfect valedictory for the society. It was recognition that the hundreds of Jewish farmers and former farmers whom the synagogue, and the Jewish community center that would be built on the empty lot next to it, would serve had achieved the independence, Jewish identity, and public respectability that the society had worked so hard to help them accomplish. Although most of Christian America may not have known of these or the other farming Jews, for the Christians who did know them their opinions of Jews in general were improved as a result of seeing these Jews farm successfully. Hirsch and Cremieux may have held grander dreams that such respectability would end all anti-Semitism, but at least bigotry dwindled where Jews farmed. With most of the old battles of acceptance won in the Catskills, Jewish farmers could concentrate on farming.

Chief among the new technological improvements that made farming easier was the introduction of two simple devices that enabled farmers to have a year-round supply of water indoors. One was a lead-sheathed, thermostatically controlled low-resistance electric heating cable taped to steel pipe. It was first used to heat soil in greenhouses and later in otherwise unheated buildings. The cable kept the water temperature above thirty-two degrees. That device came with simple instructions from the Cornell College of Agriculture's engineering department and was demonstrated to Inter-County, which supplied the cable.

The other innovation was the shallow well pump. A few deep wells were drilled close to barns and houses, but their initial drilling, casings, and submersible pumps were too expensive for most farmers. Deep well pumps also required costly large storage pressure tanks. Moreover, pumps required extensive maintenance because of their poor technology; this was expensive and inefficient and sometimes engendered a lengthy replacement period while livestock suffered from a scarcity of water. Cheap shallow-well pumps drawing from a spring and hooked to small pressure tanks could force seemingly end-

Charles Kelman, near Livingston Manor, 1940s.

less thousands of gallons through inch and a half diameter pipe under forty or fifty pounds of pressure. This was enough pressure to operate dozens of automatic waterers located even thirty feet above grade. Initially, installing such a system required applying an even more primitive technology, namely a triad of a good pick, shovel, and steel rock bar. The farmer had to bury pipe three feet into the ground (three feet being just below the maximum frost depth in those climates) to a good water source, usually a spring. By 1947 the farmer could rent or hire an operator with a circular ditching device. A little later, if he could spare the cash, he could rent a backhoe or hire an operator with one for the digging.

Automatic watering released almost eight man hours a day on a farm of 15,000 chickens, about a third of all labor hours worked per day. Less time was saved on automatic waterers for dairy herds because cattle drank at streams during daytime pasturing. But as scientific dairying moved cows into barns more of the time, automatic watering became as critical an economizer of labor time as it did for poultry farmers.[25] The extra time allowed the farmer to try to raise more products for the market.

Inter-County also sold, at cost, stock-raising hardware such as ten-gallon galvanized steel chicken-coop watering tanks and steel mash hoppers of all sizes, items that were more expensive if bought commercially. Retail prices in stores then closely followed the manufacturers' suggested prices, with little discounting. However, Inter-County, like a few midwestern farmers' co-ops, tried to discount on their own, selling most state-of-the-art farming devices and supplies at cost plus a small overhead charge. For example, within two years after the war, the new farm machinery store at the co-op sold and serviced newly developed automatic feeding belts for egg-laying operations.

The farmers discovered the virtues of the small tractor, especially the fully hydraulic, easily operated, labor-saving Ford Ferguson Model 9N which appeared first in 1939. This tractor had been available all through the war, and after the war the co-op tried to get a franchise to market them or any comparable tractor. This attempt met with about as much enthusiasm from their makers as Henry J. Kaiser and Preston Tucker received when they attempted to get American steel corporations to supply them sheets for their automobile body manufacturing stamping mills. Dairy and vegetable farms could hardly operate without tractors, and most already had them. On poultry farms, the small tractors would have saved time in hauling, digging, loading manure, and replacing horses in general. About 1948 the fiscally pressed J.I. Case Tractor and Implement Company agreed to supply the co-op with machinery, and the farm machinery division of the co-op marketed and serviced Case machines. By then a number of farmers already had bought the versatile Ford Ferguson 9N or the more conventional International or John Deere small tractors on credit from once-reluctant Christian dealers in Accord and Walden.

By this time Jewish farmers were already buying cars and trucks, not only from the Jewish pioneer auto dealers in the area, such as Laden-

Jewish woman driving a tractor, 1944.

heim in Ellenville or Lungen in Mountaindale or Schwartz in Monticello, but also from Christian-run companies. By 1940 Christian-owned
banks, lumberyards, and auto dealerships in Ellenville, Monticello, and
Liberty had extended credit to a number of Jewish farmers and hotelmen. Christian dealers had noticed that people like Ladenheim, Lungen, and Rosenthal were in the black. Used to financing tractors for use
in dairying or fruit raising, the tractor dealerships were hesitant to finance tractors to be used on poultry farms to load manure that had
been shoveled into piles from windows of multistoried chicken coops.
They overcame that hesitation by 1950, since their competitors, the

tractor dealerships in Accord, Walden, and, later, Port Jervis and Kingston, were giving credit to Jews. The tractor dealers particularly discovered Jewish farmers' creditworthiness after the co-op began selling and servicing the Case machines.

The machinery increased productive efficiency overnight. While no hard data compare the Jewish farmers' net income with the national norm, the money they plowed back into modernizing and expanding buildings after the war suggests a comfortable income. That more Jews came to take up poultry farming in the Catskills also indicates increased productivity.[26]

The boom in poultry farming was fueled by another new technology, the creation of high quality "caponettes," or roosters. About six weeks prior to slaughter the farmer implanted under the rooster's neck skin just behind the comb a pellet of disilbestrol (a female hormone) so strong that it altered the male sexually and caused him to fatten and grow remarkably. Until the Eisenhower administration found the hormone a carcinogen and outlawed its use in farm animals, this technique boomed, utilizing feed dollars efficiently and thus widening profit margins. It was time-consuming labor, however, and usually required the labor of the whole farm family plus any other cheap hands the family could hire around pellet injection time.

For a while caponette growers moved to the easier-to-use lippemone hormonal mashes (also milled on demand by the co-op) to make caponettes, but those were eventually prohibited also. The alternative was raising "heavy-breed" pullets for the New York City live poultry market, an old recourse that had failed in the past because to reach the desired four pounds such chickens ate more feed than their marketing could pay for. Furthermore, by the time they had almost reached that full weight they had so wet their litter that coccidiosis breeding in it could destroy them, ruining the entire investment in feed and chickens. To avoid this they had had to be raised in low numbers per square foot, which had, again, made production uneconomical. But with the advent of antibiotic mashes, especially those with penicillin derivatives, farmers could control coccidiosis. The heavy pullet business was then feasible, made even more so by new hybridization of the heavy breeds so that the birds gained more weight with less expense.

Barn conversions begun by Jewish farmers in 1940 gave way to new construction. Production of the pullets over a yearly three-cycle operation would run up to 20,000 fowls, which at four pounds per fowl, and at ten cents margin a pound, meant a significant $8,000 profit. The $8,000 was not net profit for the farmer and thus could not quite exceed the annual wage of a unionized urban worker. In New York City, the unionized wage worker then made about $75 per week, or about $4,000 annually, on which he supported a family that generally included a nonworking wife. Even on these prospering farms, as on farms anywhere then, a whole family had to work to generate that $8,000. Wives, and children before and after school, did the chores. They fed and milked the cows, moved manure and feed, cleaned mangers of the old rough hay and then spread it under a Holstein's belly to soften her descent to the cold concrete floor, and before supper drove home the herd for milking. They fed the chickens their mash, dumping it into

A barn previously used for hay, other crops, and dairy cattle being converted to a poultry house in Dairyland, 1940s.

Larry Batinkoff chopping wood, 1940s.

homemade wooden hoppers and spreading it evenly so that all the hens had a chance to feed. Toward evening they took down standing hoppers, pouring in cracked or whole corn kernels mixed with wheat, which reddened egg yolks.

During spring and summer, the farm children after supper drove roosting pullets from the apple trees and into range shelters. On June weekends, they hayed, storing up winter feed for the horses and cows. Within a few years this chore was made easier by tractors, bailers, and the rest of the labor-saving gear the co-op sold on liberal terms. An $8,000 income also had to cover the cost of mobile machinery. Because the New York City market seemed able to absorb practically infinite amounts of the high-quality products coming from the Jewish farmers joined in Inter-County, the wisdom of expanding production was obvious and many farmers went into debt to banks and lumberyards to add buildings. They bet on a continuing high margin, and the bet paid off for a while. In the postwar years, many family incomes came close to urban wages and in a few cases, particularly among hatcheries, even surpassed profits of some small urban businesses.

An immigration directive by President Harry Truman in 1945 and the Displaced Persons Act of 1948 allowed into the United States a sizable number of refugees from Nazism and, later, the postwar communism of Eastern Europe. About 10 percent of these Jewish refugees became farmers. They concentrated in poultry farming because this did not require proficiency in English, allowed an independence that many of these refugees had had in their occupations in Europe, and did not require a large capital investment. New Jersey became a favorite area for settlement for many of these postwar refugees.[27] The northern Catskills, in Greene and Delaware counties, with their European-like mountains and village streets, attracted Jewish refugees as summer visitors. In fact, this area of the Catskills came to have so many German and Austrian Jews that it was known as the Schnitzel Belt, in contrast to the Borscht Belt of the Russian and Polish Jews.[28] But despite its popularity with summer visitors, as in the prewar period only a few refugees from Nazism settled in the lower Catskills.

The small number of refugees who did settle in the Catskills were helped to some degree by the society. Herman Levine noted that "they all needed help—financial help from the society. Not only financial help—the society found farms for them and looked to see that the contracts were properly drawn, that they weren't overpriced and also located in places where they could adjust easily. . . . They had to find something where the English language didn't matter and where knowledge of the type of farming didn't matter. . . . It was less costly buying a poultry farm than it was any other kind of farm because you didn't need much land and you didn't need a large flock in order to make a living."[29]

Like other new farmers, and unlike the farmers of several decades earlier, the refugee farmers who did settle in the Catskills generally did not combine farming and boardinghouses. Modern farming was viewed as a full-time business, and profits usually were reinvested in the poultry business—either for broilers or for eggs.[30]

The Holocaust refugees in the Catskills needed more financial help than they received from the society, and they, like the earlier settlers, criticized the society because it offered only second mortgages. The society defended its policy as a necessary consequence of its lack of funds and noted that this policy at least had the advantage of "enabling the Society to grant a large number of loans despite the limited nature of its available funds."[31] In its twenty-five years in Ellenville, the society received about 4,000 loan applications and granted about half of them, for a total of $1 million.[32]

The lack of first mortgages was serious, regardless of the reason. Greta Engel and her husband, Ludwig, Austrian-Czech Holocaust survivors, came to the United States in 1948 with their daughter, Katerina, and son, Adolph, on a planeload of displaced Jewish farmers and rabbis, the only categories of central European Jews for which immigration officials were bending the law. As a kind of sharecropper on a run-down poultry farm in Grahamsville, New York, Engel, who before the war had been an accomplished cattle breeder and large farm owner, produced a profit within a year. He sought a farm of his own but, unable to obtain society or other financing for anything productive in the Catskills, settled for a small poultry farm over one hundred miles northwest. This farm was in New Berlin, twenty-five miles from Norwich, a dairying region where several prewar German Jews had dairy farms or were cattle dealers. The Engels produced eggs and meat birds there for almost two decades. Ludwig was also closely involved in research for Cornell University. Four decades after first entering agricultural life in the United States, their daughter, Katerina Engel Altenberg, still remembered the loneliness of farm life.[33]

Despite the Holocaust survivors' problems of financing and loneliness, Morton Shimm, who served as the society's agent in Ellenville during this time, remembered that they were successful: "The victims of the Holocaust became good farmers. . . . No disease or anything could beat them. And they worked hard, and most of them became quite wealthy in the egg business or broiler business through their sheer hard work and not taking any guff from anybody. . . . They were becoming good American citizens."[34]

The suffering of the refugees weighed heavily on the minds of the Catskill Jewish farmers, and the society continued to work hard for understanding among people. It supported, for example, the "Jew in American Life" traveling exhibit put on by the Council Against Intolerance. The *Jewish Farmer* noted with pride that Eleanor Roosevelt had visited the exhibit in New York City in October 1945.[35] The society recognized that large farms were increasing and again praised the family farm as "the backbone of our civilization . . . producing 90 percent of our food."[36] But more change was in the air.

A farm planning conference was sponsored by the society as the turbulent 1940s ended in December 1949. The society was helping farmers adjust from a wartime to a peacetime level. At the conference dairy farmers claimed that their farming was more stable and that they obtained greater satisfaction than other farmers because they worked with animals and provided a valuable food product. Growers of vegetables, fruits, and other crops admitted that they faced more hazards, such as changes in the weather, but argued that they gained just as much satisfaction and made just as much of a contribution to society. The non-poultry farmers called poultry raising "unmanly," although most admitted that they also mixed sizable flocks of poultry with their own farming.[37] The society also sponsored the twenty-seventh annual session of the night school in agriculture; the session opened in New York

Evening lecture for prospective farmers at the Jewish Educational Alliance, New York City, ca. 1950.

City in January 1951. Attendees went en masse to the New York Poultry Exhibition then at the Grand Central Palace and "created something of a sensation" as probably the largest single group of visitors to it.[38]

As the United States became embroiled in Korea in the early 1950s, increases in food production again became part of the national mobilization. Raising grain was encouraged in appropriate areas, and in the Catskills the farmers sought to be more efficient in poultry raising. Taking greater advantage of farm youths' labor before they left for war, striving even harder to prevent animal feed waste, paying closer attention to the early signs of disease in poultry, and taking even fewer chances on problems with potentially hazardous poultry house stoves were suggestions made to the poultry farmers in the national emergency.

The society published a special bulletin in 1951 reporting the advantages of various types of farming. It noted that dairy farming was an every day business requiring hard work 365 days a year and early morning and late evening hours but that it was the most stable of all the branches of farming. Vegetable farming was described as a difficult and speculative branch of agriculture, requiring a large investment in costly labor-saving devices; one advantage was that the farmer could take relatively long vacations. Fruit growing also was described as being costly and speculative but allowing vacations. The bulletin described poultry farming as best for "the inexperienced but intelligent and industrious individual with a modest capital. It requires the least amount of land. It involves somewhat less laborious work than several other branches of farming, though daily chores must be performed. Soil and climatic conditions are not as important. . . . Poultry farming is less stable than dairy farming but more so than vegetable or fruit farming."[39] The society also encouraged farmers to consider proximity to markets, schools, transportation facilities, good roads, Jewish communal life, and adequate water supply. Poultry farming was the major attraction to most prospective farmers.

By the early 1950s the Catskill Jewish poultry farms had expanded both in size and in number, supported by additional Inter-County services. But egg production from the larger flocks finally was reaching a point of oversupply, and the price of eggs was beginning to drop. Recognizing the increasing problem of market swings in egg and broiler prices, the co-op's board of directors began investigating ways to market eggs cooperatively. Their manager, Al Cohen, directed the studies.

In 1942, Cohen had succeeded Willie Berman, who resigned after what some say was anomalous red-baiting by a director. The director was an old Social Democrat who, during the time of U.S.-Soviet alliance, pursued the old ideological Bolshevik-Menshevik feud, with little enthusiasm from other board colleagues. The dispute was as much with the few board members who had uttered, or whom he perceived to have uttered, pro-Russian sympathies (sympathies hardly seditious in those war years), as with Berman. Although the board's majority supported Berman, for the sake of harmony he resigned and accepted a managerial position in New Jersey. His resignation was unfortunate and almost half a century later Al Cohen declined to comment on the incident other than to confirm that there was an unfortunate issue dividing the directors regarding Berman's retention.[40] Ironically, Berman's integrity in managing the co-op helped generate the prosperity that permitted his adversaries the leisure to pursue him. For a few months Inter-County members searched their consciences and, in self-interest, expediently ignored them. At best they believed that they had to in order to prevent their engine of success from being riven by Old World schisms.

Cohen had no part in the events leading to his appointment. He continued his predecessor's hard-headedness in serving his fellow farmers. In 1946, Joe Cohen (no relative to Al), son of a Wurtsboro small farmer, a returning war veteran with two bars, and college trained, helped Al Cohen as assistant manager.[41] Like Al, he was essentially apolitical and nonideological; together they were all business.

Their study of the possibility of the co-op's marketing its members' eggs did not promise great profits, but the Inter-County board recommended the study to the membership for adoption and the members approved it. They invested in storage, packaging, and transportation facilities. They incurred credit and plowed operating reserves into the scheme, building a modern, cork-lined refrigeration unit, and installing advanced grading, candling, and packaging machines. They were the first to use foam dozen-egg cartons, finding them more efficient than paper cartons.[42] With the cooperation of local banks the co-op sponsored a pullet-financing program. Using Federal-State Grading Service guidance, it also instituted an egg quality control program on members' farms.[43] Reauthorized by the federal Agricultural Marketing Act of 1946, the grading service, which operated on a fee-for-service basis, aimed to improve the quality of commodities as a way to increase producers' profits. The service was provided by USDA-supervised staff of the state agriculture department.

The Catskill farmers entered the collective egg marketing business reluctantly. But it was something that most other farmers' co-ops did when they organized and was necessary if they were to survive. They were in a vicious cycle. When prices for their poultry and eggs were high, the incentive to expand output or to become more efficient with existing floorspace ultimately led to investment and debt. Farmers were continuously cautioned to be "very careful as far as expansion goes, especially expansion of plant."[44] But the only viable alternative was to leave the business, an option some exercised by entering the resort business. A bulk feeding system had been invented that could greatly increase the efficiency of existing plants, but it was costly. Plant expansion, contin-

Al Cohen of Kerhonkson, later manager of the Inter-County Cooperative, ca. 1940.

gent both on mortgages and operating credit, was difficult because although Federal Land Bank mortgages might solve the construction problem, operating credit had been more difficult to obtain because one could pledge no worthwhile collateral for it. Thus producers could not avail themselves of the technology needed to stay competitive.

By 1950, two significant changes in agricultural financing solved both credit problems in acquiring bulk feeding and expanding plants. One was access to real production credit through the Federal Land Bank's Middletown Production Credit Association, one of many hundreds of such associations throughout agricultural America.[45] While these associations existed in the 1930s, like the Federal Land Bank itself, which in those days favored dairy operations, poultry farmers were not represented on the Production Credit boards and thus were not approved for benefits. That had changed by 1950.[46] The Jewish poultry farmers of the Catskills would even have someone from their community, Larry Batinkoff from Ferndale, on the board of the Middletown Production Credit Association. With the changes came significant loans for production.[47] With the loans, the farmer could in turn buy the new feeding and watering machines that eliminated his reliance on hired hands or the farm family to feed the flocks of thousands of hens. (By this time, flocks numbered up to 15,000 a year on many of the expanded places.) The credit was liberal and the terms were fair. The plan operated like a well-funded credit union: the collateral was the anticipated sale of the farm product being financed.

The other change in financing was Inter-County's ingenious project to fund quick construction of hundreds of bulk feed bins and distribution piping in new and existing poultry houses. The bins were to accommodate the new bulk feed delivery system that brought feed from the co-op's new state-of-the-art automated feed mill. The new system supplied automatic feeders with feed distributed from an elevated supply bin through manually controlled chutes. Inter-County outfitted several of its Macks and Internationals to deliver the bulk feed to the farms (these trucks each had a special blower that sent feed up to the supply bin), and plans were made to build a fully automated feed mill on the old siding in Woodridge. The co-op borrowed open-endedly from the Woodridge National Bank for the construction and sent specially trained building teams to each farm, where they erected the bins and chutes in only one day per farm. The farmer then paid a small surcharge on delivered bulk feed. Because the new system wasted less

A three-story poultry house on the Picoult family farm in Oak Ridge, 1957.

food and required less labor per bird, it almost immediately returned to the farmers the cost of bin installation. The manufacturing and delivery of feed were both more efficient in the new system.

Clifford Calhoun, who was then president of the Woodridge bank, advanced the project with Al Cohen and subsequently with the board of directors and the membership of Inter-County. That a Christian banker actively worked to help Jewish farmers showed how much things had changed in a few decades.[48]

A hefty loan from the Springfield Bank for Cooperatives in 1950 financed Inter-County's new, electronically automated mill, built adjoining the old one and capitalizing on the still-operating O&W rail delivery of raw materials.[49] The tall, windowless concrete mill and the bulk feed bins planted on hundreds of Catskill chicken coops sat like cannon aimed at their more numerous but ill-equipped adversaries in the economic war for the New York poultry and egg market. Many of the co-op's members thought their position had become invincible.

By 1950 antibiotics permitted the poultry industry to move indoors permanently so that it could be mechanized and managed with only a few hands. Because chickens are sensitive to heat an unusually hot spell of weather could cause decreases in egg production, so proper

Clifford C. Calhoun, Ellenville, 1987.

ventilation and temperature control were also important.[50] The move indoors, essentially completed in the Catskills by 1955, was facilitated by scientific nutrition, selective breeding, and knowledge gained from experience, advice from the co-op, and information sent by the State College of Agriculture's experiment station to each New York farm home. Jewish farmers by now also personally received the government documents without having to go through an agent.

Egg production soared, limited only by the cost of floor space. It was becoming a market of oversupply but not one of guaranteed bankruptcy. Well-managed, properly capitalized operations simply compensated for lowered unit profit by producing more units. But some farmers had invested more than was wise in new buildings and equipment. Their predecessors in the 1930s and 1940s had improvised building materials, but they used expensive lumberyard products, predicating their expenditure on a best case margin of profit. If the co-op's feed credit had not bailed them out, some of these farms would have been foreclosed. And because egg prices were so high in the early 1950s, a large number of newcomers had entered poultry farming. Many of these newcomers lacked financial reserves and suffered from the low prices caused by subsequent overproduction. In the Catskills, however, these failures still were relatively few.[51] In fact in 1953 the society reported that all Jewish farmers in the area had a gross annual production of $10,000 or more, whereas only 14 percent of all U.S. farmers could boast such high figures.[52]

In the wake of such prosperity, many Jewish farmers renovated their homes. Some old farmhouses came down, replaced by brand new homes. Some of the new homes were stylish "ranchers" straight out of *House Beautiful;* others were boilerplate lumberyard design, and still others were designed and built in part by the farmers themselves. Some of the old farmhouses were remodeled and usually central heat, insulation, rewiring, and modern plumbing were added. Some driveways got paved with shale trucked from a quarry and, in a few cases, were asphalted. Some farmers even painted the exteriors of their farm buildings, an improvement the thrifty, especially the Russo-Polish immigrants, never were convinced had to be made. After all, they reasoned, farm structures never got painted in the old country.

Apprehensive of the future of the poultry business, some farmers redirected their profits into building more summer rental property, chiefly bungalows, which appeared to hold promise for the future. This future meant at least a winter vacation for their owners if farming did not pay or if age limited their ability to farm.[53] Bungalows were relatively inexpensive to build, and farmers who had watched and worked with those who helped build or remodel their farm structures could use the plumbing, carpentry, and electrical knowledge they had gleaned doing this. Unlike rooming or boarding houses, bungalows could be built easily in increments and thus did not force the owner into large debt. They could be framed of the same local pine and hemlock that was used to do practically everything from framing chicken coops to girdering and flooring Inter-County's massive structure. Ann Macin remembers the typical bungalow development. With her parents, Kate and Dave Kaminsky, she moved from the Lower East Side to Greenfield Park in 1916 when she was six years old. In 1933, when she was twenty-three, she built ten bungalows on five acres given to her by her father. She bought lumber on credit and kept adding bungalows through the 1950s until she eventually had twenty-three. As of 1994, she was continuing to manage her summer bungalows. Most of her summer renters now are fairly recent Jewish immigrants from Russia, another level of ethnicity in the Catskills.[54]

In the early and mid-1950s, the resort business flourished with growing disposable urban income and the major highway modernization that brought New York City only about two hours away from the Catskills. In 1953, for example, as Sullivan County celebrated its Golden Jubilee as a resort area, the county had 538 hotels, 2,000 bungalow colonies averaging 25 bungalows each, and 1,000 rooming houses averaging 25 rooms each.[55] Sullivan County was by far the most prosperous and luxurious of the resort areas. Ulster, Greene, and Delaware counties also had good resorts, although these tended to be smaller, less deluxe, and less organized than those in Sullivan County. Long gone were the days when most guests stayed at farmhouses and bungalows and entertained themselves with such simple activities as hayrides and singing. Competition for guests was fierce, and hotels vied with each other to have the most glitter and the newest fad.[56] But even in Sullivan County, despite much competition from large hotels, many guests remained loyal to the bungalows, especially where they felt they were part of a community.[57] Enough guests preferred bungalows to keep them in business, and many of them were run by farmers or former farmers. Mothers and children still came for long periods, and fathers continued working in the city and coming on weekends or whenever their work schedule permitted. Alvin Fertel, for example, notes that his father, who had a bagel bakery in the Bronx, "would come up alone after the weekend, because he was busy on the weekend. He would come up Sunday morning and go right to sleep, usually, because he had worked a thirty-hour shift, and he'd stay as long as he possibly could."[58]

On the whole, however, diversity and expansion became the key concepts in the Catskill resort business. Entertainment ranged from small little-known groups to national stars, and Bernard Kalb reported that recreation at the resorts also covered a wide range: "In recreation, there are places that haven't much more than a pool and a casino, just as there are places that have an outdoor pool, an indoor pool, a lake, a casino, an indoor theatre, an outdoor theatre, a night club, a bridle path, a nine-hole golf course, an eighteen-hole golf course and an indoor ice-skating rink."[59]

Most resort owners lived modestly and reinvested almost everything in their resorts in a perpetual growth and improvement cycle to keep up with their competitors. The hotels were financed by all sorts of credit, among them local bank mortgages and loans, some urban bank and collateral mortgages on urban businesses, and a considerable amount of credit from local lumberyards, plumbing services, and electrical supply stores.[60] The low interest rates of these loans stimulated business expansion, in turn increased employment, and ultimately increased city workers' and businessmen's disposable personal incomes. In turn the workers and businessmen spent on the things the originally loaned money produced, and in the Catskills that was vacations at the resorts. In cities, that income bought more poultry, eggs, and milk and milk products, some of which came from Catskill farms. The new economy boomed like that of the 1920s and of the reviving postwar 1940s.

Unlike the period of the 1920s through the 1940s, however, when hotels, rooming houses, and boardinghouses were the major market for local farm products, in the 1950s the expanding hotels, except the few still offering strictly kosher dining, did not get most of their produce from local farms. By then modern refrigeration had diminished the appeal of the advertising slogan "fresh from nearby farms." Hotels could buy kosher dressed meat and poultry more readily and more economically from commercial distributors. By the middle 1950s successful caponette farmers were shipping their birds to the live New York City market where they generally commanded good prices. Some local kosher butchers bought fowls and calves directly from local producers in summer, however, and sold them to the still-thriving bungalow market. Moreover, although the hotels generally bought their eggs from the national market, some of them bought local "shell" eggs in the summer for such breakfast specialties as poached, sunny-side up, and soft-boiled dishes. (They used the less fresh product for scrambling and baking.)

Although the volume of the egg trade to the local hotels had diminished since its heyday from the 1920s through the 1940s, nonetheless it diverted enough produce to disrupt contracts made by the co-op's egg branch with city stores like New York City's upscale Gristede's chain and in fact jeopardized the continuation of such lucrative contracts.[61] The siphoning to the local resorts continued despite entreaties to the farmers by Inter-County's board members and directors, for farmers could get a nickel or dime more per dozen selling to local hotels and to local stores that supplied the rooming houses and bungalows.

To solve the problem, the board built a cooperative egg factory to supply eggs especially for the summer shortage. They pioneered an experimental plant to house several hundred thousand hens—an incredibly large number then—to be housed in cages set one on another similar to what had been known as "batteries." These cages were designed with manure removers, egg conveyor belts, and mechanical feeding and watering. The co-op consulted with the New Holland farm machinery company for advice on how to execute their machinery designs and built the structure near Woodbourne. They named it after their own egg brand, Mount Pride. They had in effect invented the modern egg factory, the prototype of egg plants that would come thirty years later. As Mel Lesser described the facility,

> Inter-County had a wholly owned subsidiary, Mt. Pride, in the hamlet of Hasbrouck near Woodbourne, with over 300,000 birds. It was an experiment, a test farm. One purpose was to supply Inter-County with eggs to

Inter-County's egg-processing facility, 1985.

meet its egg contracts when members were selling their own eggs to local resort outlets for nearly retail prices. Inter-County was invested heavily in modern egg-handling facilities and was threatened with losing outlets because farmers weren't delivering their eggs to the facility in the
summer. Another purpose of the test farm was to test strains of birds for
all of us, and to keep better records on egg size, feed conversion, and to
test feeds. We wanted to make that information public.[62]

This largesse had unfortunate consequences: the egg factories were
replicated elsewhere, as was the broiler business. When the technology proved at the experimental farm was adopted by and improved on
by egg producers nationally, the Jewish farmers of the Catskills were
in national competition for the New York egg and broiler markets
which had been theirs.

As for Mt. Pride itself, such strong manure and ammonia odors em-
anated from it that the plant was closed down in a few years by the
Woodbourne authorities as a public nuisance. Ironically, it was closed on
complaints filed by resort keepers, whose demand for summer eggs had
caused the shortage that had led to its building.[63] Ultimately the experimental poultry farm that spawned modern egg production became the
white elephant that strained Inter-County's capital resources. To it one
can trace the decline of the fortunes of Jewish farming in the Catskills.

In the beginning of the 1950s, few would have thought that the
Catskill resort business would also suffer a major reversal in the next
few years. With the mass production of air-conditioning the need to escape from hot cities in the summer decreased. For those who could afford to travel, air-conditioned Miami Beach was now bearable. A mass
market was developing for televisions too as their quality improved
and their prices became affordable. The Channel Master antenna factory built in Ellenville by the Resnicks, a Jewish farm family, illustrated
that market, and in fact one of the Resnick brothers, Joseph, conceived
of antennas while he was serving in World War II.[64] The urbanite no
longer needed the mountains for either cool air or entertainment.[65]
The small hotel keepers, the motel operators, and the bungalow owners were also caught in the cycle of construction and renovation as they
tried to hold their own for a few more years in a losing resort battle.[66]
Farmers who had built more bungalows and added more rooms suffered from both the decrease in boarders and the declining produce demands of the larger resorts. And because so many businesses in the
area were supported by the resorts, the decline in summer tourism hurt

the whole area. Although in the 1950s some industries did begin moving to rural and small-town areas in the Catskills, they could not make up for the larger losses.[67]

The Catskill Jewish farmers were increasingly competing with large, automated corporate farming funded by commercial feed companies that had foreclosed individual operators and then hired them as sharecroppers at low wages. Each year seemed worse than the one before. In 1957, the society said that year was one of the hardest years Jewish farmers had had to face since they first settled in the United States.

The egg market was affected first. With improved storage techniques eggs shipped from the Midwest tasted as good as the fresher product produced nearby. Suppliers in Delmarva (the Delaware-Maryland-Virginia Eastern Shore) and the deep South marketed their eggs more cheaply. These areas had lower wage costs and milder climates (and so lower fuel bills and flimsier buildings) and consequently were formidable competition for even an Inter-County-based low-cost production. The New York market was so large that it was specifically targeted from distant areas: "The New York and other big northeastern markets are a coveted prize for these 'newly arrived' poultry areas [the southern states] and they are trying to invade these markets by shipping at low prices."[68] The Catskills and areas in New Jersey trumpeted their claims as the "egg baskets" of their regions, but the farmers there were in trouble.[69]

Farmers raising for the live poultry market enjoyed a moderate boost in sales with the emergence in the late 1950s of kosher supermarkets and of sections in conventional supermarkets featuring kosher products. Thus such gigantic kosher poultry dressing operations as Empire bought Catskill products, packaging them for the special supermarket trade. Even so, live poultry required large-volume production to make sufficient profits to support a family beyond the barest subsistence. When competitors learned of this new lucrative niche in the live poultry markets, competition from Pennsylvania and New Jersey lowered profitability as the 1960s began.

In the early 1960s a new phenomenon began which caught the Jewish farmers of the Catskills by surprise. Younger, first- and second-generation Jews succumbed to the attraction of the supermarket, then becoming popular in urban areas and in the rapidly growing suburban areas. Becoming assimilated, casually religious, casually kosher, these younger Jews, lured by low prices and convenience, began to buy

"Egg Basket of New York State" sign, ca. 1950.

nonkosher supermarket poultry. Unlike the kosher product from butchers, this poultry came eviscerated and frozen. In the 1960s, most Catskill
farmers got out of the business of raising poultry for meat, either selling their properties for nonagricultural uses or retiring on them.

Those who stayed in the poultry business stopped raising meat birds,
but they joined with the co-op to make Catskill egg production more
competitive. Inter-County put still more energy into processing and
marketing the eggs. It enlarged refrigeration facilities and hired more
staff to process and sell the eggs formerly marketed by each farmer. It
adopted a new technique of washing and then lightly waxing eggs to
keep them from losing moisture in storage. To raise the capital for this
project the co-op depleted its reserves and still had to make loans. Although the egg operation was now modern and efficient (in fact Inter-
County even combined feed delivery and egg pickup in some of its
phases to reduce transportation costs), the operation was labor inten-
sive compared with the feed milling operation. As a result, the egg operation lost money most of the time and had to be subsidized by the

feed portion of the business. Even though the feed mill workers and truck drivers were unionized and were paid high union wages and benefits, the feed mill was so efficient and the price of commercially milled feeds was also so high that the feed operation was a financial success. Not only could the feed mill carry the egg loss, but even with the strain of Mt. Pride's closing it generated considerable dividends as well. All dividends were declared and paid even retrospectively on shares purchased at the founding of the organization.

In fact although it lost money on the egg operation for some time, the co-op's numerous benefits permitted poultry-farming members to continue prospering, some with fewer than 50,000 laying hens. For example, Mel Lesser was able to net about $20,000 a year on 25,000 layers well into the mid-1970s—a remarkable feat considering how other producers had to farm hundreds of thousands of birds, and later millions, in order to turn a profit. Lesser was typical of many other Jewish farmers, however, in that his sons did not take over the farm he offered them despite its profitabilty.[70] Others relied on the co-op to help them market and process the output of their large, newly mortgaged egg plants running 100,000 to 300,000 layers. They built Mt. Pride replicas on Route 52, from Liberty to Ellenville, and on the other roads leading out from Woodridge. As their output hit the markets, smaller scale operations could not compete and closed unless they had no debt to meet.

Shift to massive egg plants prompted some of the large operators in the co-op to request volume discounts on their feed purchases and increased voting power in proportion to the larger quantities of feed they bought.[71] At one time or another, many farm co-ops, such as the Indian River and Sunkist operations of Florida and California, the Dairymen's League, Lehigh Valley, Land of Lakes in Minnesota, Capitol Milk Producers, and various milk cooperatives in New York, Pennsylvania, and Maryland had to confront such requests by large groups within the co-op. To varying degrees in these co-ops, power to control the boards of directors passed to the larger producers if by no other means than by volume discounts. Driven by debt and low profit margins, the greater producers among Inter-County members did seek similar privileges in the 1950s, but they were resisted. Many members felt that the ideal underpinning the one-man-one-vote principle—that of all members receiving equal voice and benefits—would have been compromised had they been granted these special benefits. Abe Jaffe, president of Inter-County at its twenty-fifth anniversary in 1961, excoriated U.S. Department of Agriculture advocates of volume discounts because he believed that they "would speed the tendency of big business farming to swallow up the average family farmer." Jaffe wrote: "Our success is the direct result of a tenacious adherence to [cooperative principles]. It is the result of a steady battle against special-interest individuals and groups who seek preferential treatment and prices. It is the result of an unending battle to keep the welfare of the average member above the profits of the cooperative. So far, we have succeeded in maintaining a balance between the desirable goal of a financially strong co-op and a genuine concern with each—and especially the small—member's welfare."[72]

Members successfully opposed the volume discount until the mid-1960s, when the co-op adopted it briefly and then abandoned it.[73] Years later Jaffe remembered that, in response to the decision to offer bulk discounts to big customers, "we made a corporation of the small guys and got a discount too. We got six guys, and formed the corporation from an unused bungalow corporation charter. Eight weeks later they rescinded the $2 discount rule."[74]

Abe Jaffe and his wife retired on their Glen Wild farm that his father bought early in the century. His father, a schochet (ritual slaughterer), on arriving in Glen Wild from Lithuania in 1904, found established Jewish farmers, including the Cohen brothers on Church Road and the Solomons, Gordons, Berkmans, Goldbergs, Marcuses, and others. As noted, the Jaffe farm was directly opposite the original Gerson property, and Abe remembered the Gerson hotel of tiny rooms burning across the road around 1925.

Jaffe, a long-standing Inter-County president in its middle and late years, can confirm the history of that organization. In the nearby one-room school, when he was nine, he and his sister got typhoid fever from water contaminated by nearby outhouses. His father and his father's neighbors built the still-functioning Glen Wild stucco shul in 1924 for the congregation which had formed in 1913 and met in Jaffe's apartment opposite the Glen Wild post office. Until 1925 he had no alternating current electricity line on the sixty-acre farm his father bought for his boys in 1919; he got it only by paying the electric company the difficult amount of $125. Like many other local farmers, he used a Delco Direct Current gasoline generator before that.

Abe Jaffe's family did not belong to the Workmen's Circle even though they were socialists, and they had no medical insurance until after World War II. A Jewish physician named Cohen in Monticello made house calls by horse and buggy for $5, as did another named Roginsky in Woodridge. Abe had no toys, his amusements being the out-of-doors. He visited Woodridge three or four times a year and Monticello once a year. After the shul was built, social parties during the high holidays added to his other pleasures—he fished, skated, rode sleighs, and sometimes hunted. His father, also a mulamed (a scholar of scripture who had not sought ordination), taught Hebrew to children.

Abe attended Woodridge and then Monticello high schools, and in 1927 he enrolled at New York University's night school to study history with the aim of teaching it in a high school. Away from an area where

Abe Jaffe, Glen Wild, 1987.

people knew each other, he knew loneliness for the first time. During the day, he earned $10 a week as a cutter of ladies underwear, then he got $12, and just before the depression in 1932, he earned $32 a week as a skilled cutter. He poignantly remembered how his teaching preparation was worthless because school districts had little money for salaries.[75]

Several large poultry operators did break from the co-op, however, attracted by lower feed pricing offered by commercial millers. In leaving they sacrificed the group Blue Cross–Blue Shield medical insurance that Al Cohen and the board of directors had obtained for the membership about fifteen years earlier.

The milk market had also become very competitive. Some Catskill Jewish farmers expanded into what might be termed *industrial dairying.* Because Catskill dairy farmers primarily fed their milk-producing cows hay, not milled feed, the benefit of their membership in Inter-County was not so much the feed. Yet even in dairying, with its dependence on expensive, large tank refrigeration from which tank trucks pumped the milk, Inter-County helped by offering low-cost tractors, tractor implements, and other special dairying equipment. Inter-County also provided special rations of milled feed for calves and cows (especially pre- and postpartem cows) and medicinal dairy feeds, made on short notice. Gradually dairying used more concentrates, that is, protein-rich feed supplements, and Inter-County supplied them economically.

One Inter-County family, the Yasgurs, who operated a large modern dairy farm in Bethel, were the dairy counterpart to the poultry expansion. They met the price issue with more production. Thanks to the depression-generated federal milk marketing orders, which set base prices for milk in most of the United States, the milk production business never became as volatile as the poultry business. Good managers like the Yasgurs could make a living without being pressed to recapitalize continually. The Yasgurs had not only a large herd of registered Holstein cows and enough land to grow their own feed and fodder; they also had their own pasteurizing plant.[79] (The Yasgurs later became known beyond the Catskills for hosting the "Woodstock" folk festival in 1969.) About a dozen Catskill Jewish dairy farmers were operating by 1960, but their numbers fell when their children chose other occupations and the elders could not continue farming themselves.

The old ideological divisions that had threatened to split the co-op during the Berman affair in 1942 appeared healed by 1960. But as evidenced by the disagreement about whether members who bought in larger volumes should have more power and higher discounts, many Inter-County and fire co-op members held opposing opinions on the spirit in which the co-ops should operate. Although they were all capitalists, some felt they were pledged to a higher social order characterized by selflessness and that the co-op should perpetuate that order. In 1961, Harry Wasserman, secretary of the fire co-op, which by then was keenly property-oriented simply because it insured so many large hotels, advanced the ideological issue when he wrote:

> Cooperation does not charge that our profit system of production and distribution is malevolent, but does contend that it is bungling and extravagant because it has no way, other than by guessing, to measure, in advance of production, the kind, quantity and quality of goods which consumers want. So it produces more or less in the dark and tries to dispose of the products by acute competition, enormously expensive advertising, high pressure salesmanship and the battering down of consumers' sales resistance. Over-production and recessions necessarily occur, in cycles; and consumers pay all the bills—all the costs and all the profits.
>
> Cooperation proposes to replace this profit system, not all at once or by any revolutionary method, with another system. This cooperative system calls for reorientation—substitution of production for the service and benefit of the producers and distributors. In other words, capital and industry are to be made the servants of the people and not their masters.[76]

This was the Rochdale idea, stated in the words of a more left-oriented perspective. In an "In Memoriam" to its deceased members and friends, Inter-County thanked them for their efforts on behalf of the co-op, which "represented the finest achievement of human endeavor—man's cooperation with man for the common good."[77]

On the other side stood those represented by the secretary of Inter-County, Al Cohen, who at the 1961 annual Inter-County meeting said, "Cooperatives in this country are the greatest backbone for the retention of our capitalistic system, keeping out all 'isms's."[78] His argument that cooperatives were as important to the survival of the legitimate "ism" (capitalism) was about as tenable as Wasserman's claim that because capitalist production could not gauge consumer demand it cost consumers in the long run. In fact, the advertising extravagance that Wasserman denounced developed consumer market research and remedied much pointless production. Furthermore the agribusiness conglomerates supplanting family farming posed no threat to capitalism unless one defined capitalism as only including and benefiting small business.

Regardless of inner schism, however, the fact that co-op members thought about ideology at all then distinguished them from many other farming co-op members and from most Americans. Few except the business schools thought about political economy, a term that still rang of sedition in the 1960s. Those on the Wasserman side—such as Yaffe, Rosenberg, Miller, and the Koopermans—whose opinions stemmed from Old World socialist movements would interrupt the feeding of chickens or the reading of law to speculate on the meaning of life. If they had quiet moments, they often wrote poetry, and if they spoke or wrote publicly, they expressed their ideas in romantic terms.

The more hardheaded Inter-County members probably would not have spent their time on such musings, and their speech and writing were equally down-to-earth. But when he got home from that co-op ceremony in 1961, each Inter-County member returned to advancing his own prosperity as best as he could by refining and expanding his business. And he continued to use Inter-County precisely as Al Cohen had described it at the ceremony: as a "useful corporate organization dedicated to the principle that the services provided will give farmers economic betterment, individual ownership and survival of family-type farms."[79]

Chapter 5

Completing a Community

While all the changes had been occurring in farming, Jewish life in the Catskills also had been improving significantly. As the 1950s ended, Edward Koenig, with experience as the society's extension agent in Ellenville, could state accurately that "Jewish farm families live well, in modern homes and with modern conveniences. The various communities abound with Jewish organizations of every type and are literally beehives of activity. The automobile, the radio, television and increased incomes have brought to the farm family every comfort of city living plus the advantages of country life."[1] The shtetl-like villages and towns were generally booming. The agricultural success that followed World War II augmented the prosperity generated from the still-flourishing summer resort bungalow colonies. Thousands of customers with rising disposable incomes shopped in the towns and patronized local entertainment. The resort hotel proprietors added to the area's prosperity by purchasing many supplies locally, by hiring local building trades craftsmen for their expansions, and by staffing their maintenance crews and dining halls with local residents. Most of the craftsmen in turn spent a major part of their earnings in the local shops, many of which had Jewish proprietors.

This cycle ran for three generations in these towns, long enough to make them home also for their surrounding farmers who, even in renewed adversity, strove to hang on. Were these Amish or Mennonites or Mormons this outcome wouldn't be noteworthy because religion—a single version of it for each group—glued its followers together. The Catskill Jews, despite their diverse world views, found themselves at home. Perhaps that was owing to their individual respect for each other's politics and degrees of acculturation; perhaps it was their gradual entrance into the cultural lives, businesses, and local governments of these small towns that made the area home. These people in effect became more "empowered" in the Catskills than they would have been elsewhere.

Clothing stores, bakeries, shoe repair services, barbershops, paint stores, auto dealerships and repair shops, grocery stores, tailor shops, delicatessens, new and used furniture stores, mattress factories, stationery stores, bookstores, newsstands, pharmacies, and hardware stores all prospered. These businesses were owned by both Christians and Jews, and, although all prospered, the Jewish-owned businesses outnumbered the Christian-owned businesses. Eventually the Jews even went into banking, which, like the electric power and telephone companies, had been exclusively run by Christians.[2] A 1940 film made by a group of Ellenville merchants, most of whom were Jewish, had urged residents to buy from local merchants instead of from mail-order houses. The threat of nonlocal competition never disappeared, but it did not become serious in the twenty-five-year boom in the Catskills that followed World War II because the boom generated so much business for local merchants. Later it did become a serious issue for the small community merchants in the Catskills as it did elsewhere in the United States.[3]

Although the society had closed its office in Ellenville in 1945, it still retained an agent in the Catskills. When Israel Bernstein decided to move to Israel, he recruited as his successor a Liberty poultry farmer, Morton Shimm, who served from about 1948 until 1953. By this time the society had already been replaced by Inter-County as the center of social life and economic life for many Jewish farmers. It was different for their children, however. Most of the Jewish farm children attended schools in the towns. For these children, the schools and the town life—not the Inter-County—became the center of their social life if and when they had time off from the farm. A few young people even stayed after school to practice basketball or rehearse plays when they could be spared from the farms and could get a ride home, which for some were over twenty miles away. In adjusting to public schools, some farm youths adopted the rustic speech and manners of their peers, and most refused to speak Yiddish at home. For most of these young people, when they had time off from farm chores and school, their interests leaned no more to cultural refinement or religious studies than did those of their Christian farm peers whose tongues they emulated. In general, the tastes of these rural Jewish youth were not as sophisticated as those of their parents and grandparents.

Some of the Jewish young people in Catskill towns who had leisure time studied classical music privately, as did some of their Christian counterparts from propertied families. Visiting New York City also exposed these Jewish youths from Catskill towns to traditional Jewish urban culture, a far more intellectual influence than that of their schoolmates. By associating with the Jewish young people in the towns and with urban Jewish peers whose families were summer renters, Jewish farm youths similarly were less likely to follow a pattern of rustification. But such summer contacts were for the most part with children whose preference for music was playing the radio instead of the violin, despite their parents' wishes. Some farm children, envying the liberty of the city children up for the summer, translated that envy into hatred for city "slickers" in general and for their speech and mannerisms in particular.

Most Jewish farm youth, however, were positively influenced by the emphasis that their parents and their culture placed on education. The Jewish community continued to graduate a major share of the college-bound youths from schools in Monticello, Liberty, Grahamsville, and Ellenville, and many of them left the area permanently. A number of the Jewish farm youth also moved into the local towns and became prominent in nonfarming areas. As Herman Levine said, "You go into Ellenville and you find the judges and the lawyers and the doctors and dentists and the businessmen were formerly farm children."[4] The Jewish farm youth also generally had positive feelings about their Jewish identity, having grown up in an era of increased Jewish consciousness. Few of the children and grandchildren of the Jewish farmers were lost to the Jewish community by converting or marrying out of their faith.

The rebirth of Jewish consciousness following the Holocaust and the formation of the state of Israel brought many Jews who had abandoned formal observance of Judaism back into the fold. In the heyday of socialism in the 1930s many farmers, leaning toward atheism, had refused to live in the shuls. Others—hardly socialists or atheists—believed, or rather feared, that strict observance would hinder assimilation to "American" (i.e., Christian) society. Some of the latter, to the dismay of the J.A.S. and their more traditional relatives, adopted local rustic speech and behavior, often half-consciously. In the 1950s and 1960s, however, the notion of what S.E. Rosenberg called an "interdependence of faith" became a rallying point for the rebirth of Jewish identity.[5] The local Zionist organization in Ellenville was popular,[6] and, prompted by their prosperity and renewed faith, many Jews built and renovated synagogues in the towns and rural areas of the Catskills.

It was during this period that the society sold its Ellenville office to the Hebrew Aid Society, which subsequently became the Ezrath Israel Congregation. The congregation converted the office's old building into a home for the full-time rabbi it hired and built the Joseph Slutsky Center on part of the lot at 36 Center Street. (Its namesake, who donated the center, was owner of the prominent Nevele Hotel, which had begun as a typical farmhouse near Ellenville in 1901 and which had maintained a sizeable Holstein herd until after World War II.) The Slutsky Center, like many other Jewish centers established in America during that period, offered Jews an opportunity to explore that renewed identity. And since Route 52 from Liberty to Ellenville had been rebuilt by 1950, about half of the Jews in the Catskills could drive to it.

The center's functions in the postwar years did not involve the farmers as much as the townspeople, who had city work schedules most of the year, with evenings and holidays off. Farm families, including children, had little time for socializing.[7] For many young Jewish people on farms, chores consumed much of the time outside of school. Participation in after-school organized sports was difficult to reconcile with farm

The Joseph Slutsky Center (left) *and the old J.A.S. office, now the rabbi's residence, 1991.*

duties.[8] For some members of Jewish farm families there was some solitary hunting in the fall and fishing in streams and creeks in the spring and summer. Most did not sing and few played instruments; these required time off from farm work to practice and teachers who were not available, or who had to be driven into town, or who charged more than some of the farmers could afford. As it had always been for most Catskill Jewish farmers, it was a somewhat forlorn life, much work and little play for all the family, and even lacking the fairs of the earlier years.

In the 1950s and 1960s, prosperity required the Catskill Jewish farmers to work harder to compete in tougher markets. For those who had grown up on the left, there wasn't time to remember, let alone sing of, union hall and picket line. Gone too was the time to listen to afternoon operas and violinists, even on radio and even if one were still interested in hearing them. Now that the prosperous farmers could better afford mail delivery, they rarely ever had time to read the *New York Times*. Books assigned for school competed with work on chicken coops or haychutes. Seven-day workweeks also precluded family vacations and left little time for such simple pleasures as sightseeing drives to New York state's splendid historical markers. Summer evenings, after one chased pullets from tree roosts into wire-enclosed range shelters at dusk, or after one pastured or bedded down the milked cows, could be spent on pleasures if one could wash and dress quickly enough to use the remaining night. Winter evenings, unless one had to mind chicks or sick pullets, or polish, grade, candle, and box eggs, were free and long, but only for the adults—the children had to do homework after chores.

Even prayer took time away from work and was faithfully performed only by the orthodox. Thus even with the renewed interest in Jewishness, synagogues that had been built immediately after the war had more paying than praying farmers. There was little time for speculation on the religious and philosophical meanings of life. A few, like the orthodox Gibbers in the Monticello area, managed to take time off for prayer. To observe the Sabbath and the Jewish holidays, they relied on their Christian employees to operate their nine poultry farms. In fact in the 1950s the Gibber brothers—Morris, Isidore, and Yale—were instrumental in starting the Hebrew Day School in Monticello, a school that combined religious and secular studies.[9] But the religious observance of the Gibbers was uncommon for the busy Jewish farmers.

Most members of the Jewish farming community in the Catskills were from Eastern Europe, part of the mass migration at the turn of the century or refugees from the Holocaust, but there were a few Sephardic Jews. They spoke Ladino, Spanish, Turkish, or Greek rather than Yiddish, Russian, Polish, or German. They were descended from Spanish Jews who left during the Inquisition and went to the Ottoman Empire. They spoke mostly Ladino, a Castilian Spanish written in Hebrew, in contrast to the Ashkenazim's Yiddish, a low German written in Hebrew.

One Sephardic family in Youngsville ran a boardinghouse catering to other Sephardim. The head of that family, Leon Perez, had migrated from a farm in Silivri, Turkey, in 1921, pushed out by economic deprivations and the drafting of non-Muslim males for twenty or thirty years of military service. He went first to the Lower East Side, then to Jeffersonville twenty years later. There he ran the boardinghouse and subsequently became a farmer. His daughter Rae married a fellow immigrant from Silivri, Victor Bechar, and the two families shifted into raising chickens on a 98-acre farm. Too few to form their own synagogues, they worshiped with the Ashkenazim, sharing English and other commonalities with the Ashkenazi farmers and blending into a community faster in a rural area than they would have in urban settings.

Most Jewish Catskill farmers did find the time for the nearly ritual buffets following the midnight adjournments of the annual and semiannual Inter-County meetings at the Woodridge High gym. These buffets continued from the war's end into the 1950s and were similar to those before the war. Practically all members attended these meetings, usually with their spouses. The fare was always delicatessen—kosher hot dogs on rolls, kosher corned beef and pastrami on rye, and mustard unique to New York City delicatessens. Another New York City emblem was ubiquitous at these buffets: the ornately labeled Dr. Brown's bottles containing cream soda, ginger ale, or celery tonic. As it had for a long time, the buffet came from the general fund. By this time, however, few had impulses to squirrel away a couple of sandwiches for the children; almost everyone ate well most of the time now. The people talked as they ate, usually standing, and although more than half the speakers still had accents, their speech was now bookishly grammatical English.

These midnight adjournment buffet revels were part corporate shareholders' meetings, part country fairs, part fall bull roasts, and part cowboys' barbecues, things of which these revelers knew essentially nothing. The annual meeting was usually in the late fall or early winter, similar to the fall shows the society had supported at the Mountaindale high school a decade and a half earlier when work had slowed down following the hectic summers. That had been the time of seasonal farming before dairying went largely indoors and poultry raising totally indoors to produce a relatively steady supply of milk, eggs, and meat birds all year long. The fall and winter evenings also gave the hard-working farmers some respite, for sunrise came late that time of year and they didn't have to worry about having to rise early.

To those who might have thought about such comparisons, the co-op celebration was somewhat analagous to Succoth, the Jewish harvest holiday. But the co-op's adjournment revels were much more than the secular counterparts of the religious festivals and thanksgivings, which were mostly grateful fun and which in the 1930s through the mid-1950s were left largely uncelebrated by most of the Jewish farmers. The co-op ceremony really celebrated capital and operating budgets, credit policy, and the remedy of individual complaints. Its Jewish members ate heartily because they knew that in the events of the evening they had materially directed their own fortunes.

In the early 1950s the Inter-County revels changed. The ethnic evening delicatessen was replaced by an annual chicken barbecue at which Inter-County adopted a Cornell cooking promotion subsequently employed wherever broilers were raised in order to promote consumer demand for the barbecued product. The scheme involved constructing an unmortared pit twenty to forty feet long, three feet wide, and three feet high. Newly fashioned charcoal briquets were scattered into the pit. After the briquets were lit and became white hot, three-foot lengths of pipe were placed over them. A roll of one-by-two-inch galvanized mesh fence was extended over the pipe. The mesh fence supported the quartered broilers which were basted with a special sauce made according to the Cornell formula.[10] Farm families had to take off a summer afternoon to attend, however, and not every family could.

More formal pleasures were available on summer evenings. Farm families having the inclination and the time to dress after chores could attend the local resort hotels' variety shows on Saturday nights, usually at the invitation of the hotel owners. As the hotels expanded they began to exclude the guests staying at local kochaleins and small boardinghouses who had formerly been allowed to attend. Throughout the years the local farmers were, for the most part, welcomed by the local resort owners, many of whom had come from their ranks. Esterita Blumberg, whose family had a hotel, notes that they tried to discourage "crashers" from neighboring bungalow colonies but that "local residents were never put into that category. It was always our pleasure to share the facilities with any and all of our county folks."[11] In general, however, given the call of the fowl and the cow at five o'clock the next morning, the farmers did not take up those invitations very often.

Many would not have appreciated the entertainment anyway. They would have seen the rawer part of "show biz," vaudevillian acts that New York entertainment agencies previewed in the Borscht Belt before promoting them in the city. Typical of these acts was the ribald stand-up comedian who, in a barrage of one-liners (often about such feckless family members as mothers-in-law and spouses), satirized clichés about Jewish culture and behavior. Other comedians like Myron Cohen, who exemplified the postwar borscht comedians, told jokes about the unlettered immigrants' awkward English, making puns that would have been considered bigoted if uttered by Christians. This kind of melting pot satire was popular in the Catskills long before World War II, when immigrants who wanted to become Americanized had little patience with deviations from standard American English. Such satire was a way for both the unschooled and the formally educated to distinguish themselves from less polished fellow Jews who also sought assimilation—a simple case of the pot calling the kettle black.

But such one-liners were largely anachronistic by the postwar period except for some parochial urban islands of mispronunciation. They hardly could have entertained a Catskill Jewish farmer's child who shared the family work and the family successes. That child may have been rebellious but not because of his parents' imperfect assimilation.

As in the city vaudeville nightclub, the borscht comedian, always male, was preceded by (or, if he wasn't as famous, sometimes succeeded by) a spangled, rather mediocre female singer challenged even by her repertoire of Tin Pan Alley numbers. Sometimes a tenor tried Pagliacci, and got little applause for his pains. By about 1950, opera left the Catskill resort stages to be replaced by pop crooning in the Sinatra and Crosby mode. Sometimes someone sang something in Yiddish, but the Yiddish songs were much less frequent than in previous decades. (Once there was a harmonized duet of the traditional solo "Bei Mir Bist Du Shoene," translated "I think you pretty," sung, oddly enough, by two glittering and swaying young women about whom the song should have been sung.)

Most popular were nostalgic ballads commemorating the Yiddishe Mama. The nostalgia celebrated her domesticity but not her sweatshop years in the lung-coating trades, her struggles in strikes and demonstrations, or her endless nights stuffing and stamping envelopes for pro-union politicians. The 1950s had not yet popularized the image of the ostentatious and helpless Jewish American princess, a portrayal of Jewish women that would have been considered ludicrous if applied to Jewish farm women, who were still viewed as the strong, independent Yiddishe Mama.[12] Part myth, part reality, this cherished archetype was the reason Al Jolson's "Mammie," purportedly about a black plantation mother figure, got curtain calls in the Catskills for years.

Stage dances were cane, white gloves, top hat, fishnet stockings, and taps, rewarded by claque-generated applause or the emcee's "give 'em a hand." That eliciting of applause was designed to convince the audience that it had just witnessed the birth of a star and had gotten a special value for its coin. Sometimes a magician followed. Rarely, if ever, did classical violinists or pianists appear, and if they did they played rhapsodies, not chaconnes or sonatas. Tragedy certainly never graced those stages, a significant omission given the vogue of Shakespeare in Yiddish on New York City's Second Avenue only a decade earlier. By 1950, most Jews going to the Catskill resorts had American high school and college diplomas, but their tastes were less intellectual than their parents' and grandparents' had been. They rejected Maurice Schwartz's Second Avenue King Lear and Jascha Heifetz's virtuoso violin performances in Carnegie Hall, preferring borscht comedy's concentration on such issues as "rabbis and diets, money and sex."[13]

While the farmers remained welcome as invited guests longer than the nonpaying guests from boardinghouses, beginning in the 1950s farmer friends of the hotel owners had to call intermediaries at the big hotels for Saturday night passes. Their attendance began to decline, for most perceived the borscht shows as trivial when they had so many more important things to do. The socially aware farm Jews who did have time for nonfarm activities were involved in the co-ops and were more concerned, at least since 1937, with such weighty issues as socialism, Zionism, the Spanish civil war, Hitler and the Holocaust, and the co-operative movements as an alternative to their own financial ruin.[14]

Farmers had other cultural choices in summers. Summer-stock theaters had started in the 1930s and continued into the early 1950s. One was the Cragsmoor Playhouse, on a mountaintop near Ellenville. The other was the Woodstock Playhouse in Woodstock, near Kingston. Each produced serious American and British plays, including some Shakespeare and much Eugene O'Neill, Tennessee Williams, and Thornton Wilder. Both were over twenty miles too far away for most of the Sullivan County farmers, unless, as happened in the prosperous years, the children who could drive got a special dispensation from a sympathetic parent able to cover the evening chores. (Shows started by 8 P.M.) A few of those who had been educated did attend those theaters, but most farmers did not. Woodstock was an artist's colony and had historically had few Jewish inhabitants.[15] Cragsmoor was for the white-collar people who had had or pretended to have had some learning. Jewish farmers did not fit into either group, and neither did most Jewish summer resort guests (even those with ties). They settled for their version of vaudeville, humor reflecting their experiences in life and providing escape from their unique circumstances.[16]

Local gentry—teachers, engineers, and merchants, and established Christians, chiefly bankers—attended the playhouses. So did a few isolated, summer-estate Christian Wall Streeters and uptown professionals, and so did some "artistes," although most of those were from Woodstock. A few of the engineers and teachers were second-generation Jews, and some did not feel welcome at the ticket booth in Cragsmoor. A few Christian gentlemen farmers went, but most of the mortgaged Christians did not go. There were few gentlemen farmers of any religion in the mountains then. The few Christians in that class were mostly retired on inherited land around Stone Ridge, between Ellenville and Kingston.

The mortgaged Jewish poultrymen and dairymen were even less likely than the Jewish professionals to attend the playhouses, even if they had had the time and had been welcomed. The immigrants generally knew little about American theater. Some went anyway, ignoring the stares during intermissions. After several summers, no one paid them attention at Cragsmoor. Then the theater folded. Woodstock continued, but it was inaccessible to the Catskill farmers, most of whom lived forty or fifty miles away. Another summer stock theater in Forestburg, between Monticello and the Delaware River, ran a few seasons and featured the works of major playwrights. But Forestburg was as inaccessible as Woodstock and was patronized primarily by the inhabitants of Sullivan County west of Monticello and Liberty.[17]

The thousands of guests in summer rooming houses and bungalow colonies had found their entertainment in local movie theaters for years, and their patronage guaranteed enough income to run a number of film houses year-round. Nearly everyone saw some movies then, including the farmers who especially went in winter when they had some free time. The young people with cars explored the newly built Woodbourne drive-in after the war. Fallsburg, Woodbourne, and Monticello each had one year-round film house and Ellenville had two; and they all showed first-run Hollywood films and occasionally foreign art films. Even without a car, anyone with a few dimes and the time to walk plowed snowy roads on winter evenings in the Catskills could take in Greer Garson and Ronald Colman. If one could make a 7 P.M. show, he or she could be back in time to get enough sleep to feed and milk promptly the next morning. With a car, the 9 P.M. show was possible.

In fact, the Catskill movie theaters were kind of a New Haven try-out for films; through the 1950s distributors tested box office reaction on rural New Yorkers prior to setting prices for leases in the city itself. The summer bungalow renters and hotel guests constituted test groups of city audiences. Somehow the movie house proprietors persuaded the film distributors to try out movies even in the winter, presumably arguing for projected attendance by the guests of the few winterized hotels in the area. But unlike some of the guests at shows who were flattered by and even sometimes snobbish at knowing that they were subjects of market research, most attending the films were utterly oblivious to the fact that they saw first runs. The Jewish farming adults and teenagers who attended the films benefited from coming into contact with the city people present. But young farm children, unless taken by their parents or by older siblings or friends having drivers' licenses, saw few films. Unlike city children, few farm children lived close enough to towns with movies to walk to even if they could take the time away from chores and school work.

Most Catskill Jewish farm children, like Christians, were bused long distances to central public schools after 1937, when school centralization began in rural counties in southeastern New York. Because of the long distances, most of them could not participate in plays, interschool team sports, and extracurricular music programs. Sometimes girls had more free time than boys because they were spared some of the evening chores, but, lacking transportation home, even they usually could not capitalize on after-school activities.

As popular as football was in America then,[18] the New York state education department did not permit football in New York schools. Thus the bused farm children were spared the anguish of being excluded from that great determiner of high school popularity. But there were baseball and basketball heroes, few of whom were farmers and even fewer of whom were Jewish farmers. Few farm children knew tennis or had the opportunity to play it after school even if they knew how. As they had for decades, the boys fished and hunted a little between chores during the summers and on fall weekends. The boys and the girls sledded and ice-skated on winter weekends between chores and homework. When a roller skating rink opened near Middletown in the 1950s, thirty or more miles from many of the Jewish farms, a few of the older children would convince parents to lend a car or truck for an occasional evening there. Sometimes they also were able to go to the drive-in movies at Rock Hill, near Monticello.

Catskill Jews could also attend the area's half dozen or so left-oriented summer resorts, which featured a mixture of art, exercise, and education. The American Communist Party had been organized in Woodstock, in Ulster county, in 1921. Although a couple of these resorts had been founded in the 1930s, flourishing during the Spanish Civil War, most were started after the war. (While a significant percentage of the members and leaders of the American Communist Party were Jewish, they accounted for a small percentage of Jewish immigrants. America's labor movement, its educational and political systems, and the New Deal gave hope to most Jews that the world could be made better for working people without having to resort to radicalism.)[19]

The clientele at the leftist resorts was a mixture of members from vaguely communist-led unions in and around New York City and unaffiliated apolitical intellectuals who shared cultural and aesthetic interests with the leftists. These interests were flatly antithetical to the popular show-biz entertainment that the masses, which the left proposed to lead, learned to love. Sometimes a cultured right-leaning Zionist showed up at one of the leftist resorts, discussing common interests with political adversaries. Nearly everyone in those places not only knew the difference between yes and yeah, but said yes. Members of Teachers' Unions were a mainstay, particularly at the private proprietorships. A few necktie-wearing Jewish farmers visited the resorts on Saturday nights, hoping for fox-trots and uncomfortably sitting out the alien folk dances. But most of the Jewish farmers, even those on the political left, avoided these resorts. Like the summer guests at the borscht resorts, the meaning of life for them focused increasingly on the balance sheet.

Around campfires guests sang militantly political as well as standard folk songs invented or interpreted on site by Pete Seeger, individual Weavers, Woodie Guthrie, Paul Robeson, and Leon Bibb. Martha Schlamme sang class-conscious Yiddish material, and she, as well as Seeger and Robeson, also sang international numbers in their native tongues. One could also hear Bach and Brahms on the loudspeakers and in live performance or see Chekhov, Shaw, and O'Casey acted. Sometimes one could see scenes from *King Lear* acted by the small repertory, with help from guests and drafted dining room staff. Prior to his prominence, Joseph Papp, the New York Shakespearian, directed some of these. One could also see topically satirical skits, hear lectures on politics and art by college professors and political figures, see graphic artists teaching guests to sculpt and paint, and watch guests making pottery and sewing leather handbags from scratch.

The leftist resorts also tried stand-up comedians, such as Mel Leonard and Sam Levenson, with fairly complex routines spoofing opera, politics, and America's class structure. Levenson, for example, frequently masqueraded as an obsequious waiter and then parodied his customers after they left.[20] Ossie Davis and Ruby Dee were new talents, acting out themes from what then was called Negro history. Visiting farmers sometimes would meet elderly Anglo-Saxon D.A.R. (Daughters of the American Revolution) "angels." They spoke impeccable, measured English and, fit for parasols, seemed to be latter-day Victorians on porch rockers. A few of the visiting Jewish farmers even met famous people, rocking on those porches, such as W. E. B. DuBois and Shirley Jackson, who occasionally lectured at the resorts. College students waiting tables could be heard discussing "the meaning of life." Entertainments in those places could be viewed as an inheritance of the Second Avenue sensibility, although this would not have occurred to those attending and running events. There were similar resorts across the Hudson River, but they were too far for the Catskill farmers to travel for an evening.[21]

The times were just not right for the farmers or the locals in general to attend the left-oriented resorts. Cold War politics discouraged ideological nonconformity, and people seen there in the McCarthy period could become targets of abuse. In 1949, when Paul Robeson attempted to give two concerts in Peekskill on the east side of the Hudson River across from Orange county, he was met by over a thousand rioters yelling racist and anti-Semitic slogans and equating radicalism and Judaism.[22] By the mid-1950s practical people knew that a national reevaluation of values made obsolete and unwanted the ten- and twenty-year-old songs asking for societal change; Americans were also uninterested in the other music, art, and poetry that the left tried to advance. Attendance at the resorts waned. A few survived into the 1960s, one into the 1970s. The United States was a long way from the stock market crash, and the left was largely superfluous. Jews and Jewish farmers in America primarily who kept their ties to the left did so by giving money to defend victims of the Smith and McCarran acts and to the defense of Julius and Ethel Rosenberg without ever having visited the leftist resorts. Experiences with cooperatives in the 1930s and with Hitler in the 1940s had sensitized them to the significance of red-baiting and Jew-baiting.

In 1955, another cultural opportunity flashed briefly in the Catskills, this one grander and more accessible than the others. This was the Ellenville summer appearance of the Symphony of the Air, the reconstituting of Arturo Toscanini's NBC Symphony Orchestra.[23] It was inspired partly by the type of patronizing noblesse oblige that led Carnegie and Rockefeller to establish libraries, museums, and scholarships. But it was inspired more by its sponsors' appetites for the culture they had learned about in school or that was buried, almost forgotten, in their memories of visits with parents to Second Avenue and Carnegie Hall. These were the tastes that might have been nourished if the farmers ever had made enough profit from milk, egg, or poultry sales to afford reliable labor to cover chores for a weekend trip to New York City.

It is not clear who brought the Symphony of the Air to Ellenville. Legend has it that someone connected with the orchestra proposed to Bill Rose, a local banker, that Ellenville become a second Tanglewood, with the symphony to be housed initially in a shed and then perhaps expanded into smaller instrument ensemble buildings. Rose—educated, patron of the local summer stock theaters, deeply interested in his community's prosperity—was intrigued. He too loved classical music, and he had the prescience to suspect a dormant taste for classical music in many of the large hotel operators who were feeding their guests show biz. Most important, Rose persuaded two wealthy Jewish former farming families, the Channel Master Resnicks and the Nevele Slutskys, to organize the Catskill Civic Association, a committee of local business people to plan the festival. Resort operators, insurance agents, and a few merchants were the main contributors.[24]

The full-page local newspaper announcements soliciting support were in a language not born of staid Anglo-Saxon propriety but one from Lodz. It was the language of Elmer Rosenberg ("Shall We Organize and Exist or Compete and Destroy Ourselves?") of a quarter century earlier, the language of the restless and discontented taking collective action. Reading like a union organizing broadside, the advertisement announced a mass meeting of great urgency. Its sponsors must have presumed a readership responsive to that rhetoric; apparently there was still an audience who could identify with such rhetoric. The farmers-turned-hotelmen were utilitarian and individualistic, but many still thought collectively. Their parents' earlier agitations for unions in the city and later for co-ops during the depression still influenced them. Others who ran summer resorts, like Elmer Rosenberg, Ephraim Yaffe, and David Levinson in the Ellenville area, were not uncomfortable with the project and the radical overtones of its advertising rhetoric. The festival belonged to those who believed that the point of making money was not to make more money and that individualistic materialism was not the supreme value.

About half of the committee was Jewish, and a couple of the Jewish members were combination farmers/resort keepers. Within a few months of the committee's organizing, pledges from local businesses produced enough cash to build a fine music tent over an asphalt amphitheatre, with labor and materials partly contributed by a builder of resort tennis courts. The site was a level, pine-covered top of a great sand hill just off the Ellenville exit of the newly rebuilt Route 52. The committee named it the Empire State Music Festival in the hope of attracting state funding.[25]

Unlike Tanglewood, which did not offer opera, the Ellenville festival began in the summer of 1955 with Puccini, and casted as eminently in that genre as Tanglewood did in symphony. The first programs featured *La Boheme* and *Madame Butterfly* starring Phyllis Curtin and John Brownlee and alternated with evenings of such events as a Buxtehude chaconne, a Shostakovich symphony, a Ravel pavane, and new works conducted by their composers. Some of the conductors were well known, and others would become well known. Despite opera's absence on Borscht Belt stages, thousands attended the opening programs. The new Route 52 was jammed with guests from Monticello, Liberty, Fallsburg, Glen Wild, Woodridge, Ferndale, Loch Sheldrake, Livingston Manor, and all the other resort towns that were, on the new road, only half an hour from Ellenville. It was a kind of reunion for generations of Catskill towns' businessmen, farmers, teachers, and even plumbers, electricians, bulldozer operators, and dump truck drivers. Everyone working on the facility came and returned, time after time. Hotel and bungalow summer guests came, and so did the Cragsmoor aristocracy.

The central school board encouraged the music festival and spoke of teaching local children how to play and sing that music. People of all religions praised the music festival; there were sincere predictions of classical music surpassing show business as local entertainment. Even garish hotel advertizing on highway billboards seemed to become more understated around Ellenville.[26]

Bill Rose was ebullient at the symphony's success. The music tent was his crowning achievement, and it metaphorically brought all the community into a common tent. But the tent was destroyed by hurricanes in the opening season, and the consequent loss of revenues so crippled the symphony that it could not rebuild. Donated time and funds rebuilt the tent, but in its second season, to make a bigger box office, the festival replaced some operas with Broadway musicals, reduced the number of musicians, and decreased the orchestral performances. Despite these changes, the second festival, which began on July 4, 1956, and lasted four weeks, was highlighted by a new ballet score by Villa-Lobos, played by the Symphony of the Air. Moreover, the festival was featured in the *New York Times* as a summer attraction for boarding guests and tourists.[27]

The third and fourth seasons of the music festival featured even more Broadway shows, again for fiscal reasons. *Most Happy Fella, Brigadoon, Carousel, Where's Charley, Guys and Dolls,* and *Damn Yankees* led off the fourth season.[28] A week of symphony concerts followed, but there was to be no fifth season. Ticket sales could not raise enough revenue, and the Civic Association never got state funding. Worse than that, Bill Rose went to jail, partly for covering the seasons' deficits. His trial was practically an operatic plot itself, the drama of two hands against history. It was a revelation of how, to raise money for the festival, he financed under the table some local businesses, among them two large hotels, which repaid the debt promptly, and a local paper mill, which did not. It was alleged during the trial that his best friend ran the mill and used the loans to support a yacht and a female friend.

Jewish farmers in the area severely missed Rose. He had lent them easy credit for modern farm building, and machinery. His loans had prompted bankers in the surrounding towns to follow suit. The farms and hotels he capitalized survived him almost as testimonials to his fiscal wisdom and lack of bigotry, but the music he brought the farmers and hotelmen disappeared when he went to Danbury prison. Without Bill Rose's leadership, the music festival ended and became a local memory. Nothing came of what might have been the cultural revolution of which Harry Resnick, the committee's president, spoke. Neither Jewish nor Christian farmers saw a surge of inspiration in their children to learn to play Mozart, and, even worse, no one seemed to miss the festival that they all had enjoyed while it had lasted.[29]

Chapter 6

A Remnant Lives On

In conjunction with larger sociological and economic forces, overproduction in the poultry industry and stagnation in the growth of the dairying industry settled the fate of the Catskill Jewish farmers. Based on the number of Jewish farming members in Inter-County, there were about half as many Jewish farms in 1960 as there had been in 1940. Farms did pass to settlers' children, as exemplified by the Kross family, the Sashins of Ellenville, the Cohens of Kerhonkson, and the Gibbers of Kiamesha Lake, all of whom had second-generation sons on the 1960 Inter-County board of directors, serving more than as businessmen would on a corporate board. For those families the Inter-County co-op—though a business—still was a kind of extended family to which one gave time without expecting reward, even to the extent of mowing its lawns, as one of Morris Kross's sons felt impelled to do, when the grass grew too high.[1] But the trend of the 1920s through the 1940s, when at least one son per family returned to the farm, had ended for most families by the 1960s, as it had throughout America. When the change came to the Catskills it was more rapid and more severe than expected, and farmers were caught by surprise, unable to compete with the rapid technological changes and with the intense competition attracted from other areas of the country by the ever more profitable dairy and poultry markets. When the end came, it was usually the farmer who lost, and not the credit union or bank.[2]

Those farmers who survived left their property to only one child, because usually only one could make a living from a farm. The other children left the farm for other callings. Some Jewish young people went straight into farming upon graduation from high school, and some of

the children went to agricultural colleges and returned to farming in
the Catskills. But most did neither. Some took jobs or went into business in the city after graduation from high school, believing that city
wages or profits were higher than farm wages and that creature comforts were more attainable in the city. Some went to college for education, law, medicine, or business. Some high school graduates and some
college graduates returned to their neighborhoods to pursue nonagricultural careers. Many of the daughters married city men. Most children who left the farm then were able to find situations with which
they were content. At least until the late 1960s the American economy
generally had opportunities for mobility.

Most of the Jewish farmers and their children who left the farms in
the Catskills were more worldly than those who left farms elsewhere,
chiefly because of New York state's demanding public school curriculum and the college scholarships it provided for serious students. It was
possible for a few to get a full state scholarship for a combined under-
graduate and medical school program. (One who did was Morris Hilf
of Spring Glen, whose father milked a small herd and had used his
credit to build beautiful but heavily mortgaged summer rental bungalows and a swimming pool in his pasture.)[3] Jewish families had long
emphasized the value of a profession gained through education. Jewish farming parents were no exception to this tradition,[4] and neither
were the Jewish sons and daughters who remained on the farms. They
tried to establish good local schools and were involved in community
attempts to improve them.

Not only were the Jewish farmers well educated by this time, but
they had also been assimilated into American society. The ending of
The Jewish Farmer in December 1959 symbolized this change. Over the
years the publication had gradually decreased its Yiddish section but
had continued as a bilingual publication. But the Jewish farming youth
who remained on or returned to farms were now so acculturated that
there was no need for a foreign language publication. In its final edition, it noted that, except for one publication in Argentina, it was the
only Yiddish language agricultural journal in the world. While the society acknowledged that the publication had circulation and financial
problems, it also pointed out that *"The Jewish Farmer* is the only surviving agricultural paper in the United States which has a non-English
section. In fact, there were at one time about twenty agricultural papers with foreign language sections in this country and now the last

Pincus Hilf, Oscar Hilf, Sam Marcus (front, left to right), *Sam Resnick, and Israel Steinberg* (back) *loading hay, Spring Glen, ca. 1948.*

one, *The Jewish Farmer*, is itself going to close. . . . Every segment of our farming population is now so Americanized that there is no need for a foreign language publication."[5]

To those Jewish farmers who remained in the Catskills, the 1960s were the beginnings of a major change. Pearl Trotsky Levine, who had been secretary to the editor of *The Jewish Farmer* and had then married Herman Levine, described the situation of the Jewish farm woman in that period when the demands of raising a family and keeping a house had decreased and women had not yet begun to pursue careers as ends in themselves:

> What effect did modernization of farm life have on the Jewish farm woman? Released from some of the drudgery she began looking about, seeking ways to make use of her new found leisure. First to attract her attention was her own community. She joined with other farm women in their efforts to provide better recreational and educational facilities for themselves and their children. . . . They joined their husbands in agricultural meetings and in their efforts to provide centers where they might enjoy a more abundant life and where their children might receive a Jewish education. . . . They organized or joined already existing chapters of Hadassah, ladies auxiliaries, sisterhoods, and other national organizations. . . . [They] helped raise funds by means of dinners, dances and similar affairs.[6]

Levine noted that the Jewish farm woman still gave first attention to her home, family, and farm work. In addition to canning, freezing, preserving, and storing food, many of the women still helped on the farm by feeding chickens, collecting eggs, delivering eggs to local stores, running errands, and keeping the farm books. Life on the farm was not as rough in the 1960s as it had been, but it still required hard work. Many urbanites have difficulty conceiving of middle-class and even affluent women helping with farm chores, but for farm women it was all part of a family joint enterprise. Morton Shimm concurred that "the Jewish farm wife was a hard worker. She had to be because it was a rough existence to make ends meet. And some of the ones who later became very well known and affluent, those wives also worked on the farm."[7]

Both of the co-ops that had been so important to the Jewish farmers celebrated anniversaries in the 1960s. The Inter-County Farmers' Cooperative Association celebrated its twenty-fifth year in 1961. At the anniversary meeting its members concluded that the next decade would be the most critical for agriculture and that there was a danger that the family farm would be replaced by giant corporate farms. Two years later the Associated Co-operative Fire Insurance Companies celebrated its fiftieth anniversary. The year before it had begun writing homeowners' policies,[8] and its annual meetings were still "gatherings of many hundreds of friends."[9] Mel Lesser, president of Inter-County, its sister organization, praised the fire co-op's record as helping to prove that democracy in industry was not only possible, "but absolutely necessary, if the fruits of man's ingenuity and toil are to be enjoyed by mankind and not by a favored few."[10] Lesser pledged Inter-County's

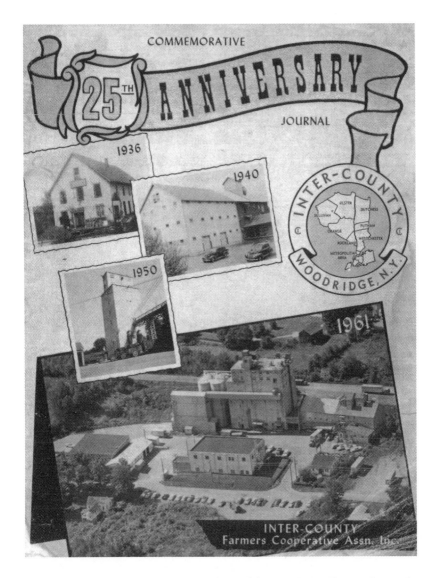

Front page of the twenty-fifth anniversary edition of the Inter-County Farmers Cooperative Association, 1961, showing the expansion in buildings as the co-op grew. The association served the needs of both the Jewish and the non-Jewish communities for half a century.

continued cooperation in aiming for a democratic and peaceful world, just as his predecessor had two years earlier.[11]

The old cooperative spirit was still alive in some of the members. Joe Kooperman declared that it was through Inter-County that his "vision of man's horizons broadened and revealed a tomorrow that is full of hope and promise of a better and more secure life for all of us" and that through the co-op he had had "a rare—a very rare—opportunity of witnessing democracy in action on the industrial field."[12] Esterita Blumberg, speaking on behalf of the fire co-op, called on its members to continue to cooperate to "flourish in a renaissance that unites humanity."[13]

The spirit also reached Washington in the words and votes of a local Jewish farm boy who went to Congress. As a liberal Democrat, Joseph Y. Resnick represented New York's traditionally conservative Republican twenty-seventh Congressional district in Washington during the Johnson administration, bringing *nachus* (pride in the accomplishments of one's children) to the Catskill Jewish farmers. In Resnick, one could see the values that they exemplified. He supported efforts to end discrimination, poverty, hunger, and unemployment and programs to support farmers, working mothers, the father's role in the family, cultural pluralism, and bilingual education for foreign-language-speaking children.

Resnick noted in the *Congressional Record* that he was born and raised on a farm, and he argued for better conditions for farmers:

> My father was an egg farmer. To me these farmers are not statistics or IBM numbers. They are my next door neighbors, people I grew up with, and so I know their problems for my family shared them. . . . Production statistics do not point up the harsh facts of life for the farmworker. Statistics do not show that the farmworker has no unemployment compensation coverage, hospitalization; or that the gap between industrial wages and farm wages is constantly widening, or in fact, that in certain areas of my state farmers must let their crops wither in the field for lack of workers—workers who have moved to the factory. Why should a man continue as a farmworker, exposed to all the extremes of weather and climate, when he can go to work in a factory, in a nearby overcrowded city, and receive all the fringe benefits visited on the industrial employee—and at two or three times the hourly wage on a farm?[14]

Not all of the Jewish farmers of the Catskills were struggling in the 1960s. Sullivan County led the state in poultry and egg production, and other Catskill Jewish farmers continued to prosper. Many of the newer

Larry and Rae Batinkoff, 1991.

farmers were college graduates with sophisticated agricultural training.[15] Abe Marcus of Woodbourne, a former construction worker, had
bought a run-down farm after World War II and had struggled to succeed. By 1966, his three sons had fully automated the farm, introduced
a multistory solar poultry house, and developed the farm into one of
the largest and best in the area. Larry Batinkoff of Ferndale, whose father was one of the many who had worked outside the farm to supplement the farm income, had developed his farm into one of the best
breeding operations in the county. Morris Kross of Dairyland, a third-
generation farmer and a graduate of Cornell's agricultural college, had
won many prizes for his registered Holstein cattle. Joe Brill, who had
bought 140 neglected acres in 1940 and trained Victory Cadets in
World War II, was one of the outstanding cattle breeders in New York
state. The Gibber brothers of Kiamesha Lake, graduates of Cornell Agricultural College, operated nine farms and their own feed mill.[16] There
were many other such success stories.

But even as success continued, inevitable changes were coming. As the 1960s ended, Herman J. Levine and Benjamin Miller, who together had spent seventy-nine years with the Jewish Agricultural Society, recognized the "over-riding sociological and economic" trends that threatened the future of farming. Urbanization, mechanization, technological competition, higher education of their children, increasing incomes, changing tastes, and improving transportation that changed vacation spots were all forces that no co-op or individual could overcome. In addition, there was the old problem that had always threatened farmers: periodic recessions even in good times. Levine and Miller, stalwarts of Jewish agriculture, concluded that "it is not unfair to say that one has to be either a rich man or a son of a farmer in order to become an agriculturist."[17] As the 1960s ended and the 1970s began, most Jewish farmers in the Catskills were not rich, were not part of corporate farming ventures, and were not joining parents on a farm profitable enough to support three generations of a family.[18]

The history of Morton Shimm, who had farmed, had then been the society's extension agent for half a decade, and then had farmed again, illustrated many of the changes in Jewish farming. He was born in the Bronx, where his parents and grandparents lived after immigrating from near Vilna, Lithuania, around 1900. Shimm's father started with a pushcart, then entered the fur business, prospered, and moved the family to New Rochelle in Westchester County, where Morton grew up. His father had an interest in small farming, and it was in New Rochelle that Morton Shimm became interested in farming: "What got me interested in agriculture was the fact that on our small acreage—it wasn't an acreage really—we had fruit trees. My father liked chickens, so we had a few chickens to give us fresh eggs. I got interested in raising pigeons, and raised both homing pigeons as a hobby, I raced them, and raised the mick type pigeon for scrobs. I actually killed them and dressed them. I think that's how I got my interest in poultry husbandry. . . . and of course I remember the wonderful fruit trees and grape arbors that we had."[19]

Shimm wanted to attend Cornell to become a veterinarian, but he couldn't get into the program. Because most Jewish veterinarians worked with small animals, Cornell assumed that he would too, and it wanted to train vets to work with larger animals such as cattle and horses for the nearby farming areas. Instead of becoming a veterinarian, Shimm studied poultry at Cornell and worked on farms during the summers.

While at Cornell, he met and married the daughter of a Catskill dairy farmer. He worked in the city for a short time after graduation in 1938, and in 1939, in a Model-A Ford, went to the Catskills to begin his farming career. He began by renting part of a farm and some chicken coops in White Sulfur Springs in Sullivan County, rented a large farm in Duchess County for a year and a half, and bought a sixty-acre farm in foreclosure in Liberty. In 1948, when he was selected as the society's extension agent, he sold his farm and, after serving as extension agent, became a turkey farmer. From 1963 until 1969 he managed Max Brender's mechanized farm with 220,000 laying hens, the largest mechanized farm in New York state at the time.

Shimm described the impact on Jewish farmers of the trend toward larger farming in the 1960s:

> The [big corporate farms] survived because they were part of an integrated plan where a hatchery and a feed mill would farm out chicks to farmers in the area who couldn't make it by themselves, who didn't have the capital. That's the reason I went out of the turkey business. I had a fine turkey business in New York state, and we made pretty darn good profits the first few years. But then it got to the point where even if you raised the best birds and were a good grower you couldn't make any money. Only the people in the integrated operations would make it. . . . And that's what happened in the egg business, in the turkey business, in the poultry industry in America, it was taken over by integrated operations.[20]

The famous Woodstock Festival, held on August 15–17, 1969, coincided with the closing of the Catskills Jewish farmers' heyday. The festival had originally been scheduled for Woodstock in northern Ulster County, the artistic town that had historically been lukewarm at best to Jews. But the town banned the festival after planning was well advanced. While retaining the name of Woodstock because it had already been publicized as such, the festival was held instead on the 600-acre farm of Max Yasgur, a Jewish farmer, near the little town of Bethel in Sullivan County. The county approved the festival, after some opposition, largely because the heavily Jewish entertainment industry in the county recognized its publicity value and saw that it would help the county move beyond its Borscht Belt image—an image the area was trying to de-emphasize in order to attract a larger market.[21] Thus a festival named after a town that was not friendly to Jews and several score miles away actually took place on a Jewish-owned farm in a biblically named town (in Hebrew *Bethel* means "house of God") in the Jewish

Woodstock peace symbol and monument, erected 1984, Bethel.

Catskills. In an odd way, it was a tribute to the generous spirit that these Jewish farmers exemplified, and it was fitting that they accommodated a group that, like themselves, stood on the perimeter of society. Alf Evers insightfully noted this philosophical connection between the two groups: "Influential Sullivan people were often sons or grandsons of immigrants to the Lower East Side. They had done well in the existing American society, yet retained much of the emphasis on human values and change in ways of living and feeling their Socialist grandfathers had debated in East Side coffee houses."[22]

In the early 1970s, the Catskill Jewish farmers' long-standing special relationship with the New York City market finally surrendered to national market forces. With the producers went the breeders supplying them, and with the breeders went the industry. So many left the business so rapidly that legal and financial matters were difficult to resolve. Who had recoverable assets to pay debts was as uncertain as the state of some debt payments and of certain titles. As more and more farmers left, those remaining called on Inter-County for more credit than it could extend, and in the process many friendships were strained. Evers observed that by 1972 "owners of old family farms are finding it easier and more profitable to sell to speculators or to subdivide and unload bit by bit on weekend and summer people than to go on farming. The incursion on so much of the region's fertile valleys by reservoirs and broad highways has gone far to reduce the appeal of farming."[23] David Wagner, who was the grandson of an Eastern European immigrant who had come to Sullivan County in the late 1920s and built a boardinghouse farm, and who had himself lived most of his life on a farm and had later taken charge of Inter-County's egg production, said in 1973 that "there was a time when I couldn't tell you the names of all the Jewish farmers—it would have taken me hours. Now I could sit down and write you a list."[24]

By 1975 several egg operations much larger than Mt. Pride— heavily mortgaged, fully automated, and highly productive—had sprung up almost overnight in Wurtsboro and North Branch. Others were built in Pennsylvania, and somewhat smaller operations continued producing in central Connecticut. The result was further attrition of the Catskill farmers; some of the small producers practically abandoned their properties just as others had previously abandoned some of the small hotels, bungalow colonies, and rooming houses. By 1980 the number of Inter-County members had declined so far that their annual meetings could have filled its board room.[25] When asked to describe the decline of Inter-County, Joe Cohen, who had succeeded Al Cohen as manager in 1972, noted:

> The number of Inter-County members fell, although the feed business stayed relatively high until some of the members set off on their own to mill feed. They were big operators. We went down to approximately 120 patrons (members and non-member buyers), less than half of what we had in the 1950s and 1960s. In the late 1970s, about 40 were dairymen, 50 had horse farms or farms with miscellaneous small farm animals, and the rest

were poultrymen. In the late 1960s about 90 percent of our purchasers produced eggs, but then it went to about 50 percent, with the rest dairy, horse-
feed, broilers, ducks, and some turkey. . . . Feed tonnage peaked in the late
1960s when we had four hundred to five hundred members.[26]

In 1976, the Catskill Center for Conservation and Development was
formed by long-time residents who were concerned not so much by increasing development as by "its renegade nature: land sold, sometimes
sight unseen, on slopes a goat could not navigate; building sites lying a
mile from any utility line, huge tracts carved and developed without
the slightest regard to pollution, erosion, wildlife, natural history or
even, in some cases, health and safety."[27]

For even as small farmers and boardinghouse and bungalow keepers
were leaving the Catskills in droves, a new wave of residents was flooding in. The population in Sullivan County, for example, increased 23
percent from 1970 to 1980, its growth fueled by low interest rates and
land prices. New York City people came seeking second homes; non-
establishment religious groups came seeking "land for isolation and
summer retreats, and painters, sculptors, musicians, and other artists
seeking inexpensive studios were major segments of new residents."
Artists from Manhattan and Brooklyn "virtually took over" the Sullivan
County farming village of Mountaindale.[28] In a postscript to his earlier
work, Alf Evers wryly noted that "the newly awakened viewer of the
Catskill scene would surely have been puzzled at the clusters of trailers
and A-frame dwellings which by 1980 had taken over many a cow pasture."[29] As John G. Mitchell said in the late 1970s, "Second homes for
urban refugees [had] risen at every bend of a back-country road" in
some areas of the Catskills.[30] Some Jewish farmers, like some Christian
farmers, had participated in this conversion of farm land to summer
homes during the 1970s and 1980s. Only periodic high interest rates
and economic cycles had kept the conversion from being more rapid.

Visitors to Ulster Heights, Woodbourne, Woodridge, Liberty, Loch
Sheldrake, and surrounding towns in 1980 would also have seen the
painful side of the change. They would have driven past endless hulks
of small hotels and rooming houses, abandoned summer bungalows,
paintless, leaning barns, and collapsing two- and three-story chicken
coops, all waiting for collapse from their own rot or for destruction by
vandals, none worth the effort to tear them down.[31] The trees that had
sprung up around their entrances and the rust eating away the roof
feed bins were at least a decade old.

Visitors also would have seen the product of the new capital: the industrial egg factories, some dairy farms, the Inter-County's vast egg handling plant built to contend with the national market. The plant was administered by orthodox Jews in Chasidic garments. In July and August one would see young bearded Chasidim (literally "pious" or "holy ones") in caftans and broad hats, their wives and daughters in full dresses and kerchiefs despite the heat. They determinedly walked the shoulders of Route 42 between Woodbourne and Fallsburg and other areas, looking as if they had stepped out of history to disprove both Hirsch's and the Lodz socialists' theories that to survive, particularly as farmers, Jews had to Westernize, to shed their caftans, round hats, and fervent rituals.

They were like hippies or other activists who made bold statements in their appearance and customs, but probably few of these Chasids thoroughly understood how they would have been received on these roads a century earlier if the more secular Jewish farmers and resort keepers had not preceded them in large numbers. These Chasidim occupied some of the former resorts, packed as tightly as guests had been in the 1920s and 1930s. They arrived from heated Brooklyn not by the O&W, which had closed even as a freight line by 1954, but in station wagons packed with children.

Visitors in 1980 would also have observed the stucco or clapboard shtetl-like synagogues still operating and in some towns actually prospering. They also would have seen a couple of brick temples such as the one in Monticello with a Reformed congregation. At any of those one could have found a few farmers, some of them quite young, at a Friday minyan. Industrial farming had finally given them some leisure along with debt.

Entertainment had changed too. In Ellenville, where a movie house had done business until the late 1970s, there was a struggling year-round repertory theater. Like the old Cragsmoor and the house that survived Woodstock, this theater produced serious plays, but spats and parasols were not typical summer dress here and its winter patrons were primarily local public school children.

A horse-racing track in Monticello, which had opened in 1958, as the Empire State Music Festival was failing, was still popular. Local residents, area resort owners, and New York City investors had already lavished a generation of money and energy on the track in search of the perfect profitable vehicle to provide public recreation. The half-

Congegration Ezrath Israel, Ellenville, 1987.

mile harness racing track had lost money the first year, largely because the racing plant was not finished and because the New York Quickway (Route 17), which went right past the track, was also unfinished. As a result traffic would back up several miles on the highway and through Monticello, making it difficult and frustrating for would-be patrons to get to it. By the second year both were finished.[32] Major resort hotels such as Grossinger's, the Windsor and Pines at South Fallsburg, the Tamarack at Greenfield Park, the Nevele at Ellenville, and Kutsher's at Monticello offered guests visits to the track as part of their packages. In fact the track later changed its opening time to 9 P.M. so that hotel guests could finish dinner. The Quickway was widened to six lanes a decade later.[33]

The venture was a continuing success and had one of the fastest tracks for pari-mutuel harness racing, an indoor paddock, Sunday matinees, and several restaurants.[34] The track's main significance for the local Jewish farmers was that it provided a market for locally grown hay for horses. Another local success that had flourished in the midst of the farmers' hard times was the Resnicks' Ellenville Channel Master television antenna factory, but in 1984, it closed, a victim of cable television and competition from other manufacturers.[35]

Chasidic camp between Fallsburg and South Fallsburg, a sign of the changing times, 1991.

But the Resnick family, like other Jewish individuals and families that had been in the Catskills since its farming heyday, continues its contribution to the community. Louis, Harry's oldest brother, has funded local scholarships for Jewish and non-Jewish farm children. In 1988, Louis and his wife, Mildred, began their support of the Distinguished Lecture Series and the annual Holocaust Memorial Lecture at The College at New Paltz, SUNY, and in 1993 they endowed the Louis and Mildred Resnick Institute for the Study of Modern Jewish Life at the college. Continuing the values that the Jewish farmers had brought to the Catskills, the Resnick Institute's goals included "a deeper understanding of Jewish civilization and Jewish life, the integration of cam-

Louis and Mildred Resnick, Ellenville, 1987.

pus and community, and the encouragement of interfaith dialogue."[36] Lawyer Joe Kooperman, that shepherd of Robert's Rules, also established a scholarship fund for high school graduates who had low grades but were willing to try to make a fresh start in college.[37] The fund was set up by Inter-County and named the Joe Kooperman Educational Fund. It was administered by Mel Lesser, the Inter-County board member who, even in those competitive times, profited on 50,000 laying hens. Funds were donated by local businesses (for example, the Poultrymen's Cooperative Hatchery released its funds on hand to the schol-

Joseph and Ethel Kooperman, 1987.

arship program in honor of Kooperman), and a fund-raiser was also held. The fund had some successful recipients which Kooperman considered as much of a triumph as the founding of Inter-County.[38]

But for others the picture was much more bleak. In the mid-1980s the same visitors could start north in Parksville, go down to Ellenville, go past Kerhonkson and up toward Kingston, then back down to Wurtsboro, and on to Port Jervis. They would see, sitting mutely, abandoned homes and inns and hundreds of cinder-block ghosts of chicken coops, even better built, better outfitted, and better ventilated than their decaying predecessors, some of them less than a decade old. Some were huge, windowless, a hundred by three hundred feet in size, and on wet warm days they reeked, reminders of the industry recently housed there. Homes on these properties were dark at night. If visitors had walked into these farm buildings and homes, they would have seen the remnants, sometimes a decade old, of their former inhabitants' last day: unremoved manure on the chicken coop floors, feathers, waterers, feeders, old mash, torn pillows, old blankets, old newspapers dating back to the time when people had lived and worked in these shells.

Like all farms in America, Catskill farms were pressured by the ever-increasing production of bigger operations. In 1900, 37.5 percent of the people in the United States were in farm occupations; by 1940, it was 17 percent; by 1950, 12 percent; by 1960, 6 percent; by 1970, 3.6 percent; and by 1980, under 3 percent.[39] By 1988, the total percentage of the American population on farms was 1.9, with another small decrease in 1989.[40] In 1935, there were 6.8 million farms in the United States, the highest number. It had decreased to 2.4 million in 1983, on a little less land. In 1935, the average farm was about 155 acres; by 1983, 432 acres.[41] By 1989, the number of farms had further decreased to 2.2 million. The number of dairy farms, for example, had decreased from 2.8 million in 1955 to 205,000 in 1989.[42]

The consolidation of farms has been encouraged, directly and indirectly, by the federal government. For example, in 1960, Earl Butz, who later would serve as secretary of agriculture from 1971 to 1976 under Presidents Nixon and Ford, stated that the decrease in the farm population was good.[43] In 1988 Marvin Cetron and Owen Davies wrote that "the Reagan administration showed Washington's power and willingness to destroy independent farms when, a week after the 1988 presidential election, it mailed out foreclosure threats to some eighty thousand delinquent farm-loan recipients."[44]

The idea that government policies aim to preserve small family farms is a myth,[45] and this policy has been worse for Jewish farmers than for many non-Jewish farmers because, like the few African-American farmers, they generally have had small farms.[46] In 1920, as Jewish farmers were beginning in the Catskills, there were 926,000 farms operated by African-Americans in America. (African-Americans were the most farm-based of the ethnic groups in the United States.) By 1954, this number was reduced to 427,000, less than half as many as in 1920. By 1987, however, these farms had dwindled to 23,000, or only 5 percent of the 1954 total.[47]

Today visitors can drive the roads of lower Ulster County and most of Sullivan County and see a whole century of Jewish farm culture in artifact. If visitors know where to look, they can even see a few Jewish poultrymen and dairymen still working their Catskill properties. If they were to engage the Jewish farmers in conversations on Rosh Hashanah or Yom Kippur, about the only time they can be found in shul, they would discover that these farmers are inwardly praying for the same thing for which most other American farmers pray—higher profits. They may hear the farmers anguish over the fact that Inter-County, salvation to Catskill farmers for half a century, had to lay off staff as an ominous response to falling demand for feed. Some were bitter that they had to resort to supplying the Monticello race track's horse farms as the only way to be able to mill cow and chicken feed.

Those visitors could talk to one of the remaining Jewish farmers, David Levitz, whose history exemplified that of others in the region. A lifelong dairyman, Levitz was born on his father's farm on Beaver Dam Road, part of the border of Ulster and Sullivan counties, close to Grahamsville. Immigrating in 1906, his father, a city house painter, bought the sixty acres for $600, clean of buildings, and in 1910 built a house in the local fashion of native pine and hemlock. His father married in 1912, brought his bride there, and was a part-time painter, part-time farmer. Neither Levitz's father nor his neighbors—the Krosses, the Bucholtzes, the Tennenbaums, or the Wagners—settled with the aid of the society; it was the society that found them immediately after World War I. Levitz's parents kept a few cows for home milk, strove for self-sufficiency, and survived the depression because their indebtedness was minimal. Their income subsequently was augmented by

David Levitz family farm, 1987.

upbreeding their herd by artificial insemination and by the blessings of Inter-County's low prices.

Growing up, David worked the farm as did any other farm youth; he milked and hayed, walked two miles each way to a one-room school through the eighth grade, and subsequently had one year of high school. He learned Hebrew for his Bar Mitzvah from an itinerant instructor at a local Ulster Heights synagogue where, as in Europe, the farmer elders prayed without rabbis. They convened when necessary, not in a zealous discovery of ritual for its own sake but because they wanted to practice a convention whose worth they did not dream of questioning.

In 1934, when David Levitz was twenty-two, his family decided to become serious dairy farmers. They built their own modern barn from plans, equipped it with the best gear then available, and stocked it with a herd of fifteen, the average number for the industry then. They sold twenty-gallon cans of milk to creameries as did the hundreds of similar mountain suppliers, the milk ultimately going to New York City by the O&W. By 1940, David took over the farm, continued to upbreed his herd, and expanded the barn to accommodate the larger cows created by upbreeding. Enamored by the success of local poultrymen profiting from Inter-County's low prices and good management on one hand and from the expanding demand of the New York poultry and egg markets on the other, David put up a chicken house in 1945 that complemented his dairying very well. For almost thirty years the combination worked well, giving him and his wife, Rose, and their children a decent net income. Riding the crest of apparently endless prosperity, they refinanced to build one of the splendidly modern middle-sized poultry structures mushrooming in the mountains.

For awhile the operation paid a profit, but by 1979 the advent of hugely efficient megafarms highly capitalized by industrial finance produced a national oversupply of eggs that converted Levitz's profits to losses. In one year he lost a dollar on each of his 12,000 laying hens. He, like others around then, emptied his poultry buildings. Having expanded his Holstein herd to forty, and having bred them up to an average yield of 13,000 pounds of milk per year each, he survived on his milk check. But even then, in the oversupply of milk at the time, milk prices fell. The milk brokering co-op went under, taking his check with it. Still paying off the vacant poultry buildings, he and his wife survive on the small net of the milk checks plus his small salary as a director in the successor to the fire insurance co-op.

Except for David Levitz and Morris Kross, his nearby neighbor in Dairyland and fellow director at Inter-County, there are few remaining Catskill Jewish dairymen.[48] Except for two or three egg farmers who run huge operations, like Meyer Kaplan's K-Brand Farms in Glen Wild and Hy Frank's vast integrated feedmill-to-egg operation in North Branch (which filed for bankruptcy in 1987), and for a dozen or so survivors of the 1960s size operation, there are no longer Catskill Jewish egg farmers. In 1986, Joe Cohen noted that the overwhelming majority of the clientele at Inter-County were non-Jewish. The factors that led to the decline of Inter-County were affecting farming in general in the United States.

A few Jewish farmers who specialized in raising heavy-breed poultry and broilers for large kosher processors such as Manor Poultry operated in the late 1980s. They relied heavily on Inter-County feed and credit to make their narrow "spread," that is, profit per pound, but they are no longer supplied with chicks by the other former Inter-County members who used to do this. Individuals who were breeders for fifteen to forty years such as Max Brender, Isadore Gibber, Larry Batinkoff, and Harold Hecht are no longer breeding. On Hecht's building, there are a few faded logos on once-painted walls of abandoned cinder-block coops. By the late 1980s, many farmers had gotten part-time jobs to supplement their farm incomes.[49]

When the board of directors and remaining members of the Inter-County Farmers' Cooperative Association, Incorporated, agreed to lease the feed mill (with an option to buy) to the cooperative conglomerate AGWAY in 1988, it seemed that it would be dissolved. In its last years, it had been milling only two-thirds of the volume of its peak years, and a major part of those closing years' volume consisted of a variety of feeds including horse and dairy feed.[50] For fifty-one years Inter-County had merged Eastern European socialist values with the entrepreneurial values of capitalism. Ironically, since the 1960s AGWAY had been the reincarnation of the Grange League Federation the affiliate of which, the Accord Farmers Co-operative Association, the Jewish farmers had not found receptive to their interests nearly half a century earlier. After the mill was leased to AGWAY, Inter-County became only a paper corporation, taking in rent, dissolving assets, and distributing the proceeds as patronage refunds to stockholders on the basis of seniority and volume of purchases. The lease to AGWAY then fell apart, and Inter-County regained management with the goal of selling off its property.[51]

When the Jewish Agricultural Society had closed its office in El-lenville in 1945, it did so with a record of success and in the knowledge that it was succeeded by even more relevant and successful Jewish-led organizations, the most significant of which was Inter-County. When Inter-County closed in 1988, it had a record of success, but it was not followed as the society had been. The drastic decrease in the farming population in the United States, particularly among small family farms, the industrialization of farms, and the professionalization of the Jew-ish community all combined to lead to different circumstances. The most famous Jewish farm of the Catskills, Max Yasgurs' where Wood-stock had been held in 1969, epitomized this change. Most of the farm has been sold, and country homes now occupy much of the former farmland. About 2,000 people make a pilgrimage each year to remem-ber the Woodstock festival; 22,000 went in 1989 to commemorate its twentieth anniversary. Major plans were made for the twenty-fifth an-niversary of Woodstock in August 1994.[52]

As the 1980s ended, the Cooperative Extension Service began to sponsor in Sullivan County an annual Down on the Farm Day so that visitors could see how farming works. Egg University, Meyer Kaplan's humorously named egg farm in Glen Wild, also offered tours of its fa-cilities. In Callicoon, the Apple Pond Farming Center offered educa-

Meyer Kaplan's sign, "Egg U. The College of Higher Eggucation," Glen Wild, 1987.

tional tours, wagon rides, haying, logging, sheep-herding, bee-keeping, and other farm activities. Other farms in the Catskills were open to the public, with many activities oriented to city children. The farmers, Jewish and Christian, who remember milking cows and doing numerous other labor-intensive chores were amused to see how much the urban children were fascinated by these activities.[53]

Jewish farming in the Catskills has been affected not only by changes in farming but also by changes in the Jewish population in New York. By 1990, the Jewish population of Ellenville was estimated to be 1,600, having grown from 540 in 1937 to 800 in 1948 and 1,100 in 1960. But in other parts of the Catskills Jewish population growth has been more uneven. For example, Monticello had an estimated Jewish population of 1,350 in 1937 which had decreased to 1,200 by 1948, had increased to 2,400 by 1960, but was the same in 1990 as it had been in 1960. Liberty had 600 Jews in 1937 and the same number in 1948, but then that number had increased to 2,100 by 1960 and remained at 2,100 in 1990. South Fallsburg was estimated to have a Jewish population of 1,100 in 1948, but the estimate stayed the same for 1960 and 1990. From 1948 to 1960, the number of Jews in Mountaindale decreased from 250 to 150, in Parksville from 225 to 140, in Kerhonkson from 575 to 350, in Woodridge from 400 to 300, in Livingston Manor from 150 to 125, and in Woodbourne it stayed the same at 200. None of these villages and small towns were even listed in the 1990 American Jewish Year Book.[54]

Jewish farmers in the Catskills are not counted separately from the overall number of Jewish residents, but the number of Jewish farmers decreased even more than did that of the total Jewish population. The towns have maintained more of their Jewish population than the farms have by absorbing some Jewish former farmers, some children of Jewish farmers, and some new Jewish residents. Some of the larger Jewish communities, such as Ellenville and Monticello, even have somewhat new synagogues, but farmers play a relatively small part in these Jewish communities. Orange County, to the south of Sullivan County and closer to New York City, has consistently had more Jews in its population, but few of these are farmers. As the number of farming Jews decreases more, suburbanization creeps closer to the heart of the Jewish Catskills.[55]

Sullivan County's population as a whole continued to grow in the 1980s, having a 6.3 percent increase from 65,155 to 69,277. Ulster

County's population increased by 4.5 percent, from 158,158 to 165,304. As with its Jewish population, however, Orange County had the largest growth in the area, increasing 18.5 percent from 259,603 to 307,647.[56] Regardless of whether these increases are due to creeping suburbanization or other sources, they do not include large increases in the number of Jews in the Catskills. And hardly ever does one of these new Jewish residents become a farmer. By 1990, there were signs that the Catskill area was possibly beginning another phase in the classic American pattern of ethnic sucession. By 1990, African-Americans accounted for 23.9 percent of Monticello's population, 21.6 percent of South Fallsburg's population, 12.5 percent of Ellenville's population, and 12.5 percent of Liberty's population.[57] Hispanics accounted for 23.6 percent of Ellenville's population, 15.9 percent of Monticello's population, 12.6 percent of Livington Manor's population, 12.1 percent of South Fallsburg's population, and 9.4 percent of Liberty's population.[58] Parts of the Catskills were now referred to as the Spanish Alps, just as they had earlier been called the Jewish Catskills. In fact in August 1991 Latinos United by Cultural Heritage and Awareness (LUCHA) celebrated its first year of existence with a picnic in Monticello.[59]

New York City, the source of the earlier Jewish migration to the Catskills, is no longer a source. Increasing numbers of Jews are moving not only out of New York City but out of New York state, largely to the Sunbelt. In 1960, 45.8 percent of the Jews in the United States lived in New York state, but by 1990 that percentage had decreased to 30.8 percent, their destinations primarily Florida and California. In 1960, California had 9.6 percent of the total U.S. Jewish population, but by 1990 that figure had increased to 15.4 percent. Florida had 2 percent in 1960 but 9.5 percent by 1990.[60]

As it has for northeasterners in general, southeast Florida in particular has a special attraction for current and former Catskill residents, many of whom attend the annual "Ellenville Get Together" held each January near Fort Lauderdale, Florida, within easy driving distance of the Miami Beach and Palm Beach areas. The event attracts several hundred people, many with roots in the Jewish farming of the Catskills. Attendees include "snowbirds" or retirees spending their winters in Florida, retirees now living permanently in Florida, and children and grandchildren of Catskill residents. Other Jews have retired in smaller numbers in various parts of Florida and on the east coast of the United States. Jewish farmers and their descendants, many of whom left the

Gertrude and William Badner, 1987.

Catskills because of the bad farming conditions or the Jewish love of learning, now leave their marks in many areas.

A century and a decade since Czar Alexander's III's pogrom, the Catskill Jewish cemeteries hold farmers and townspeople, chicken farmers and butchers. Some never surrendered their ideals; some held only the ideal of gain. Some, feigning to be hardheaded business people seven days a week, secretly wrote verse or wanted to. These lives spanned ages in less than a century. Some of the cemeteries, like the Jeffersonville Jewish Cemetery, which has horses grazing nearby, provide a fitting final resting place for these Jewish farmers and citizens of rural towns. Some are tended in perpetual care, but some of the smaller ones might be neglected in another generation and come to resemble the moss-stoned resting places of the long-ago owners of the Catskill farmhouses that Jews bought. A century of cemetery markers—the earlier ornately scrolled in Hebrew only, after the European fashion, the later stones simpler, with Ashkenazi names in English—all would be as strange to the twenty-second century viewer as the Sephardic cemetery in Newport, Rhode Island, was to Longfellow when he wrote, "How strange it seems! These Hebrews in their graves. . . . The very

Melvin Lesser, 1991.

names recorded here are strange, of foreign accent, and of different climes; Alvarez and Rivera interchange with Abraham and Jacob, of old times."[61]

Yet the twentieth century benefited from the Catskill Jewish farms even in their demise as it benefited from the demise of small farms throughout the country. Moreover the individuals migrating from the farms benefited also. In discussing the vast number of black youth who also are leaving farms, Loren Schweninger stated that "the recent decline, despite its signaling the end of a phenomenon, symbolizes a new

The Jeffersonville Jewish cemetery, near Youngsville, 1991.

beginning for younger blacks who are entering a wide variety of professions and business fields or securing more highly paying jobs in towns and cities."[62] Exiting the farms, Jewish, black, and others, were individuals who had experienced the discipline of hard work and had tackled and solved fairly large problems daily—debt servicing, civil and mechanical engineering, disease control, wholesale marketing, and labor efficiency among them. They were easily prepared to handle the small problems of daily city life.

The century of Jewish farming in the Catskills proved the Jewish Agricultural Society's points: that Jews could farm seriously and profitably, that in doing so they could assimilate in all areas of American society but religion, and they could gain the respect of Christians. The society did not regret to discover that because of the contributions of Inter-County and other organizations, halfway into that farming century the society itself became expendable to those efforts.

Without the shtetl cultures around Catskill towns, Jewish farming would not have survived. The Jewish town businesses and families were sources of credit, essential services, and, for some farmers, socializing and prayer. The towns indirectly accounted for the fire and feed co-ops, for if the towns had not had many Jews, most Jews farming near them would not have stayed around long enough to build

Former synagogue, now a hardware store, Accord, 1991.

these co-ops. But if the Jewish farmers of the Catskills had not had the sense to subordinate their disparate political doctrines to their mutual need in business, they would have ruined the cooperation critical to their success. Then and now, as David Levitz argues, the federal government's responsibility to the farmers is to appreciate their differences from other small businesses and to assist them accordingly. President Roosevelt's New Deal farm credits, and especially his credits for farm cooperatives, helped farmers, and particularly the Catskill Jewish farmers, prosper. The Catskill Jewish farmers prospered more than much of agricultural America because they had a vision of cooperation, of mutual help, and they saw how these New Deal programs could help further that vision.

The ultimate hope of Cremieux and Hirsch, to curb anti-Semitism by westernizing the Eastern European Jew as a farmer and thus to improve the European Christian opinion of Jews in general, was made moot by Hitler. Jewish success in farming the Catskills and elsewhere hardly changed Christian opinions in places other than where the Jews themselves farmed. But the world's millions of rural poor, some of them in the United States, might profit from knowing how Catskill

Former synagogue, built in the late 1920s by an Orthodox rabbi who had a rooming house next door; now a private home, Granite, 1991.

Jews farmed their way out of adversity for the better part of a century, working hard, learning, inventing, skimping, investing, borrowing, producing, establishing credibility and credit, dealing with sympathetic Christian bankers who learned to respect them, and meeting their primary needs collectively in the Rochdale cooperative fashion. It is a tale not of rugged individualism but of rugged individuals.

Appendix

Interviews

Interviewee	*Interviewer*	*Date*
Katerina Engel Altenberg	Clarence B. Steinberg	November 4, 1989
Gertrude Badner	Clarence B. Steinberg	August 19, 1987
William Badner	Clarence B. Steinberg	August 19, 1987
Lawrence Batinkoff	Abraham D. Lavender	December 27, 1990
Rae Batinkoff	Abraham D. Lavender	December 27, 1990
Rae Perez Bechar (Behar)	Abraham D. Lavender	December 12, 1989
Clifford Calhoun	Clarence B. Steinberg	August 14, 1987
Albert J. Cohen	Abraham D. Lavender	August 6, 1987
Miriam Cohen	Abraham D. Lavender	August 6, 1987
Joseph Cohen	Clarence B. Steinberg	October 3, 1986
Joseph Cohen	Clarence B. Steinberg	November 27, 1989
Greta Engel	Clarence B. Steinberg	November 4, 1989
Ruth L. Frankenstein	Abraham D. Lavender	January 3, 1990
Ruth L. Frankenstein	Abraham D. Lavender	June 21, 1992
Bruce W. Gerson	Abraham D. Lavender	June 18, 1992
David Gerson	Abraham D. Lavender	June 22, 1992
Frances S. Gerson	Abraham D. Lavender	June 21, 1992
Morris Gibber	Abraham D. Lavender	January 5, 1990
Abraham Jaffe	Clarence B. Steinberg	May 4, 1987
Ethel Kooperman	Clarence B. Steinberg	August 14, 1987
Joseph Kooperman	Clarence B. Steinberg	August 14, 1987
Melvin Lesser	Clarence B. Steinberg	August 20, 1988
Herman J. Levine	Abraham D. Lavender	July 22, 1982
Herman J. Levine	Abraham D. Lavender	July 23, 1982
Herman J. Levine	Abraham D. Lavender	July 26, 1982
David Levitz	Clarence B. Steinberg	October 2, 1986
Ann Kaminsky Macin	Abraham D. Lavender	February 19, 1990

Louis Resnick	Clarence B. Steinberg	August 14, 1987
Morton Shimm	Abraham D. Lavender	May 25, 1988
Jack Siegel	Clarence B. Steinberg	August 20, 1988
Mrs. Robert Stapleton	Abraham D. Lavender	November 23, 1993

Note: Two people, interviewed on May 3, 1987, by Clarence Steinberg, requested anonymity.

Notes

Chapter 1: Jews and the Farming Tradition

1. Mendes, "Agriculture: Historical Aspects," 262.

2. See, for example, Exodus 23:16, Leviticus 1–3, and Deuteronomy 16:9; Davidson, *Our Jewish Farmers and the Story of the Jewish Agricultural Society;* Arkin, "Farming in Biblical Times," 20–24; Novak, "Maimonides and Agriculture," 47–48.

3. Carol Rosenberg, "Pig Bowl: Secular Majority vs. Ultra-Orthodox Minority," 33a; Herscher, *Jewish Agricultural Utopias in America, 1880–1910,* 115–21; Morris, *On the Soil of Israel: Americans and Canadians in Agriculture,* 14, 248; Willner, *Nation-Building and Community in Israel,* 33, 41, 42; Engel, "North American Settlers in Israel," 172.

4. Fishman, *The Jews of the United States,* 33, 36.

5. Rischin, *The Promised City: New York's Jews, 1870–1914,* 20, 33, 270.

6. Howe, *World of Our Fathers.*

7. *Hester Street* is a sentimental adaptation of Abraham Cahan's *Yekl: A Tale of the Ghetto.* See also Friedman, *Hollywood's Image of the Jew.*

8. Forman, "Some Adopted Americans," 51–52, quoted in Rischin, *The Promised City.*

9. Rischin, *The Promised City,* 83.

10. Dawidowicz, *The Golden Tradition: Jewish Life and Thought in Eastern Europe,* 46–47.

11. Berk, *Year of Crisis, Year of Hope,* 171.

12. Menes, "The Jewish Labor Movement," 336.

13. Sorin, *The Prophetic Minority,* 77.

14. Cahan, "The Russian Jew in America," 133.

15. Berk, *Year of Crisis, Year of Hope,* 172.

16. Rochlin and Rochlin, *Pioneer Jews: A New Life in the Far West,* 70–72; Libo and Howe, *We Lived There Too,* 282–97.

17. The Jewish Agricultural Society, *Jews in American Agriculture,* 7.

18. Ibid.; Stuart Rosenberg, *The New Jewish Identity in America,* 45.

19. Marcus, *Early American Jewry: The Jews of New York, New England, and Canada, 1649–1794*, 1:42–44.

20. Reznikoff and Engelman, *The Jews of Charleston: A History of an American Jewish Community*, 7.

21. The Jewish Agricultural Society, *Jews in American Agriculture*, 12; Sharfman, *Jews on the Frontier: An Account of Jewish Pioneers and Settlers in Early America*, 70.

22. Sharfman, *Jews on the Frontier*, 58–60; Reznikoff and Engelman, *The Jews of Charleston*, 36–40; Evans, *The Provincials: A Personal History of Jews in the South*, 56.

23. Sharfman, *Jews on the Frontier*, 175.

24. Korn, *The Early Jews of New Orleans*, 62.

25. Marcus, *Early American Jewry: The Jews of Pennsylvania and the South, 1655–1790*, 2:218–19.

26. Sharfman, *Jews on the Frontier*, 109.

27. Korn, *The Early Jews of New Orleans*, 170.

28. Grossman, *The Soil's Calling*, 98.

29. Schappes, *A Documentary History of the Jews in the United States, 1654–1875*, 141; Jewish Agricultural Society, *Jews in American Agriculture*, 16.

30. Dawidowicz, *The Golden Tradition*, 24–35.

31. Green and Zerivitz, *Mosaic: Jewish Life in Florida*, 9–10.

32. Also see Liebman and Liebman, *Jewish Frontiersmen*, and Adler, "Moses Elias Levy and Attempts to Colonize Florida," 18.

33. Schappes, *A Documentary History*, 195.

34. U.S. Bureau of the Census, *1840 Census of Ulster County*.

35. Robinson, "Agricultural Activities," 56; Davidson, *Our Jewish Farmers*; U.S. Bureau of the Census, *1840 Census of Ulster County*, 267.

36. See Eisner, "Ellenville—The Community in the Catskills with the Earliest Established Jewish Families."

37. Goodwin and Levine, "A Historical Review of Farming by Jews in New York," 11.

38. Shpall, "Jewish Agricultural Colonies in the United States," 120–46; Schappes, *A Documentary History*, 346; Jewish Agricultural Society, *Jews in American Agriculture*, 16, 17, 19.

39. Rosenthal, "Agricultural Colonies in Russia," 255; Robinson, "Agricultural Activities of the Jews in America," 39.

40. Robinson, "Agricultural Activities," 29; Nirenberg, "Folksongs in the East European Tradition," 2.

41. Cahan, "The Russian Jew in the United States," 135; Rosenthal, "Agricultural Colonies in Russia," 255.

42. Rosenthal, "Agricultural Colonies in Russia," 256.

43. Rischin, *The Promised City*, 22–23.

44. Dawidowicz, *The Golden Tradition*, 30.

45. Sorin, *The Prophetic Minority*, 28.

46. Berk, *Year of Crisis, Year of Hope*, 129.

47. Halkin, "Am Olam," 2:862.

48. Berk, *Year of Crisis, Year of Hope*, 128–29.

49. Jewish Agricultural Society, *Jews in American Agriculture*, 27; Levy, "Rural Settlements: Western States," 403.

50. Robinson, "Agricultural Activities of the Jews in America"; see also H.J. Levine, "Jewish Farming in the Mid-West," 86–87; Dawidowicz, *The Golden Tradition*, 48–49; Shpall, "Jewish Agricultural Colonies in the United States," 120–146; Brandes, *Immigrants to Freedom: Jewish Communities in Rural New Jersey Since 1882*, 24–27; Joseph, *History of the Baron de Hirsch Fund*; and Norman, "The Baron de Hirsch Fund," 485.

51. Quoted in the Jewish Agricultural Society, *Jews in American Agriculture*, 25.

52. Halkin, "Am Olam," 2:862.

53. Berk, *Year of Crisis, Year of Hope*, 176.

54. Ibid., 174.

55. Jewish Agricultural Society, *Jews in American Agriculture*, 26.

56. Elkin, *Jews of the Latin American Republics*, 128.

57. Straus, "Baron Maurice de Hirsch," 414–15.

58. Ibid., 416.

59. Grossman, *The Soil's Calling*, 112–13.

60. Jewish Agricultural Society, *Jews in American Agriculture*, 15.

61. Elkin, *Jews of the Latin American Republics*, 128.

62. Malin, "The Background of the First Bills to Establish a Bureau of Markets, 1911–12," 116, 128.

63. "Aid for Immigrants," *New York Times*, 9.

64. Herscher, *Jewish Agricultural Utopias in America 1880–1910*, 107–18; Shankman, "Happyville, The Forgotten Colony," 3–19; Isaacs, "Ghetto to Farmland: A Failed Dream," 2–3.

65. Marinbach, *Galveston: Ellis Island of the West*, 42, 114, 184, 189.

66. Davidson, "The Jews in Agriculture in the United States," 101.

67. Dubrovsky, review of *Back to the Soil* by R.A. Goldberg, 191.

68. Jewish Agricultural and Industrial Aid Society, *Annual Report for the Year 1906*, 18.

69. "Exiled Jews in New Jersey," *New York Times*, 4.

70. Soltes, "The Yiddish Press," 266, 268.

71. Metzker, *A Bintel Brief*, 93.

72. Brandes, *Immigrants to Freedom*, 280; Patt, *The Jewish Scene in New Jersey's Raritan Valley, 1698–1948*; Dubrovsky, "Farmingdale, New Jersey: A Jewish Farm Community," 485–97; Dubrovsky, "Der Yiddisher Farmer," 5–7.

73. Brandes, *Immigrants to Freedom,* 333; Herman J. Levine, interview with Abraham D. Lavender, July 23, 1982. Karlin discusses the hardships of Long Island Jewish farmers in his "American Farmer."

74. Levine and Miller, *The American Jewish Farmer,* 63.

Chapter 2: Settling in "The Mountains"

1. Rudolph, *From a Minyan to a Community: A History of the Jews of Syracuse;* Kohn, *The Jewish Community of Utica, New York, 1847–1948;* Rosenberg, *The Jewish Community in Rochester, 1843–1925;* Pool and Pool, *An Old Faith in the New World,* 481–82; Feldman, "Nineteenth Century Jewish Gravesite," 35.

2. Brooks, *A Catskill Flora and Economic Botany,* 1; Scheller, *The Hudson River Valley;* Evers, *The Catskills,* 43; Mitchell, *The Catskills: Land in the Sky,* 438.

3. Evers, *The Catskills,* 659, 690.

4. "Jewish Agricultural Unit Shows Sanitation Exhibit," *Kingston Daily Freeman.*

5. Evers, *The Catskills,* 456.

6. Wakefield, *To the Mountains by Rail.*

7. Helmer, *O.&W.: The Long Life and Slow Death of the New York, Ontario & Western Ry,* 1–29; Wakefield, *To the Mountains,* 8.

8. Helmer, *O.&W.,* 51, 67.

9. Wakefield, *Coal Boats to Tidewater;* Shaughnessy, *Delaware and Hudson,* 1–29; Sanderson, *The Delaware and Hudson Canalway.*

10. Wakefield, *To the Mountains,* 5–6; Levenson, "No Hebrews Taken," 14.

11. Elliott, *Centreville to Woodridge,* 39.

12. Wakefield, *To the Mountains,* 68, 71.

13. Evers, *The Catskills,* 25.

14. Blumberg, "Those Were the Days," September 1993, 18; Webster, reproduction of the log of the canal boat *Iowa* on the Delaware and Hudson Canal, Sept. 7 to 23, 1891; Wakefield, *To the Mountains,* 35.

15. Wakefield, *To the Mountains,* 17, 181, 182–84; DeLisser, *Picturesque Catskills—Greene County.*

16. Goodwin and Levine, "A Historical Review," 12.

17. Interviews with Bruce W. Gerson, June 18, 1992, with Frances S. Gerson, June 21, 1992, and with David Gerson, June 22, 1992; U.S. Bureau of the Census, *1900 Census of Sullivan County,* 293b.

18. Abraham Jaffe, interviewed by Clarence Steinberg, May 4, 1987; Wakefield, *To the Mountains,* 167–70; Helmer, *O.&W.,* 62, 67, 42; DeLisser, *Picturesque Catskills—Greene County.*

19. Quoted in Wakefield, *To the Mountains,* 80.

20. U.S. Bureau of the Census, *1990 Census of Sullivan County,* 293b; interviews with Bruce W. Gerson, June 18, 1992, with Frances S. Gerson, June 21, 1992, and with David Gerson, June 22, 1992.

21. Miller and Roher, *50 Golden Years;* Gold, "Jewish Agriculture in the Catskills, 1900–1920," 31–49.

22. Gold, "Jewish Agriculture in the Catskills, 1900–1920," 35.

23. Herman J. Levine, interview with Abraham D. Lavender, July 22, 1982.

24. H.J. Levine, "The Jewish Farmers' Contributions to Ellenville's Growth," 52.

25. Rhine, "Race Prejudice at Summer Resorts," 527.

26. Evers, *The Catskills,* 691.

27. "The Anti-Hebrew Crusade," *New York Times,* 1.

28. Evers, *The Catskills,* 467, 476–79, 516–19.

29. Davidson, "A Glimpse at Jewish Life in the Mountains."

30. Evers, *The Catskills,* 663, 695; Blumberg, "Those Were the Days," December 1992, 21.

31. Miller and Roher, *50 Golden Years,* 27–30.

32. Jewish Agricultural and Industrial Aid Society, *Annual Report for the Year 1908,* 17–18.

33. Goodwin and H.J. Levine, "A Historical Review"; Robinson, "Agricultural Activities of the Jews in America."

34. Fishman, *The Jews of the United States,* 38.

35. U.S. Bureau of the Census, 1990 and 1910 censuses of Sullivan and Ulster counties.

36. See Lavender, "United States Ethnic Groups in 1790: Given Names as Suggestions of Ethnic Identity," 36–66, and Lavender, "Hispanic Given Names in Five United States Cities: Onomastics as a Research Tool in Ethnic Identity," 105–25.

37. U.S. Bureau of the Census, 1900 and 1910 censuses of Ulster County.

38. Rischin, *The Promised City,* 29.

39. Davidson, "Jewish Farm Movement," 2.

40. Goodwin and Levine, "A Historical Review," 14.

41. Jewish Agricultural and Industrial Aid Society, *Annual Report for the Year 1910,* 29.

42. Ibid., 30–31.

43. Nass, "I Remember," 73.

44. Strauss, "When the All-Inclusive Weekly Rate Was $9," xx-3.

45. Foster, "The Magic Words in the Catskills: 'More, More, More,' " xx-33.

46. Kanfer, *A Summer World,* 75.

47. Miller and Roher, *50 Golden Years,* 28.

48. Ibid., 29.

49. Jewish Agricultural and Industrial Aid Society, *Annual Report for the Year 1908,* 19.

50. "Notable Event in Ellenville,"*Ellenville Journal;* "New Synagogue Dedicated," *Ellenville Journal,* 45; Miller and Roher, *50 Golden Years,* 76.

51. Jewish Agricultural and Industrial Aid Society, *Annual Report for the Year 1906*, 8.

52. Ibid., *1911*, 29.

53. Yaffe, "The Leurenkilll Farmers Start a Hebrew School," 59.

54. Ibid.

55. This interviewee requested anonymity.

56. Jewish Agricultural and Industrial Aid Society, *Annual Report for the Year 1915*, 44.

57. Wakefield, *To the Mountains*.

58. Cowling, *A Short Introduction to Consumers' Co-Operation*, 26.

59. Malin, "The Background of the First Bills to Establish a Bureau of Markets," 112.

60. Cowling, *A Short Introduction to Consumers' Co-Operation*, 26.

61. Alanne, *Fundamentals of Consumer Cooperation*, 95.

62. Shulman, *The New Country: Jewish Immigrants in America*, 9.

63. Jewish Agricultural and Industrial Aid Society, *Annual Report for the Year 1910*, 36–37; ibid., *1911*, 28–29.

64. Ibid., *1914*, 47.

65. "Creditable Enterprise: Jewish Farmers' Creamery Association Ready for Business," *Ellenville Journal*, May 25, 1916.

66. Atkinson, *Big Eyes: A Story of the Catskill Mountains*, 71.

67. Malin, "The Background of the First Bills," 114.

68. Blumberg, *Fifty Years Working Together*, 9.

69. Ibid., 77; Cosor and Cosor, "Elmer Rosenberg," 81.

70. Abraham Jaffe, interview with Clarence Steinberg, May 4, 1987.

71. Blumberg, *Fifty Years Working Together*, 31.

72. Anonymous interviewee; Letter from Theodore Norman to Harry Wasserman, January 3, 1963, reprinted in Blumberg, *Fifty Years Working Together*, 29.

73. Goodwin and Levine, "A Historical Review," 19.

74. Blumberg, *Fifty Years Working Together*, 35.

75. Ibid., 9.

76. Strisik, "Cooperatives—Old and New."

77. The society is recognized as the pioneer of cooperative agricultural credit in the United States.

78. Jewish Agricultural and Industrial Aid Society, *Annual Report for the Year 1912*, 23–24; *Annual Report for the Year 1913*, 50–51.

79. Gertrude Badner, interview with Clarence Steinberg, August 19, 1987; Miller and Roher, *50 Golden Years*, 29.

80. Morris Gibber, interview with Abraham D. Lavender, January 5, 1990; Kanfer, *A Summer World*; Evers, *The Catskills*; Simons, *Jewish Times*, 274; Fertel, quoted in Simons, *Jewish Times*, 295.

81. Gold, "Jewish Agriculture in the Catskills," 36; Wadler, quoted in Simons, *Jewish Times*, 278.

82. Herman J. Levine and Gertrude Badner, interviews with Clarence Steinberg, August 19, 1987; Morton Shimm, interview with Abraham D. Lavender, May 25, 1988.

83. Atkinson, *Big Eyes*, 41.

84. Herman J. Levine, interview with Abraham D. Lavender, July 23, 1982.

85. Ann Kaminsky Macin, interview with Abraham D. Lavender, February 19, 1990; Wadler, quoted in Simons, *Jewish Times*, 277.

86. "Federation to Meet in New York City," *Mountain Hotelman*, 1.

87. Albert J. Cohen, interview with Abraham D. Lavender, July 22, 1982.

88. Gertrude Badner, interview with Clarence Steinberg, August 19, 1987.

89. Herman J. Levine, interview with Abraham D. Lavender, July 23, 1982.

90. Lavender, *Ethnic Women and Feminist Values*, 86.

91. S. Cohen, "The Woman's Part," 4.

92. Jewish Agricultural Society, *Annual Report for the Year 1924*, 54.

93. Jewish Agricultural and Industrial Aid Society, *Annual Report for the Year 1917*, 7–8.

94. Fishman, *The Jews of the United States*, 55.

95. Miller and Roher, *50 Golden Years*, 27–31.

96. Herman J. Levine, interview with Abraham D. Lavender, July 22, 1982.

97. Shepard and Levi, *Live and Be Well*, 97.

98. Anonymous interviewee.

99. In the Catskills, one was issued, for example, to the Siegel family around 1925 with the help of Joe Kooperman, the then-Woodridge lawyer retained by the fire insurance co-op. The Siegels had come from Port Chester, New York, with their four sons and one daughter to a 110-acre farm and a 20-cow herd on the Irish Cape Road between Ulster Heights and Napanoch in 1916. (Jack Siegel, interview with Clarence Steinberg, August 20, 1988.)

100. Ethel Kooperman, interview with Clarence Steinberg, August 14, 1987; Davidson, *Our Jewish Farmers*, 104–5.

101. Anonymous interviewee.

102. Jewish Agricultural and Industrial Aid Society, *Annual Report for the Year 1909*, 10.

103. Ibid., *1919*, 37–38.

104. Frankenstein, "Herman J. Levine," 173.

105. Albert J. Cohen, interview with Abraham D. Lavender, August 6, 1987.

106. Louis Resnick, interview with Clarence Steinberg, August 14, 1987.

107. Miller and Roher, *50 Golden Years*, 29, 30, 50.

108. Louis Resnick, interview with Clarence Steinberg, August 14, 1987.

109. Lawrence Batinkoff, interview with Abraham D. Lavender, December 27, 1990.

110. Fishman, *The Jews of the United States,* 42.

111. Ibid., 59.

112. B. Miller, "50 Years of 'The Jewish Farmer'," 71.

113. Sulzberger, "In Defense of the Immigrant," 35.

114. Jewish Agricultural and Industrial Aid Society, *Annual Report for the Year 1920,* 16.

115. "Offers Prizes for Jewish Farmers," *New York Times,* May 9, 1927, 38.

116. Letter from H.J. Levine to Gabriel Davidson, November 9, 1923.

117. Goodwin and Levine, "A Historical Review," 21.

118. Letter from H.J. Levine to Gabriel Davidson, July 20, 1927.

119. David Levitz, interview with Clarence Steinberg, October 2, 1986.

120. Herman J. Levine, interview with Abraham D. Lavender, July 26, 1982.

121. Anonymous interviewee.

122. Anonymous interviewee.

123. David Levitz, interview with Clarence Steinberg, October 2, 1986; Gertrude Badner, interview with Clarence Steinberg, August 19, 1987.

124. Jewish Agricultural Society, *Annual Report for the Year 1924,* 55.

125. Louis Resnick, interview with Clarence Steinberg, August 14, 1987; Waldinger, *Through the Eye of the Needle,* 53.

126. Abraham Jaffe, interview with Clarence Steinberg, May 4, 1987; Albert J. Cohen, interview with Abraham D. Lavender, August 6, 1987; Louis Resnick, interview with Clarence Steinberg, August 14, 1987.

127. Jack Siegel, interview with Clarence Steinberg, August 20, 1988.

128. Letter from Charles Morrison to Herman J. Levine, April 4, 1929.

129. Davidson, *Our Jewish Farmers,* 96; Herman J. Levine, interview with Abraham D. Lavender, July 23, 1982.

130. Jewish Agricultural Society, *Annual Report for the Year 1928,* 30.

131. Lavender, "Disadvantages of Minority Group Membership."

132. Quoted in Davidson, *Our Jewish Farmers,* 96.

133. "Burglars Vandalize Kerhonkson Center," *Ellenville Journal,* March 3, 1977.

134. Evers, *The Catskills,* 650, 677, 681.

135. "Says Jews Are Becoming Farmers," *New York Times,* November 21, 1927, 7.

136. *World Almanac and Book of Facts,* "Election Returns."

137. Anonymous interviewee.

138. Clifford Calhoun, interview with Clarence Steinberg, August 14, 1987.

139. Elliott, *Centreville to Woodridge,* 62.

140. Ruth L. Frankenstein, interview with Abraham D. Lavender, June 21, 1992; Mrs. Robert Stapleton, interview with Abraham D. Lavender, November 24, 1993.

141. Miller and Roher, *50 Golden Years,* 33; playbill for *Dus Emese Glick (Lebensbild).*

142. Lawrence Batinkoff, interview with Abraham D. Lavender, December 27, 1990.

143. Albert J. Cohen, interview with Abraham D. Lavender, August 6, 1987.

144. Frankenstein, "Herman J. Levine," 180.

145. Abraham Jaffe, interview with Clarence Steinberg, May 4, 1987.

146. Anonymous interviewee.

147. Blumberg, "Those Were the Days," 16.

148. Yaffe, "The Leurenkill Farmers Start a Hebrew School," 59.

149. "Naturalization Mass Meetings," *Ellenville Journal,* April 8, 1926.

150. Frankenstein, "Pearl T. Levine—H.J. Levine's Wife."

151. Frankenstein, "Herman J. Levine," 178.

Chapter 3: Surviving the Depression

1. Greider, *Secrets of the Temple,* 294.

2. K. Phillips, *The Politics of Rich and Poor,* 106; letter from Charles Morrison to Herman J. Levine, April 4, 1929.

3. Jewish Agricultural Society, *Annual Report for the Year 1932;* Warbasse, "Why Be a Farmer?", 2.

4. Jewish Agricultural Society, *Annual Report for the Year 1932,* 9.

5. Barone, *Our Country: The Shaping of America From Roosevelt to Reagan,* 43–49.

6. Jewish Agricultural Society, *Annual Report for the Year 1930,* 13.

7. Davidson, *The Jewish Agricultural Society,* 31.

8. Kanfer, *A Summer World,* 71; Shepard, "About Long Island," 5; Fertel, quoted in Simons, *Jewish Times,* 294 .

9. Gertrude Badner, interview with Clarence Steinberg, August 19, 1987; S. Cohen, "The Woman's Part," 4.

10. Jewish Agricultural Society, *Annual Report for the Year 1931,* 30.

11. Lawrence Batinkoff, interview with Abraham D. Lavender, December 27, 1990.

12. Davidson, *The Jewish Agricultural Society,* 30–34.

13. Davidson, "The Jews in Agriculture in the United States," 109.

14. Davidson, *The Jewish Agricultural Society,* 31.

15. "Farmer and Hotelman," *Mountain Hotelman,* 12.

16. Davidson, "Letters from Readers," 3.

17. "Time to Call A Halt," *Mountain Hotelman*, 12.

18. Jewish Agricultural Society, *Annual Report for the Year 1931*, 30.

19. Louis Resnick, interview with Clarence Steinberg, August 14, 1987.

20. Ethel Kooperman and Joseph Kooperman, interview with Clarence Steinberg, August 14, 1987.

21. Ann Kaminsky Macin, interview with Abraham D. Lavender, February 19, 1990.

22. Herman J. Levine, interview with Abraham D. Lavender, July 22, 1982.

23. Ethel Kooperman and Joseph Kooperman, interview with Clarence Steinberg, August 14, 1987.

24. Jack Siegel, interview with Clarence Steinberg, August 20, 1988.

25. Albert J. Cohen, interview with Abraham D. Lavender, August 6, 1987.

26. Louis Resnick, interview with Clarence Steinberg, August 14, 1987; Albert J. Cohen, interview with Abraham D. Lavender, August 6, 1987.

27. Louis Resnick, interview with Clarence Steinberg, August 14, 1987.

28. Ibid.

29. Jewish Agricultural Society, *Annual Report for the Year 1930*, 22.

30. Ibid., 29.

31. "One Year Old," *Mountain Hotelman*, 6.

32. Moran, "Helen Aldrich: The Lady Who Is the Voice of the Valley," 12G.

33. Letter from Sam Hyman to Herman J. Levine, November 27, 1930; "Help!" *Mountain Hotelman*, 1; "Good News for Dirt Road Farmers and Hotelman," *Mountain Hotelman*, April 25, 1930, 1.

34. Goodwin and Levine, "A Historical Review of Farming by Jews in New York," 22.

35. "Transportation for School Children," *Mountain Hotelman*, October 10, 1930, 6.

36. "Sullivan County Good-Will Movement Inaugurated," *Mountain Hotelman*, March 14, 1930, 6; "Jew, Catholic, Protestant Meeting," *Mountain Hotelman*, March 28, 1930, 1, 3; "Religious Discrimination in Schools," *Mountain Hotelman*, April 24, 1931; "Prejudice and Bigotry," *Mountain Hotelman*, April 22, 1932.

37. "Sullivan County Good-Will Movement Inaugurated," *Mountain Hotelman*, March 14, 1930, 6.

38. "Jew, Catholic, Protestant Meeting," *Mountain Hotelman*, March 28, 1930, 1.

39. Ibid.

40. "Sullivan County Good-Will Movement Inaugurated," *Mountain Hotelman*, March 14, 1930, 6; "Jew, Catholic, Protestant Meeting," *Mountain Hotelman*, March 28, 1930, 1.

41. Herman J. Levine, interview with Abraham D. Lavender, July 26, 1982.

42. "Religious Discrimination in Schools." *Mountain Hotelman,* April 24, 1931.

43. Frankenstein, "Herman J. Levine," 179–80; "Herman Levine Senior Member of Ellenville Trustees' Board," *Ellenville Press,* August 2, 1945.

44. Letter from H.J. Levine to Gabriel Davidson, May 23, 1933.

45. Blumberg, "Those Were the Days," July 1993, 16.

46. "Giving Thanks," *Mountain Hotelman,* December 5, 1930, 6.

47. Stovall, "History of the Ku Klux Klan," 1508.

48. Davidson, "The Jews in Agriculture in the United States," 131.

49. "Save the Community Centers." *Mountain Hotelman,* October 10, 1930, 6.

50. Yaffe, "Save Our Basic Agricultural Industry—Dairying," 6.

51. Yaffe, "Milk Sanitation," 6.

52. Jewish Agricultural Society, *Annual Report for the Year 1928,* 25; ibid., *1929,* 23; and ibid., *1930,* 24.

53. Davidson, *The Jewish Agricultural Society,* 25.

54. Herman J. Levine, interview with Abraham D. Lavender, July 23, 1982.

55. Jewish Agricultural Society, *Annual Report for the Year 1924,* 49.

56. Davidson, "A Tribute to Dr. Goodwin on His Seventy-Fifth Birthday," 1.

57. Goodwin and Levine, "A Historical Review," 22.

58. Jewish Agricultural and Industrial Aid Society, annual reports for the years 1919–21; Jewish Agricultural Society, *Annual Report* for the years 1922–33.

59. Abraham Jaffe, interview with Clarence Steinberg, May 4, 1987; Louis Resnick, interview with Clarence Steinberg, August 14, 1987.

60. Jewish Agricultural Society, *Annual Report for the Year 1956,* 24.

61. Ibid.

62. Gertrude Badner, interview with Clarence Steinberg, August 19, 1987.

63. Albert J. Cohen, interview with Abraham D. Lavender, August 6, 1987.

64. Jewish Agricultural Society, *Annual Report for the Year 1931,* 30.

65. Ibid., *1933,* 29.

66. David Levitz, interview with Clarence Steinberg, October 2, 1986.

67. Abraham Jaffe, interview with Clarence Steinberg, May 4, 1987.

68. Albert J. Cohen, interview with Abraham D. Lavender, August 6, 1987; Levine and Miller, *The American Jewish Farmer in Changing Times,* 71, 73.

69. Waldinger, *Through the Eye of the Needle,* 109.

70. Howe, *A Margin of Hope.*

71. Blumberg, *Fifty Years Working Together,* 43.

72. Rosenberg, "Shall We Organize and Exist or Compete and Destroy Ourselves?" 1.

73. Kaplow, "From the First President of Inter-County," 12.

74. Joyce Wadler, quoted in Simons, *Jewish Times,* 283.

75. Ibid.; B. Miller, "Inter-County's Unrecorded History," 13.

76. Berman, "Looking Back 25 Years," 14.

77. B. Miller, "Inter-County's Unrecorded History," 13.

78. Berman, "Looking Back 25 Years," 14.

79. Ibid.

80. Ibid., 26.

81. Goodwin and Levine, "A Historical Review," 23.

82. Berman, "Looking Back 25 Years," 14; B. Miller, "Inter-County's Unrecorded History," 26.

83. Inter-County Farmers Cooperative Association, "A Brief Statistical History of Inter-County," 6. Fifty years later, in 1987, Abe Jaffe would remember that "the Land Bank was wonderful to the co-op [Inter-County]. It would finance anything that was justified. The Roosevelt administration made the difference in the Land Bank. The changes [for more liberal credit and for the Bank for Cooperatives] were installed in the New Deal." (Abraham Jaffe, interview with Clarence Steinberg, May 4, 1987).

The Jewish farmers of the Catskills were admirers of the economic innovations of Franklin Delano Roosevelt, the patrician from Dutchess County, only a few score miles across the Hudson River, and they expressed their appreciation for him through the ballot box. Roosevelt's own home county, his fellow oldline Protestant Americans, had voted against him in 1932, some even using words close to class-traitor to describe him. To the north of Sullivan County, Delaware County, with a small Jewish population, had voted over two to one for Hoover. Outside of New York City, which gave Roosevelt a resounding victory, only four New York counties had given him a majority in 1932: Albany County and neighboring Rensselaer County, the state capital area where Roosevelt had served as governor and where there was a strong Democratic organization, Franklin County with a strong Democratic past, and Sullivan County, the heart of the Jewish farming area. The Jewish farmers of the Catskills heavily influenced these results (election returns, *World Almanac and Book of Facts*). Joyce Wadler recounts an amusing anecdote: "When I was little, like when I was in kindergarten, I remember somebody asking me what religion I was. I said 'Jewish Democrat.' That's what we absolutely were. There was no separation. It was like FDR had made it . . . so Jews didn't lose their farms; you didn't lose your farm during the Depression" (quoted in Simons, 282). Not all Jewish farmers were that fervent, but most strongly supported Roosevelt. About the time they were having their first annual meeting, the Jewish farmers of Sullivan County again helped Roosevelt win the county, one of only seven of fifty-seven outside of New York City that Roosevelt won (election returns, *World Almanac and Book of Facts*).

84. Fuchs, *The Political Behavior of American Jews,* 129.

85. Levine and Miller, *The American Jewish Farmer in Changing Times,* 73.

86. Ibid., 71.

87. U.S. Department of Agriculture, *Compilation of Statutes,* 76.

88. Selzer, *Kike,* 168.

89. Dimont, *The Jews in America,* 167.

90. J. Kooperman, "Democracy in Industry," 9.

91. B. Miller, "Inter-County's Unrecorded History," 13.

92. Leviticus 14:13.

93. Jewish Agricultural Society, *Annual Report for the Year 1930,* 30, and *Annual Report for the Year 1939,* 32.

94. Ethel Kooperman and Joseph Kooperman, interview with Clarence Steinberg, August 14, 1987.

95. Jewish Agricultural Society, *Annual Report for the Year 1935,* 24.

96. Goodwin and Levine, "A Historical Review," 22.

97. Frankenstein, "Herman J. Levine," 169.

98. "Jewish Agricultural Unit Shows Sanitation Exhibit," *Kingston Daily Freeman,* September 10, 1940.

99. Jewish Agricultural Society, *Annual Report for the Year 1937,* 24, and ibid., 1939, 31.

100. Morton Shimm, interview with Abraham D. Lavender, May 25, 1988.

101. Albert J. Cohen, interview with Abraham D. Lavender, August 6, 1987.

102. Jewish Agricultural Society, *Annual Report for the Year 1935,* 7; ibid., *1936,* 28; ibid., *1939,* 32.

103. "Forty Years of Dedicated Service," *Jewish Farmer,* 144; Herman J. Levine, interview with Abraham D. Lavender, July 23, 1982. In July 1940 the *Middletown Times Herald* described one Holocaust victim who had settled in the Catskills in Orange County and who was typical of many refugees. Romeo D. Levy was Belgian by birth and education but had spent most of his business life in Amsterdam. His wife was a native of Holland, and each of them spoke French, Dutch, German, and English. The farm of sixty acres, which had chickens, ducks, and geese, was close enough to New York City to allow him to continue some brokerage business. Its sweeping view of the Shawangunk Mountains was much like the rolling hills of the Ardennes in Belgium and reminded him of his home in Belgium. ("Former Amsterdam Broker Builds New Life on Farm," 44; Parsons, "Starting from Scratch," 26–28).

104. "The Refugee Problem," *The Jewish Farmer,* 143.

Chapter 4: Prosperity and Its Challenges

1. Nelson, "Farms and Farming Communities," 86.

2. Jewish Agricultural Society, *Annual Report for the Year 1941,* 29. Cooperatives also continued in other areas. For example, the Ellenville Cooperative

Freezer Locker project was expanding, and the society planned a facility that would have 600 lockers and bulk storage (H.J. Levine, "News and Views," 3).

3. Wickard, "What Are the Farmers Doing to Help the War Effort?" 155.

4. "Cooperative Plan on Poultry Pushed," *New York Times*, 12.

5. Morton Shimm, interview with Abraham D. Lavender, May 25, 1988.

6. Jewish Agricultural Society, *Annual Report for the Year 1944*, 13.

7. "Farmers to Have Jamaican Helpers," *Ellenville Journal*, 8.

8. "Camp Hayden Now 'Little Jamaica'," *Ellenville Journal*, 3.

9. Jewish Agricultural Society, *Annual Report for the Year 1944*, 13.

10. "J.A.S. Training for Farm Service Develops Amity," *Jewish Farmer*, 1–2.

11. "E.H.S. Students to Work on Farms." *Ellenville Press*, 39.

12. "Facts for Farmers," *Jewish Farmer*, 2.

13. Jewish Agricultural Society, *Annual Report for the Year 1944*, 14.

14. Burdett, *Victory Garden Manual*, 1, 5.

15. Jewish Agricultural Society, *Annual Report for the Year 1942*, 12.

16. "Reviews Trek of Jews to the Land," *Jewish Farmer*, 1.

17. "Jewish Farmers Pitch In," *Jewish Farmer*, 1.

18. "Jewish Farmers Active on Food Front," *Jewish Farmer*, 58.

19. Lord, "What Happened in Agriculture," 247.

20. Melvin Lesser, interview with Clarence Steinberg, August 20, 1988.

21. Jewish Agricultural Society, *Annual Report for the Year 1945*, 23.

22. Levine and Miller, *The American Jewish Farmer in Changing Times*, 38.

23. "Large Number of Jewish DP's Have Settled on Farms," *Jewish Farmer*, 1.

24. Jewish Agricultural Society, *Annual Report for the Year 1945*, 22.

25. Ibid., *1948*, 18.

26. Morton Shimm, interview with Abraham D. Lavender, May 25, 1988.

27. Shepard and Levi, *Live and Be Well*, 41.

28. Severo, "Rash of Fires in Catskills Points Up Growing Decline," 31, 38.

29. Herman J. Levine, interview with Abraham D. Lavender, July 22, 1982.

30. Goodwin and Levine, "A Historical Review," 24.

31. Jewish Agricultural Society, *Jews in American Agriculture*, 60.

32. Jewish Agricultural Society, *Annual Report for the Year 1945*, 23.

33. Katerina Altenberg and Greta Engel, interviews with Clarence Steinberg, November 4, 1989.

34. Morton Shimm, interview with Abraham D. Lavender, May 25, 1988.

35. "Mrs. Roosevelt Was Here," *Jewish Farmer*, 119.

36. Davidson, "Farmers' Accomplishments—Source of Uplift," 1.

37. "Dairy Farming Favored at J.A.S. Forum," *Jewish Farmer*. Poultry farming was in fact well suited to the Catskills because of the area's long winters and poor soil.

38. "Farm Aspirants Go to J.A.S. School," *Jewish Farmer*.

39. "Mobilization for Duty on the Farm Front," *Jewish Farmer,* 2; Jewish Agricultural Society, special bulletin.

40. Berman, "Looking Back," 25; Albert J. Cohen, interview with Abraham D. Lavender, August 6, 1987.

41. Kaplow, "From the First President of Inter-County," 12; Jaffe, "President's Message," 1.

42. Albert J. Cohen, interview with Abraham D. Lavender, August 6, 1987.

43. A.J. Cohen, "A Look at the Co-op: Past, Present and Future," 4; Scanlan, "Congratulations from Washington," 10.

44. Norman, "Poultry Outlook," 62.

45. Stokes, *Credit to Farmers: The Story of Federal Intermediate Credit Banks and Production Credit Associations,* 100–140; Lawrence Batinkoff, interview with Abraham D. Lavender, December 27, 1990.

46. Ethel Kooperman and Joseph Kooperman, interview with Clarence Steinberg, August 14, 1987; David Levitz, interview with Clarence Steinberg, October 2, 1986.

47. Lawrence Batinkoff, interview with Abraham D. Lavender, December 27, 1990.

48. Clifford C. Calhoun, interview with Clarence Steinberg, August 14, 1987.

49. Doe, "As Your Banker," 8.

50. Jewish Agricultural Society, *Annual Report for the Year 1952,* 12.

51. Ibid., *1955,* 7.

52. "Jewish Farmers Continue Upswing," *New York Times,* 40.

53. Gertrude Badner, interview with Clarence Steinberg, August 19, 1987.

54. Ann Kaminsky Macin, interview with Abraham D. Lavender, February 19, 1990.

55. Kalb, "Catskill Birthday," XX–13.

56. Kalb, "Where Hotelmen Improve on Nature," XX–7.

57. Strauss, "A Bungalow in the Hills," XX–9.

58. Kalb, "The Vacationland Rip Van Winkle Built," XX–6; Fertel, quoted in Simons, *Jewish Times,* 294.

59. Kalb, "Catskill Birthday," XX–13.

60. McCandlish Phillips, "Sullivan County Accents Activity, Glamour," XX–6.

61. Albert J. Cohen, interview with Abraham D. Lavender, August 6, 1987.

62. Melvin Lesser, interview with Clarence Steinberg, August 20, 1988.

63. Albert J. Cohen, interview with Abraham D. Lavender, August 6, 1987.

64. "Sees Continued Growth in TV Antenna Industry," *Ellenville Journal,* 1.

65. Kanfer, *A Summer World,* 227.

66. Strauss, "The Catskills 'Revolution,' " XX–5.

67. Evers, *The Catskills,* 722.

68. Norman, "Annual Report of the General Manager, 1958," 69.

69. Jewish Agricultural Society, *Annual Report for the Year 1957,* 69; also see Brandes, *Immigrants to Freedom,* and Dubrovsky, *The Land Was Theirs.*

70. Albert J. Cohen, interview with Abraham D. Lavender, August 6, 1987; Melvin Lesser, interview with Clarence Steinberg, August 20, 1988.

71. Jaffe, "President's Message," 1; Jaffe, interview with Clarence Steinberg, May 4, 1987.

72. Jaffe, "President's Message," 1.

73. David Levitz, interview with Clarence Steinberg, October 2, 1986.

74. Abraham Jaffe, interview with Clarence Steinberg, May 4, 1987.

75. Abraham Jaffe, interview with Clarence Steinberg, May 4, 1987.

76. Wasserman, "Cooperatives and the Future," 15.

77. Inter-County Farmers Cooperative Association, "In Memoriam," 24.

78. A.J. Cohen, "A Look at the Co-Op: Past, Present, and Future," 25.

79. Ibid.

Chapter 5: Completing a Community

1. Koenig, "Jewish Farmers in New York State," 85.

2. Video conversion, courtesy of J. Bernard Slutsky, Rockville Center, New York City.

3. Lavender, *A Coat of Many Colors,* 8.

4. Melvin Lesser, interview with Clarence Steinberg, August 20, 1988; Herman J. Levine, interview with Abraham D. Lavender, July 26, 1982.

5. S.E. Rosenberg, *The New Jewish Identity in America,* 263.

6. "Ben Miller Heads Local Zionists," *Ellenville Journal,* 1.

7. For a while, a Zionist organization of America (ZOA) youth group met there, and a few members were from farm families.

8. Abraham Jaffe, interview with Clarence Steinberg, May 4, 1987; Louis Resnick, interview with Clarence Steinberg, August 14, 1987.

9. Morris Gibber, interview with Abraham D. Lavender, January 5, 1990.

10. Albert J. Cohen, interview with Abraham D. Lavender, August 6, 1987.

11. Kanfer, *A Summer World,* 128; Blumberg, "Those Were the Days," March 1993, 18.

12. Lavender, "Jewish College Women."

13. Kanfer, *A Summer World,* 106.

14. Still idealistic, most Jewish farmers in the Catskills resembled the Amish in that they too were alienated, ideologically committed farmers, but in other ways they were different. The unworldly Amish wanted to keep twentieth-century technology at bay and to remain isolated, but the Jewish farmers, pledged to and involved in worldliness, welcomed it. At any Inter-County meeting, at least until the mid-1950s, concerns for the world outside

of the Catskills emerged in debate enough to remind them of the days of Union Square's ideologues and socialist parades. Although they no longer had time to pursue these ideals, the values underpinning them remained.

15. Evers, *The Catskills*, 1–2.

16. See Spalding, *Encyclopedia of Jewish Humor*.

17. Morton Shimm, interview with Abraham D. Lavender, May 25, 1988.

18. Calhoun, *Sport, Culture, and Personality*, 236.

19. Fuchs, *The Political Behavior of American Jews*, 130.

20. Kanfer, *A Summer World*, 226.

21. Leviatin, *Followers of the Trail: Jewish Working-Class Radicals in America.*

22. Kanfer, *A Summer World*, 198.

23. Terwilliger, "Empire State Festival" collection.

24. "J.A.S. 1956 Report Strikes Somber Note," *Jewish Farmer*, 106.

25. Terwilliger, "Empire State Festival" collection.

26. "J.A.S. 1956 Report Strikes Somber Note," *Jewish Farmer*, 106.

27. Schwartz, "Two Ways of Seeing the Catskills," XX–7.

28. Schwartz, "Music, Scenery and Fishing in the Catskills," XX–9.

29. Terwilliger, "Empire State Festival" collection.

Chapter 6: A Remnant Lives On

1. Inter-County Farmers Cooperative Association, "What Some Charter Members and 'Old Timers' Are Doing Now," 23; letter to Clarence Steinberg, from E. Kooperman, August 26, 1988.

2. Lawrence Batinkoff, interview with Abraham D. Lavender, December 27, 1990.

3. Davis, "Changing Times Come to the Catskills Resorts," 3F; Clarence Steinberg, personal recollection.

4. See Levine and Miller, *The American Jewish Farmer in Changing Times*, 92.

5. " 'Jewish Farmer' Says Farewell to Its Readers," *Jewish Farmer*, 1.

6. P. Levine, quoted in Levine and Miller, *The American Jewish Farmer in Changing Times*, 91; "He Aided Jewish Immigrants in U.S.," *Town and Village* (New York City).

7. Morton Shimm, interview with Abraham D. Lavender, May 25, 1988.

8. Blumberg, *Fifty Years Working Together*, 23.

9. Ibid., 36.

10. Lesser, "Co-Op Neighbor," in Blumberg, *Fifty Years Working Together*, 100.

11. Wasserman, "Cooperatives and the Future," 15.

12. J. Kooperman, "Democracy in Industry," 9.

13. Blumberg, *Fifty Years Working Together*, 111.

14. Resnick, *The Congressional Record,* August 19, 1965, 21055; May 24, 1966, 11290.

15. Max Brender, quoted in Levine and Miller, *The American Jewish Farmer in Changing Times,* 71.

16. Ibid., 71–74.

17. Ibid., 97.

18. Ibid.; B. Miller, "Inter-County's Unrecorded History," 13.

19. Morton Shimm, interview with Abraham D. Lavender, May 25, 1988.

20. Ibid.

21. Weinraub, "Catskill Vacation Resorts Draw Many Ethnic Groups," 37.

22. Evers, *The Catskills,* 711–12.

23. Ibid., 718.

24. Quoted in Shenker, "Borscht Belt Farms Reap Laughs, Mostly," A3.

25. David Levitz, interview with Clarence Steinberg, October 2, 1986.

26. Joseph Cohen, interview with Clarence Steinberg, October 3, 1986.

27. King, "How Conscience Tamed a Land of Ticky-Tacky," B-1.

28. Lyons, "Catskills Reawakening after a Long Sleep," 25–26.

29. Evers, *The Catskills,* 724.

30. Mitchell, *The Catskills,* 100.

31. Evers, *The Catskills,* 724.

32. Strauss, "A Day and Night at the Races," XX-3.

33. Strauss, "Monticello Raceway Marking a Milestone," XX-3.

34. Sullivan County Catskills Office of Public Information, *Sullivan County Catskills Travel Guide,* 6.

35. Williams, "Catskills Village Facing an Industrial 'Disaster'."

36. Sorin, "Eli Evans Enthralls Audience at Opening Resnick Lecture," 41; "Resnicks Endow SUNY Institute for Study of Modern Jewish Life," *Jewish Star,* 5.

37. Lowry, "He Thinks It's Smart To Aid the Average," 12.

38. Ethel Kooperman and Joseph Kooperman, interview with Clarence Steinberg, August 14, 1987; Poultrymen's Cooperative Hatchery, Minutes of July 18, 1973.

39. "Agriculture," *World Almanac and Book of Facts 1993,* p. 122.

40. U.S. Bureau of the Census, *Rural and Rural Farm Population: 1990.*

41. Taylor, "Agriculture," 257.

42. Samuelson, "The Absurd Farm Bill," 51.

43. Conrat and Conrat, *The American Farm: A Photographic History,* 225.

44. Cetron and Davies, *American Renaissance,* 212.

45. Samuelson, "The Absurd Farm Bill," 51.

46. "Black Dairyman Completes a Half Century in the Business," *Dairyman's Digest,* 10–11, 24; Kilbanoff, "The Black Farmer Is Leaving the Land."

47. Billips, "Black Farmers, Their Numbers Falling, Have Tougher Row to Hoe," 12.

48. David Levitz, interview with Clarence Steinberg, October 2, 1986.

49. Soth, "Slowly Strengthen Rural America," 6.

50. Joseph Cohen, interview with Clarence Steinberg, October 3, 1986.

51. Ibid., November 27, 1989; Inter-County Farmers Cooperative Association, "Account Statement of Estate of Irving Steinberg."

52. Solomon and Sparkman, "The Faithful Brace for Battle at Rock Music's Sacred Site," 61; Della Cava, "Bethel '94 lives in the '60s Spirit."

53. Michaels and Barile, *The Hudson Valley and Catskill Mountains.*

54. Seligman and Swados, "Jewish Population Studies in the United States," 651–89; Liskofsky, "Jewish Population Estimates of Selected Cities," 71–76; Chenkin, "Jewish Population in the United States, 1960," 53–63; Kosmin, Ritterband, and Scheckner, "Jewish Population in the United States, 1987," 222–41; Kosmin and Scheckner, "Jewish Population in the United States, 1990," 207–8.

55. Kosmin and Scheckner, "Jewish Population," 207–8.

56. Andriot, *Population Abstract of the United States,* 545–46.

57. U.S. Bureau of the Census, 1990 censuses of Sullivan and Ulster counties, New York.

58. U.S. Bureau of the Census, 1990 censuses of Sullivan and Ulster counties, New York.

59. Gref, " 'Latinos United' Celebrate First Year," 1-A.

60. Kosmin and Scheckner, "Jewish Population," 207–8.

61. Longfellow, "The Jewish Cemetery at Newport," 121.

62. Schweninger, "A Vanishing Breed: Black Farm Owners in the South, 1651–1982," 55.

Bibliography

Adler, Cyrus, ed. *The American Jewish Year Book*. Philadelphia: Jewish Publication Society of America, 1900.

Adler, Joseph Gary. "Moses Elias Levy and Attempts to Colonize Florida." In *Jews of the South*, edited by Samuel Proctor, Louis Schmier, and Malcolm Stern, 17–29. Macon, Ga.: Mercer University Press, 1984.

"Aid for Immigrants." *New York Times*, April 6, 1890, 9.

Alanne, V.S. *Fundamentals of Consumer Cooperation*. Superior, Wisconsin: Cooperative Publishing Association, 1948.

Andriot, John L., ed. *Population Abstract of the United States*, Vol. 1. McLean, Va.: Andriot Associates, 1983.

"The Anti-Hebrew Crusade: Not So Extensive in the Catskills as Reported." *New York Times*, May 7, 1889, 1.

Arkin, Marcus. "Farming in Biblical Times." *Jewish Affairs*, December 1957, 20–24.

Atkinson, Oriana. *Big Eyes: A Story of the Catskill Mountains*. Cornwallville, N.Y.: Hope Farm Press, 1980.

Barone, Michael. *Our Country: The Shaping of America from Roosevelt to Reagan*. New York: Free Press, 1990.

"Ben Miller Heads Local Zionists." *Ellenville Journal*, July 1, 1943, 1.

Berk, Stephen M. *Year of Crisis, Year of Hope: Russian Jewry and the Pogroms of 1881–1882*. Westport, Conn.: Greenwood Press, 1985.

Berman, William. "Looking Back 25 Years." In *25th Anniversary Commemorative Journal*, edited by Inter-County Farmers Cooperative Association, 14. Woodridge, N.Y.: Inter-County Farmers Cooperative Association, 1961.

Bernheimer, Charles, ed. *The Russian Jew in the United States*. Philadelphia: John C. Winston Co., 1905.

Best, Gary Dean. "Jacob H. Schiff's Galveston Movement: An Experiment in Immigrant Deflection, 1907–1914." *American Jewish Archives* 30, no. 1 (April 1978): 43–79.

Bigart, Jacques. "Alliance Israelite Universelle." In *The Jewish Encyclopedia*, edited by Isidore Singer, 413–22. New York: Ktav, 1964. Originally published 1901.

Billips, Mike. "Black Farmers, Their Numbers Falling, Have Tougher Row to Hoe." *Chicago Tribune,* November 15, 1992, 7–12.

"Black Dairyman Completes a Half Century in the Business." *Dairyman's Digest* 17 (North Central Region Edition), September 1986.

Blumberg, Esterita R., ed. *Fifty Years Working Together.* Fallsburg, N.Y.: Fallsburg Printing Company, 1963.

———. "Those Were the Days." *Jewish Star,* December 1992, 20–21.

———. "Those Were the Days." *Jewish Star,* March 1993, 18.

———. "Those Were the Days." *Jewish Star,* June 1993, 16.

———. "Those Were the Days." *Jewish Star,* July 1993, 16–17.

———. "Those Were the Days." *Jewish Star,* September 1993, 18–19.

Brandes, Joseph. *Immigrants to Freedom: Jewish Communities in Rural New Jersey Since 1882.* Philadelphia: University of Pennsylvania Press, 1971.

Brender, Max. Quoted in Herman J. Levine and Benjamin Miller, *The American Jewish Farmer in Changing Times.* New York: Jewish Agricultural Society, 1966.

Brodsky, Alyn. "The Catskill as a Jewish Eden." Review of *A Summer World,* by Stefan Kanfer. *Miami Herald,* December 10, 1989, 7M.

Brooks, Karl L. *A Catskill Flora and Economic Botany.* Albany: University of the State of New York, 1979.

Burdett, James H. *Victory Garden Manual.* Chicago: Ziff-Davis Publishing Company, 1943.

"Burglars Vandalize Kerhonkson Center." *Ellenville Journal,* March 3, 1977, 1, 9.

Cahan, Abraham. *The Rise of David Levinsky.* New York: Harper and Row, 1966.

———. "The Russian Jew in America." *Atlantic Monthly,* July 1898, 128–39.

———. "The Russian Jew in the United States." In *The Russian Jew in the United States,* edited by Charles Bernheimer, 32–40. Philadelphia: John C. Winston Co., 1905.

———. *Yekl: A Tale of the Ghetto.* New York, 1896.

Calhoun, Donald W. *Sport, Culture, and Personality.* Champaign, Ill.: Human Kinetics Publishers, 1987.

Campbell, Louisa, ed. *New York State.* New York: Prentice Hall, 1985.

"Camp Hayden Now 'Little Jamaica'." *Ellenville Jounal,* May 20, 1943, 3.

The Catskills—Today. Fort Lee, N.J.: Esprit Promotions International, Inc. 1989. Film.

Cetron, Marvin, and Owen Davies. *American Renaissance: Our Life at the Turn of the 21st Century.* New York: St. Martin's Press, 1989.

Chenkin, Alvin. "Jewish Population in the United States, 1960." In *The American Jewish Year Book,* edited by Morris Fine and Milton Himmelfarb, 53–63. New York: American Jewish Committee, 1961.

Cohen, Albert J. "A Look at the Co-Op: Past, Present, and Future." In *25th Anniversary Commemorative Journal,* edited by Inter-County Farmers Cooperative Association, 4, 25. Woodridge, N.Y.: Inter-County Farmers Cooperative Association, 1961.

Cohen, Joseph. "A Place in the Sun." In *25th Anniversary Commemorative Journal*, edited by Inter-County Farmers Cooperative Association, 5. Woodridge, N.Y.: Inter-County Farmers Cooperative Association, 1961.

Cohen, Sara. "The Woman's Part." *Mountain Hotelman*, April 25, 1930, 4.

Cole, Mrs. Fred. Letter to Herman J. Levine, November 25, 1930.

Conrat, Maisie, and Richard Conrat. *The American Farm: A Photographic History*. Boston: California Historical Society, San Francisco/ Houghton Mifflin, 1977.

"Cooperative Plan on Poultry Pushed." *New York Times*, June 1, 1945, 12.

Cosor, Frances, and Benjamin Cosor. "Elmer Rosenberg." In *Fifty Years Working Together*, edited by Esterita R. Blumberg, 80–81. Fallsburg, N.Y.: Fallsburg Printing Company, 1963.

Cowling, Ellis. *A Short Introduction to Consumers' Co-Operation*. Antigonish, Nova Scotia: Saint Francis Xavier University, 1937.

"Creditable Enterprise: Jewish Farmers' Creamery Association Ready for Business." *Ellenville Journal*, May 25, 1916.

"Dairy Farming Favored at J.A.S. Forum." *Jewish Farmer* 42, no. 12 (December 1949): 1.

Darin-Drabkin, H. *Patterns of Cooperative Agriculture in Israel*. Tel Aviv: Israel Institute for Books, 1962.

Davidson, Gabriel. "A Glimpse at Jewish Life in the Mountains." *Mountain Hotelman*, April 1933.

———. "Farmers' Accomplishments—Source of Uplift." *Jewish Farmer* 38, no. 12 (December 1945): 1.

———. *The Jewish Agricultural Society: Report of the Managing Director for the Period 1900–1949*. New York: Jewish Agricultural Society, 1950.

———. "Jewish Farm Movement." *Ellenville Journal*, August 2, 1923.

———. "The Jews in Agriculture in the United States." In *The American Jewish Year Book*, edited by Harry Schneiderman, 99–134. New York: American Jewish Committee, 1935.

———. "Letters from Readers." *Mountain Hotelman*, September 12, 1930, 3–4.

———. *Our Jewish Farmers and the Story of the Jewish Agricultural Society*. New York: L.B. Fischer, 1943.

———. "A Tribute to Dr. Goodwin on His Seventy-Fifth Birthday." *Jewish Farmer* 51, no. 4 (April 1958): 1.

Davis, Peter. *The Rise and Fall of the Borscht Belt*. Villon Films, New York: 1988.

Davis, William A. "Changing Times Come to the Catskills Resorts." *Miami Herald*, October 2, 1988, 3F.

Dawidowicz, Lucy S. *The Golden Tradition: Jewish Life and Thought in Eastern Europe*. Boston: Beacon Press, 1967.

DeLisser, R. Lionel. *Picturesque Catskills: Greene County*. Cornwallville, N.Y.: Hope Farms Press, 1983.

Della Cava, Marco R. "Bethel '94 Lives in the '60s Spint." *USA Today,* August 12, 1994, 1D.

Dimont, Max. *The Jews in America: The Roots and Destiny of American Jews.* New York: Simon and Schuster, 1978.

Doe, J. Roberts. "As Your Banker." In *25th Anniversary Commemorative Journal,* edited by Inter-County Farmers Cooperative Association, 8. Woodridge, N.Y.: Inter-County Farmers Cooperative Association, 1961.

"Drive Completed by Talmud Torah." *Ellenville Journal,* June 24, 1943, 8.

Dubrovsky, Gertrude. "Der Yiddisher Farmer." *Reform Judaism* 18, no. 1 (Fall 1989).

―――. "Farmingdale, New Jersey: A Jewish Farm Community." *American Jewish Historical Quarterly* 66 (June 1977): 485–97.

―――. *The Land Was Theirs: Jewish Farmers in the Garden State.* Tuscaloosa: University of Alabama Press, 1992.

―――. Review of *Back to the Soil: The Jewish Farmers of Clarion, Utah, and Their World,* by Robert Alan Goldberg. *American Jewish Archives* 1002, no. 2 (Fall/Winter 1990): 189–95.

Dunphy, Robert J. "What's Doing in Sullivan County," *New York Times,* June 10, 1979, X-15.

"E.H.S. Students to Work on Farms." *Ellenville Press,* June 8, 1944, 39.

Eisner, Rabbi Herman. "Ellenville—The Community in the Catskills with the Earliest Established Jewish Families." Ellenville, N.Y.: photocopy, 1957.

Elkin, Judith Laikin. *Jews of the Latin American Republics.* Chapel Hill: University of North Carolina Press, 1980.

Elliott, Erna W. *Centreville to Woodridge: The Story of a Small Community.* Woodridge, N.Y., 1976.

Engel, Gerald. "North American Settlers in Israel." In *The American Jewish Year Book,* edited by Morris Fine and Milton Himmelfarb, 161–87. New York: American Jewish Committee, 1970.

Evans, Eli. *The Provincials: A Personal History of Jews in the South.* New York: Atheneum, 1973.

Evers, Alf. *The Catskills: From Wilderness to Woodstock.* Woodstock, N.Y.: The Overlook Press, 1982.

"Exiled Jews in New Jersey." *New York Times,* July 11, 1891, 4.

"Facts for Farmers." *Jewish Farmer* 36, no. 3 (March 1943): 1–2.

"Farm Aspirants Go to J.A.S. School." *Jewish Farmer* 44, no. 1 (January 1951): 3, 6.

"Farmer and Hotelman." *Mountain Hotelman,* May 9, 1930, 12.

"Farmers to Have Jamaican Helpers." *Ellenville Journal,* June 17, 1943, 8.

"Federation to Meet in New York City." *Mountain Hotelman,* March 11, 1932, 1.

Feldman, Bert. "19th Century Jewish Gravesite Could Become Communal." *Jewish Star,* September 1992, 35.

Fine, Morris, ed. *The American Jewish Year Book.* New York: American Jewish Committee, 1950.

Fine, Morris, and Milton Himmelfarb, eds. *The American Jewish Year Book.* New York: American Jewish Committee, 1961.

———. *The American Jewish Year Book.* New York: American Jewish Committee, 1970.

Fishman, Priscilla, ed. *The Jews of the United States.* New York: Quadrangle, 1973.

Forman, Allen. "Some Adopted Americans." *American Magazine* 9 (November 1888).

"Former Amsterdam Broker Builds New Life on Farm." *Middletown Times Herald,* July 10, 1940.

"Forty Years of Dedicated Service: Mr. Herman J. Levine." *Jewish Farmer* 52, no. 11 (November 1959): 1, 144.

Foster, Lee. "The Magic Words in the Catskills: 'More, More, More'." *New York Times,* March 5, 1972, XX-1, 33, 34.

Frankenstein, Ruth J. "Herman J. Levine, Manager of the Jewish Agricultural Society." American Jewish Personalities. *American Jewish Archives* 1002, no. 2 (Fall/Winter 1990): 167–81.

———. "Pearl T. Levine—H.J. Levine's Wife." Unpublished paper, 1990.

Friedenwald, Herbert, ed. *The American Jewish Year Book.* Philadelphia: Jewish Publication Society of America, 1910.

Friedman, Lester D. *Hollywood's Image of the Jew.* New York: Ungar, 1982.

Fuchs, Lawrence H. *The Political Behavior of American Jews.* Glencoe, Ill.: Free Press, 1956.

Gerard, Helene. "Yankees in Yarmulkes: Small-Town Jewish Life in Eastern Long Island." *American Jewish Archives* 38, no. 1 (April 1986): 23–56.

"Giving Thanks." *Mountain Hotelman,* December 5, 1930, 6.

Gold, David. "Jewish Agriculture in the Catskills, 1900–1920." *Agricultural History* 55, no. 1 (January 1981): 31–49.

Goldberg, Robert Alan. *Back to the Soil: The Jewish Farmers of Clarion, Utah, and Their World.* Salt Lake City: University of Utah Press, 1986.

Goodman, Jack, ed. *While You Were Gone: A Report on Wartime Life in the United States.* New York: Simon and Schuster, 1946.

"Good News for Dirt Road Farmers and Hotelman." *Mountain Hotelman,* April 25, 1930, 1.

Goodwin, Edward A., and Herman J. Levine. "A Historical Review of Farming by Jews in New York." In *Report of the General Manager 1956,* edited by the Jewish Agricultural Society, 10–31. New York: Jewish Agricultural Society, 1957.

Granott, A. *Agrarian Reform and the Record of Israel.* London: Eyre and Spottiswoode, 1956.

Green, Henry Alan, and Marcia Kerstein Zerivitz, *Mosaic: Jewish Life in Florida.* Coral Gables, Fla.: Mosaic, 1991.

Gref, Barbara. "'Latinos United' Celebrate First Year." *Sullivan County Democrat,* August 13, 1991, 1-A, 12-A.

Greider, William. *Secrets of the Temple.* New York: Simon and Schuster, 1987.

Grimes, Paul. "Escaping to the Catskills: Battleground with New Targets." *New York Times,* January 15, 1978, XX-1.

Grossman, Vladimir. *The Soil's Calling.* Montreal: Eagle Publishing Co., 1938.

Halkin, Hillel. "Am Olam." In *Encyclopaedia Judaica,* edited by Cecil Roth, 2:862. Jerusalem: Keter Publishing House, 1971.

Harkin, Frank. "We Call it Utopia, U.S.A." *New York Times,* May 18, 1969, II-18.

"He Aided Jewish Immigrants in U.S." *Town and Village.* May 19, 1977.

Helmer, William F. *O.&W.: The Long Life and Slow Death of the New York Ontario & Western Ry.* Berkeley: Howell-North, 1959.

"Help!" *Mountain Hotelman,* March 14, 1930, 1.

"Herman Levine Senior Member of Ellenville Trustees' Board." *Ellenville Press,* August 2, 1945.

Herscher, Uri D. *Jewish Agricultural Utopias in America, 1880–1910.* Detroit: Wayne State University Press, 1981.

Higham, John. *Send These to Me: Immigrants in Urban America.* Baltimore: Johns Hopkins University Press, 1984.

Howe, Irving. *A Margin of Hope.* San Diego: Harcourt Brace Jovanovich, 1982.

———. *World of Our Fathers.* New York: Simon and Schuster, 1976.

Hyman, Sam. Letter to Herman J. Levine, November 27, 1930.

Inter-County Farmers Cooperative Association, Inc. Account Statement of Estate of Israel Steinberg, December 20, 1989.

———. "A Brief Statistical History of Inter-County." In *25th Anniversary Commemorative Journal,* edited by Inter-County Farmers Cooperative Association, 6. Woodridge, N.Y.: Inter-County Farmers Cooperative Association, 1961.

———. "In Memoriam." In *25th Anniversary Commemorative Journal,* edited by Inter-County Farmers Cooperative Association, 24. Woodridge, N.Y.: Inter-County Farmers Cooperative Association, 1961.

———. "What Some Charter Members and 'Old Timers' Are Doing Now." In *25th Anniversary Commemorative Journal,* edited by Inter-County Farmers Cooperative Association, 23. Woodridge, N.Y.: Inter-County Farmers Cooperative Association, 1961.

Isaacs, Ellyn. "Ghetto to Farmland: A Failed Dream." *Newsday,* October 10, 1981, 2–3.

Jaffe, Abe. "President's Message." In *25th Anniversary Commemorative Journal,* edited by Inter-County Farmers Cooperative Association, 1. Woodridge, N.Y.: Inter-County Farmers Cooperative Association, 1961.

———. "The President's Message." In *Fifty Years Working Together,* edited by Esterita R. Blumberg, 20–21. Fallsburg, N.Y.: Fallsburg Printing Company, 1963.

Jaffe, Abe, and Jack Millstein. "Inter-County Cooperative Extends Greetings." *The Jewish Farmer* 51, no. 5 (May 1958): 92.

"J.A.S. 1956 Report Strikes Somber Note." *Jewish Farmer* 50, no. 8 (August 1957): 1–2.

"J.A.S. Training for Farm Service Develops Amity." *Jewish Farmer* 37, no. 7 (July 1944): 1–2 .

"J.A.S. Welcomes New Class of Farm Seekers." *Jewish Farmer* 33, no. 1 (January 1940): 11.

"Jew, Catholic, Protestant Meeting." *Mountain Hotelman,* March 28, 1930, 1, 3.

Jewish Agricultural and Industrial Aid Society. *Annual Report of the General Manager.* New York: Jewish Agricultural and Industrial Aid Society, 1906–21.

Jewish Agricultural Society. *Annual Report of the General Manager.* New York: Jewish Agricultural Society, 1922–58.

———. *Jews in American Agriculture: The History of Farming by Jews in the United States.* New York: Jewish Agricultural Society, 1954.

———. Special bulletin. New York: Jewish Agricultural Society, 1951.

"Jewish Agricultural Unit Shows Sanitation Exhibit." *Kingston Daily Freeman,* September 10, 1940.

Jewish Encyclopedic Handbooks. *The Jewish People: Past and Present.* New York: Marstin Press, 1955.

"Jewish Farmers Active on Food Front." *Jewish Farmer* 38, no. 5 (May 1945): 58.

"'Jewish Farmer' Says Farewell to Its Readers." *Jewish Farmer* 52, no. 12 (December 1959): 157.

"Jewish Farmers Conference." *Mountain Hotelman,* October 24, 1930, 2.

"Jewish Farmers Continue Upswing." *New York Times,* June 26, 1953, 40.

"Jewish Farmers Pitch In." *Jewish Farmer* 37, no. 4 (April 1944): 1.

"Jews Are Seen Turning to Farm." *New York Times,* February 15, 1935, 12.

"Jews Prove Successful Farmers with Help of Agricultural Society." *Middletown Times Herald,* August 17, 1935.

Johnson, Dirk. "Catskill Resorts Woo Young Set." *New York Times,* August 11, 1986, B-1–2.

Joseph, Samuel. *History of the Baron de Hirsch Fund.* Philadelphia: Jewish Publication Society, 1953.

Kalb, Bernard. "Catskill Birthday." *New York Times,* May 10, 1953, XX-13.

———. "The Vacationland Rip Van Winkle Built." *New York Times,* June 14, 1953, XX-6.

———. "Where Hotelmen Improve on Nature." *New York Times,* June 14, 1953, XX-7.

Kanfer, Stefan. *A Summer World: The Attempt to Build a Jewish Eden in the Catskills.* New York: Farrar Straus Giroux, 1989.

Kaplow, Harry. "From the First President of Inter-County." In *25th Anniversary Commemorative Journal,* edited by Inter-County Farmers Cooperative Association, 12. Woodridge, N.Y.: Inter-County Farmers Cooperative Association, 1961.

Karlin, Jacob. "American Farmer." New York: National Broadcasting Company, 1982.

Kilbanoff, Hank. "The Black Farmer Is Leaving the Land." *Philadelphia Inquirer,* June 5, 1987.

King, Wayne. "How Conscience Tamed a Land of Ticky-Tacky." *New York Times,* July 18, 1989, B-1.

Kleiman, Dena. "2-Hour Commutes and Ladies Nights." *New York Times,* August 21, 1988, I-46.

Koenig, Edward. "Jewish Farmers in New York State." *Jewish Farmer* 51, no.5 (May 1958): 85.

———. "New York State News." *Jewish Farmer* 50, no. 4 (April 1957): 51.

Kohn, S. Joshua. *The Jewish Community of Utica, New York, 1847–1948.* New York: American Jewish Historical Society, 1959.

Kooperman, Ethel. Letter to Clarence B. Steinberg, August 26, 1988.

Kooperman, Joseph. "Democracy in Industry." In *25th Anniversary Commemorative Journal,* edited by Inter-County Farmers Cooperative Association, 9. Woodridge, N.Y.: Inter-County Farmers Cooperative Association, 1961.

———. Review of *Our Jewish Farmers,* by Gabriel Davidson. *The Inter-County Co-Op Bulletin,* May 1944, 4; June 1944, 3.

Korn, Bertram Wallace. *The Early Jews of New Orleans.* Waltham, Mass.: American Jewish Historical Society, 1969.

Kosmin, Barry, and Jeffrey Scheckner. "Jewish Population in the United States, 1990." In *The American Jewish Year Book,* edited by David Singer and Ruth R. Seldin, 204–24. New York: American Jewish Committee, 1991.

Kosmin, Barry, Paul Ritterband, and Jeffrey Scheckner. "Jewish Population in the United States, 1987." In *The American Jewish Year Book,* edited by David Singer and Ruth R. Seldin, 222–41. New York: American Jewish Committee, 1988.

Landsman, Isaac. "Catskill, Playground of Jewish Masses." *The American Hebrew,* August 31, 1928.

"Large Number of Jewish DP's Have Settled on Farms." *Jewish Farmer* 49, no. 7 (July 1956): 1.

Lavender, Abraham D. "Disadvantages of Minority Group Membership: The Perspective of a 'Nondeprived' Minority Group." *Ethnicity* 2, no. 1 (March 1975): 99–119.

———. *Ethnic Women and Feminist Values: Toward a New Value System.* Lanham, Md.: University Press of America, 1986.

———. "Hispanic Given Names in Five United States Cities: Onomastics as a Research Tool in Ethnic Identity." *Hispanic Journal of Behavioral Sciences* 10, no. 2 (June 1988): 105–25.

———. "Jewish College Women: Future Leaders of the Jewish Community." *Journal of Ethnic Studies* 5, no. 2 (Summer 1977): 81–90. Reprinted in Abraham D. Lavender, ed., *A Coat of Many Colors.*

———. "The Sephardic Revival in the United States: A Case of Ethnic Revival in a Minority-within-a-Minority." *Journal of Ethnic Studies* 3, no. 3 (Fall 1975): 21–31.

———. "United States Ethnic Groups in 1790: Given Names as Suggestions of Ethnic Identity." *Journal of American Ethnic History* 9, no. 1 (Fall 1989): 36–66.

Lavender, Abraham D., ed. *A Coat of Many Colors: Jewish Subcommunities in the United States.* Westport, Conn.: Greenwood Press, 1977.

Leshner, Ben. "Letter to Harry Wasserman." In *Fifty Years Working Together,* edited by Esterita R. Blumberg, 64. Fallsburg, N.Y.: Fallsburg Printing Company, 1963.

Lesser, Melvin. "Co-Op Neighbor: Inter-County." In *Fifty Years Working Together,* edited by Esterita R. Blumberg, 100. Fallsburg, N.Y.: Fallsburg Printing Company, 1963.

Levenson, Gabe. "Catskill Resorts Still the Place to Relax." *Miami Jewish Tribune,* April 26–May 2, 1991, 10B.

———. "No Hebrews Taken." *Jewish Week and The American Examiner,* December 23, 1983.

Leviatin, David. *Followers of the Trail: Jewish Working-Class Radicals in America.* New Haven: Yale University Press, 1989.

Levine, Darwin. "Pioneering in the Early 1900's." *Jewish Farmer* 51, no. 5 (May 1958): 88–91.

Levine, Herman J. "The Jewish Farmers' Contributions to Ellenville's Growth." In *50 Golden Years: The Ellenville Hebrew Aid Society 1907–1957,* edited by Mrs. Ben Miller and Daniel S. Roher, 52–53. Ellenville, N.Y.: Ellenville Hebrew Aid Society, 1959.

———. "Jewish Farming in the Mid-West." *Jewish Farmer* 51, no. 5 (May 1958): 86–87.

———. Letters to Gabriel Davidson, November 9, 1923, July 20, 1927, and May 23, 1933.

———. "News and Views." *The Inter-County Co-Op Bulletin,* May 1944.

Levine, Herman J., and Benjamin Miller. *The American Jewish Farmer in Changing Times.* New York: Jewish Agricultural Society, 1966.

Levine, Pearl. Quoted in Herman J. Levine and Benjamin Miller. *The American Jewish Farmer in Changing Times.* New York: The Jewish Agricultural Society, 1966.

Levine, Robert M. *Tropical Diaspora: The Jewish Experience in Cuba.* Gainesville: University Press of Florida, 1993.

Levy, Rabbi A. R. "Rural Settlements: Western States." In *The Russian Jew in the United States,* edited by Charles Bernheimer, 392–403. Philadelphia: John C. Winston Co., 1905.

Libo, Kenneth, and Irving Howe. *We Lived There Too*. New York: St. Martin's Press, 1984.

Liebman, Malvina W., and Seymour B. Liebman. *Jewish Frontiersmen*. Miami Beach: Jewish Historical Society of South Florida, 1978.

Lipman, Jacob G. "Rural Settlements: Eastern States." In *The Russian Jew in the United States*, edited by Charles Bernheimer, 376–91. Philadelphia: John C. Winston Co., 1905.

Lipset, Seymour Martin. "A Unique People in an Exceptional Country." *Society* 28, no. 1 (November/December 1990): 4–13.

Liskofsky, Sidney. "Jewish Population Estimates of Selected Cities." In *The American Jewish Year Book*, edited by Morris Fine, 71–76. New York: American Jewish Committee, 1950.

Longfellow, Henry Wadsworth. "The Jewish Cemetery at Newport." In *The Oxford Book of American Verse*, edited by F. O. Mathiessen, 121–23. New York: Oxford University Press, 1950.

Lord, Russell. "What Happened in Agriculture." In *While You Were Gone: A Report on Wartime Life in the United States*, edited by Jack Goodman, 230–48. New York: Simon and Schuster, 1946.

Lowry, Bill. "He Thinks It's Smart to Aid the Average." *Sunday Record* (Middletown, New York), August 23, 1981, 12.

Lurie, H.L. "Jewish Communal Life in the United States." In *The Jewish People: Past and Present*, edited by Jewish Encyclopedic Handbooks, 187–242. New York: Marstin Press, 1955.

Lyons, Richard D. "Catskills Reawakening After a Long Sleep." *New York Times*, July 25, 1981, 25–26.

Malin, James C. "The Background of the First Bills to Establish a Bureau of Markets, 1911–12." *Agricultural History* 6, no. 3 (July 1932): 107–29.

Marcus, Jacob Rader. *Early American Jewry: The Jews of New York, New England, and Canada, 1649–1794*. Volume 1. Philadelphia: Jewish Publication Society of America, 1951.

———. *Early American Jewry: The Jews of Pennsylvania and the South 1655–1790*. Vol. 2. Philadelphia: Jewish Publication Society of America, 1953.

Marinbach, Bernard. *Galveston: Ellis Island of the West*. Albany: State University of New York Press, 1983.

Marshall, Louis. "In Defense of the Immigrant." In *The American Jewish Year Book*, edited by Herbert Friedenwald, 19–98. Philadelphia: Jewish Publication Society of America, 1910.

Mendes, Frederick de Sola. "Agriculture: Historical Aspects." In *The Jewish Encyclopedia*, edited by Isidore Singer, 262–66. New York: Ktav, 1964.

Menes, Abraham. "The Jewish Labor Movement." In *The Jewish People: Past and Present*, edited by Jewish Encyclopedic Handbooks, 334–90. New York: Marstin Press, 1955.

Metzker, Isaac, ed. *A Bintel Brief.* Garden City, N.Y.: Doubleday and Company, 1971.

Meyer, Eugene L. "A Good Old Boy from Molczadz." *Washington Post,* October 31, 1985, C-1, C-5.

Michaels, Joanne, and Mary Barile. *The Hudson Valley and Catskill Mountains.* New York: Crown, 1988.

Miller, Benjamin. "50 Years of 'The Jewish Farmer'." *Jewish Farmer* 51, no. 5 (May 1958): 71–74.

———. "Inter-County's Unrecorded History." In *25th Anniversary Commemorative Journal,* edited by Inter-County Farmers Cooperative Association, 13, 26. Woodridge, N.Y.: Inter-County Farmers Cooperative Association, 1961.

Miller, Mrs. Ben, and Daniel S. Roher, eds. *50 Golden Years: The Ellenville Hebrew Aid Society 1907–1957.* Ellenville, N.Y.: Ellenville Hebrew Aid Society, 1959.

Mitchell, John G. *The Catskills: Land in the Sky.* New York: The Viking Press, 1977.

"Mobilization for Duty on the Farm Front." *Jewish Farmer* 44, no. 1 (January 1951): 2.

Moran, Rick. "Helen Aldrich: The Lady Who Is the Voice of the Valley." *Sullivan County Democrat,* August 13, 1991, 7G–15G.

Morris, Yaakov. *On the Soil of Israel: Americans and Canadians in Agriculture.* Israel: Association of Americans and Canadians in Israel, 1965.

Morrison, Charles. Correspondence to Herman J. Levine, April 4, 1929.

"Mrs. Roosevelt Was Here." *Jewish Farmer* 38, no. 10 (October 1945): 119.

Nass, Jonas. "I Remember." In *Fifty Years Working Together,* edited by Esterita R. Blumberg, 73. Fallsburg, N.Y.: Fallsburg Printing Company, 1963.

"Naturalization Mass Meetings." *Ellenville Journal,* April 8, 1926.

Nelson, Lowry. "Farms and Farming Communities." In *American Society in Wartime,* edited by William Fielding Ogburn, 82–104. Chicago: University of Chicago Press, 1943.

"New Synagogue Dedicated." *Ellenville Journal,* September 15, 1910.

Niger, Samuel. "Yiddish Culture." In *The Jewish People: Past and Present,* edited by Jewish Encyclopedic Handbooks, 264–307. New York: Marstin Press, 1955.

Nirenberg, Miriam. Booklet accompanying a Yiddish folksong record, "Folksongs in the East European Tradition, from the Repertoire of Miriam Nirenberg." New York: YIVO Institute of Jewish Research, 1986.

Norman, Theodore. "Annual Report of the General Manager, 1958." *The 1958 Annual Report and The Jewish Farmer,* May, 1959, 68–70.

———. "The Baron de Hirsch Fund Since 1935." N.p., n.d.

———. "The Jewish Agricultural Society During the Past 50 Years." *Jewish Farmer* 51, no. 5 (May 1958): 47–48.

————. Letter to Harry Wasserman, reprinted in *Fifty Years Working Together,* edited by Esterita R. Blumberg, 29. Fallsburg, N.Y.: Fallsburg Printing Company, 1963.

————. "Poultry Outlook." *Jewish Farmer* 42, no. 6 (June 1950): 62.

"Notable Event in Ellenville." *Ellenville Journal,* April 29, 1909.

Novak, David. "Maimonides and Agriculture." *Jewish Spectator* 45 (Spring 1980): 47–48.

"Offers Prizes for Jewish Farmers." *New York Times,* May 9, 1927, 38.

Ogburn, William Fielding, ed. *American Society in Wartime.* Chicago: University of Chicago Press, 1943.

"Oldest Links." *New York Times,* June 12, 1966, XX-3.

"One Year Old." *Mountain Hotelman,* January 16, 1931, 6.

Orni, Efraim. *Agrarian Reform and Social Progress in Israel.* Jerusalem: Keren Kayemeth Leisrael, 1972.

Ornstein-Galicia, Jacob L. "An American Jewish Family's Farm Odyssey." *American Jewish Archives* 41, no. 1 (Spring/Summer 1989): 53–76.

Parsons, Beatrice. "Starting from Scratch." *National Grange Monthly,* October 1956, 26–28.

Patt, Ruth Marcus. *The Jewish Scene in New Jersey's Raritan Valley, 1698–1948.* New Brunswick, N.J.: Jewish Historical Society of Raritan Valley, 1978.

Peck, Abraham, ed., *The American Jewish Farmer: An Exhibit Sponsored by the American Jewish Archives.* Cincinnati: American Jewish Archives, 1986.

Phillips, Kevin. *The Politics of Rich and Poor.* New York: Random House, 1990.

Phillips, McCandlish. "Sullivan County Accents Activity, Glamour." *New York Times,* May 6, 1956, XX–6.

Pool, David de Sola, and Tamar de Sola Pool. *An Old Faith in the New World.* New York: Columbia University Press, 1955.

"A Poultrymen's League." *Mountain Hotelman,* January 2, 1931, 6.

Poultrymen's Cooperative Hatchery, Inc. Minutes of July 18, 1973.

"Prejudice and Bigotry." *Mountain Hotelman,* April 22, 1932.

"The Refugee 'Problem'." *Jewish Farmer* 33, no. 12 (December 1940): 143.

Reik, Theodor. *Jewish Wit.* New York: Gamut Press, 1962.

"Religious Discrimination in Schools." *Mountain Hotelman,* April 24, 1931.

Resnick, Joseph Y. *The Congressional Record,* August 19, 1965; May 4, 24, June 2, August 15, 1966; August 3, 1967. Washington, D.C.: Government Printing Office.

————. Letter to Israel Steinberg, January 22, 1965.

————. *This Special Valley.* Ellenville, N.Y.: Privately printed, 1964.

"Resnicks Endow SUNY Institute for Study of Modern Jewish Life." *Jewish Star,* August 1993, 5.

"Reviews Trek of Jews to the Land." *Jewish Farmer* 39, no. 4 (April 1946): 1, 47.

Reznikoff, Charles, and Uriah Z. Engelman. *The Jews of Charleston: A History of an American Jewish Community.* Philadelphia: Jewish Publication Society of America, 1950.

Rhine, Alice Hyneman. "Race Prejudice at Summer Resorts." *Forum* 3 (1887): 527.

Rischin, Moses. *The Promised City: New York's Jews, 1870–1914.* New York: Harper and Row, 1970.

Robinson, Leonard. "Agricultural Activities of the Jews in America." In *The American Jewish Year Book,* edited by Herbert Friedenwald, 3–89. Philadelphia: Jewish Publication Society of America, 1910.

Rochlin, Harriet, and Fred Rochlin. *Pioneer Jews: A New Life in the Far West.* Boston: Houghton Mifflin, 1984.

Rosenberg, Carol. "Pig Bowl: Secular Majority vs. Ultra-Orthodox Minority." *Miami Herald,* December 6, 1990, 33.

Rosenberg, Elmer. "Shall We Organize and Exist or Compete and Destroy Ourselves?" *Mountain Hotelman,* March 11, 1932, 1, 5.

Rosenberg, Stuart E. *The Jewish Community in Rochester 1843–1925.* New York: Columbia University Press, 1954.

————. *The New Jewish Identity in America.* New York: Hippocrene Books, 1985.

Rosenthal, Herman. "Agricultural Colonies in Russia." In *The Jewish Encyclopedia,* edited by Isidore Singer, 252–56. New York: Ktav, 1964.

Rosten, Leo C. *The Education of H*Y*M*A*N K*A*P*L*A*N.* New York: Harcourt-Brace, 1977.

Roth, Cecil, ed. *Encyclopaedia Judaica.* Jerusalem: Keter Publishing House, 1971.

Rudolph, B. G. *From a Minyan to a Community: A History of the Jews of Syracuse.* Syracuse: Syracuse University, 1970.

Ruxin, Robert H. "The Jewish Farmer and the Small-Town Jewish Community: Schoharie County, New York." *American Jewish Archives* 29, no. 1 (April 1977): 3–21.

Samuelson, Robert J. "The Absurd Farm Bill." *Newsweek,* August 6, 1990, 51.

Sanderson, Dorothy Hurlbut. *The Delaware & Hudson Canalway.* Ellenville, N.Y.: Rondout Valley Publishing Company, 1974.

Sarna, Jonathan D. "The Roots of Ararat: An Early Letter from Mordecai M. Noah to Peter B. Porter." *American Jewish Archives* 32, no. 1 (April 1980): 52–58.

"Save the Community Centers." *Mountain Hotelman,* October 10, 1930, 6.

"Says Jews Are Becoming Farmers." *New York Times,* November 21, 1927, 7.

Scanlan, John J. "Congratulations from Washington." In *25th Anniversary Commemorative Journal,* edited by Inter-County Farmers Cooperative Association, 10. Woodridge, N.Y.: Inter-County Farmers Cooperative Association, 1961.

Schappes, Morris, ed. *A Documentary History of the Jews in the United States, 1654–1875.* New York: Citadel Press, 1950.

Scheller, William G. *The Hudson River Valley.* Helena, Mont.: American Geographic Publishing, 1988.

Schneiderman, Harry, ed. *The American Jewish Year Book.* Philadelphia: Jewish Publication Society of America, 1924.

———. *The American Jewish Year Book.* Philadelphia: Jewish Publication Society of America, 1937.

Schneiderman, Harry, and Morris Fine, eds. *The American Jewish Year Book.* Philadelphia: Jewish Publication Society of America, 1949.

Schoener, Allon, ed. *Portal to America: The Lower East Side 1870–1925.* New York: Holt, Rinehart and Winston, 1967.

Schwartz, Marvin. "Music, Scenery and Fishing in the Catskills." *New York Times,* June 8, 1958, XX–9.

———. "Two Ways of Seeing the Catskills." *New York Times,* June 10, 1956, XX–7.

Schweninger, Loren. "A Vanishing Breed: Black Farm Owners in the South, 1651–1982." *Agricultural History* 63, no. 3 (Summer 1989): 41–57.

"Sees Continued Growth in TV Antenna Industry." *Ellenville Journal,* December 29, 1955, 1.

Seligman, Ben B., and Harvey Swados. "Jewish Population in the United States." In *The American Jewish Year Book,* edited by Harry Schneiderman and Morris Fine, 651–89. Philadelphia: Jewish Publication Society of America, 1949.

Selzer, Michael, ed. *Kike.* New York: World Publishing, 1972.

Severo, Richard. "Rash of Fires in Catskills Points Up Growing Decline." *New York Times,* July 27, 1976, 31, 38.

Shankman, Arnold. "Happyville, the Forgotten Colony." *American Jewish Archives* 30 (April 1978): 3–19.

Sharfman, Rabbi I. Harold. *Jews on the Frontier: An Account of Jewish Pioneers and Settlers in Early America.* Chicago: Henry Regnery Co., 1977.

Shaughnessy, Jim. *Delaware & Hudson.* Berkeley: Howell-North, 1967.

Shenker, Israel. "Borscht Belt Farms Reap Laughs, Mostly." *Washington, D.C., Evening Star and Daily News,* July 3, 1973, A3.

Shepard, Richard F. "About Long Island." *New York Times,* June 15, 1980, (L.I. ed.) XX–2.

Shepard, Richard F., and Vicki Gold Levi. *Live and Be Well: A Collection of Yiddish Culture in America.* New York: Ballantine Books, 1982.

Shpall, Leo. "Jewish Agricultural Colonies in the United States." *Agricultural History* 25 (July 1950): 120–46.

Shulman, Abraham. *The New Country: Jewish Immigrants in America.* New York: Charles Scribner's Sons, 1976.

Silver, Joan Macklin. *Hester Street.* Midwest Films, 1974. Film.

Simons, Howard. *Jewish Times: Voices of the American Jewish Experience.* Boston: Houghton Mifflin Company, 1988.

Singer, David, and Ruth R. Seldin, eds. *The American Jewish Year Book.* New York: American Jewish Committee, 1988.

———. *The American Jewish Year Book.* New York: American Jewish Committee, 1991.

Singer, I.J. *The Brothers Ashkenazi.* New York: Grosset and Dunlap, 1936.

Singer, Isidore, ed. *The Jewish Encyclopedia.* New York: Ktav, 1964.

Sive, David. "The Undiscovered Charms of the Catskills." *New York Times,* May 10, 1959, XX-7.

Sklare, Marshall, ed. *The Jew in American Society.* New York: Behrman House, 1974.

Solomon, Jolie, and Robin Sparkman. "The Faithful Brace for Battle at Rock Music's Sacred Site." *Newsweek,* September 6, 1993, 61.

Soltes, Mordecai. "The Yiddish Press—An Americanizing Agency." In *The American Jewish Year Book,* edited by Harry Schneiderman, 165–372. Philadelphia: Jewish Publication Society of America, 1924.

Sorin, Gerald. "Eli Evans Enthralls Audience at Opening Resnick Lecture." *Jewish Star,* September 1993, 41.

———. *The Prophetic Minority: American Jewish Immigrant Radicals, 1880–1920.* Bloomington: Indiana University Press, 1985.

Soth, Lauren. "Slowly Strengthen Rural America." *Illinois Agri-News,* November 14, 1986, 6.

Spalding, Henry D., ed. *Encyclopedia of Jewish Humor.* New York: Jonathan David Publishers, 1969.

Steinberg, Israel. "I Inaugurate a President." *Middletown Times Herald Record,* January 20, 1965.

Stetka, Steven N. "The Land of Opportunity." *New York Times,* May 18, 1969, II–18.

Stokes, William N., Jr. *Credit to Farmers: The Story of Federal Intermediate Credit Banks and Production Credit Associations.* Washington, D.C.: Farm Credit Administration, 1973.

Stovall, Mary E. "History of the Ku Klux Klan." In *Encyclopedia of Southern Culture,* edited by Charles Reagan Wilson and William Ferris, 1507–8. Chapel Hill: University of North Carolina Press, 1989.

Straus, O.S. "Baron Maurice de Hirsch." 1901. Reprinted in *The Jewish Encyclopedia,* edited by Isidore Singer, 414–16. New York: Ktav, 1964.

Strauss, Michael. "A Bungalow in the Hills." *New York Times,* June 10, 1956, XX–9.

———. "Busy Catskills Take Spring in Their Stride." *New York Times,* April 3, 1966, XX–11.

———. "The Catskills 'Revolution.'" *New York Times,* June 7, 1959, XX–5.

————. "Catskills Turn to Tennis." *New York Times,* June 12, 1966, XX–3.

————. "Catskill Switch." *New York Times,* June 5, 1960, XX–3.

————. "A Day and a Night at the Races." *New York Times,* June 5, 1960, XX–3.

————. "Monticello Raceway Marking a Milestone." *New York Times,* May 7, 1967, XX–3.

————. "Round Skyscraper in Ulster Country." *New York Times,* May 18, 1965, XX–5.

————. "When the All-Inclusive Weekly Rate Was $9." *New York Times,* June 12, 1966, XX–3.

Strisik, Philip R. "Cooperatives—Old and New." *Jewish Farmer* 37, no. 2 (February 1944): 22.

Sullivan County Catskills Office of Public Information. *Sullivan County Catskills Travel Guide.* Monticello, 1990.

"Sullivan County Good-Will Movement Inaugurated." *Mountain Hotelman,* March 14, 1930, 6.

Sulzberger, Cyrus. "In Defense of the Immigrant." In *The American Jewish Year Book,* edited by Herbert Friedenwald, 19–98. Philadelphia: Jewish Publication Society of America, 1910.

Sweet Lorraine. New York: Angelika Artists, 1987. Film.

Taylor, Hal R. "Agriculture." In *Funk & Wagnalls Encyclopedia,* edited by Norma H. Dickey, 245–58. New York: Funk & Wagnalls, 1986.

Terwilliger, Kathrine, curator. "Empire State Festival" collection in Ellenville, New York, Public Library.

"Time To Call a Halt." *Mountain Hotelman,* May 9, 1930, 12.

"Transportation for School Children." *Mountain Hotelman,* October 10, 1930, 6.

U.S. Bureau of the Census. *1840 Census of Ulster County, New York, Wawarsing Township.* Washington, D.C., 1840.

————. *1900 Census of Sullivan County, New York, Thompson Township.* Washington, D.C., 1900.

————. *1900 Census of Ulster County, New York, Wawarsing Township.* Washington, D.C., 1900.

————. *1910 Census of Ulster County, New York, Wawarsing Township.* Washington, D.C., 1910.

————. *Rural and Rural Farm Population: 1990.* Washington, D.C.: Government Printing Office.

————. *Sullivan County, Ulster County, Delaware County, Greene County, Orange County Censuses.* 1940–1990.

U.S. Department of Agriculture. *Compilation of Statutes Relating to the Agricultural Marketing Service and Closely Related Activities.* Washington, D.C.: 1986.

Wakefield, Manville. *Coal Boats to Tidewater.* Grahamsville, N.Y.: Wakefair Press, 1981.

————. *To the Mountains by Rail.* Grahamsville, N.Y.: Wakefair Press, 1970.

Waldinger, Roger D. *Through the Eye of the Needle: Immigrants and Enterprise in New York's Garment Trades.* New York: New York University Press, 1986.

Warbasse, J.P. "My View on Being a Farmer." *Mountain Hotelman,* April 25, 1930, 1–2.

———. "Why Be a Farmer?" *Mountain Hotelman,* March 14, 1930.

Wasserman, Harry. "Cooperatives and the Future." In *Twenty-fifth Anniversary Commemorative Journal,* edited by Inter-County Farmers Cooperative Association, 15. Woodridge, N.Y.: Inter-County Farmers Cooperative Association, 1961.

———. "The Secretary's Message." In *Fifty Years Working Together,* edited by Esterita R. Blumberg, 22–23. Fallsburg, N.Y.: Fallsburg Printing Company, 1963.

Webster, Albert L. Reproduction of the log of the canal boat *Iowa* on the Delaware and Hudson Canal, September 7 to 23, 1891 in Webster, *Then and Now.* High Falls, N.Y.: D & H Canal Historical Society, December 4, 1971.

Weinraub, Bernard. "Catskill Vacation Resorts Draw Many Ethnic Groups." *New York Times,* August 7, 1969, 37.

Wickard, Claude R. "What Are the Farmers Doing to Help the War Effort?" In *America Organizes to Win the War,* 141–60. New York: Harcourt, Brace and Company, 1942.

Williams, Lena. "Catskill Village Facing an Industrial 'Disaster'." *New York Times,* April 1984.

Willner, Dorothy. *Nation-Building and Community in Israel.* Princeton: Princeton University Press, 1969.

Wilson, Charles Reagan, and William Ferris, eds. *Encyclopedia of Southern Culture.* Chapel Hill: University of North Carolina Press, 1989.

Winsberg, Morton D. *Colonia Barón Hirsch: A Jewish Agricultural Colony in Argentina.* Gainesville: University of Florida Press, 1963.

World Almanac and Book of Facts. New York: Scripps Howard Company, published annually, 1893–1992.

Yaffe, Ephraim. *A Good Old Age.* Ellenville, N.Y.: Privately printed, 1974.

———. "The Leurenkill Farmers Start a Hebrew School." In *50 Golden Years: The Ellenville Hebrew Aid Society 1907–1957,* edited by Mrs. Ben Miller and Daniel S. Roher, 59. Ellenville, N.Y.: Ellenville Hebrew Aid Society, 1959.

———. "Milk Sanitation." *Mountain Hotelman,* February 13, 1931.

———. "Save Our Basic Agricultural Industry—Dairying." *Mountain Hotelman,* September 26, 1930.

YIVO Institute for Jewish Research. "Folksongs in the East European Tradition, from the Repertoire of Miriam Nirenberg." New York: YIVO Institute, 1986.

Index

Photo Credits

About the Authors

Abraham D. Lavender is an Associate Professor of Sociology and Anthropology at Florida International University in Miami, Florida, where he has been since 1988. He previously taught sociology and Judaic studies at the University of Maryland, St. Mary's College of Maryland, and the University of Miami. He has A.B. and M.A. degrees in psychology from the University of South Carolina in Columbia and a doctorate in sociology from the University of Maryland with a dissertation on Jewish identity. He is the author of *A Coat of Many Colors: Jewish Subcommunities in the United States*, *Ethnic Women and Feminist Values*, *French Huguenots: From Mediterranean Catholics to White Anglo-Saxon Protestants*, and over thirty articles in academic journals such as *Contemporary Jewry*, *Jewish Social Studies*, *Ethnicity*, *Journal of Ethnic Studies*, *Journal of American Ethnic History*, and *Review of Religious Research*. He grew up on a tobacco, cotton, and corn farm in the village of New Zion, South Carolina.

Clarence Steinberg has worked for the United States Department of Agriculture's Agricultural Marketing Service since September 1986 as a public affairs specialist. He taught Medieval and Renaissance English language and literature at the University of Maryland, College Park, between 1968 and 1975, and holds a doctorate in these disciplines from the University of Pennsylvania. While studying there, he taught English composition and surveys at Delaware Valley College of Science and Agriculture (formerly the National Farm School) in Doylestown, Pennsylvania. He attended Cornell University College of Agriculture for two years, and subsequently received an A.B. from City College of New York and an M.A. from the University of Connecticut, Storrs. He grew up on a dairy and poultry farm near Ellenville, New York, during the Great Depression and World War II, attending the Ellenville public schools. His father was a founder of Inter-County Farmers' Cooperative Association.

Abraham D. Lavender, New Zion, South Carolina, ca. 1957.

Clarence B. Steinberg, Ellenville, New York, ca. 1942.